DK small business *guides*

managing
your
finances

DK small business *guides*

managing your finances

COLIN BARROW

A Dorling Kindersley Book

Dorling Kindersley

LONDON, NEW YORK, SYDNEY, DELHI, PARIS,
MUNICH, JOHANNESBURG

Senior Art Editor Jamie Hanson
DTP Designer Julian Dams
Production Controller Michelle Thomas

Managing Editor Adèle Hayward
Senior Managing Editor Stephanie Jackson
Senior Managing Art Editor Nigel Duffield

Produced for Dorling Kindersley by
Grant Laing Partnership
48 Brockwell Park Gardens,
London SE24 9BJ

Managing Editor Jane Laing
Project Editor Alison Bolus
Project Art Editor Christine Lacey
Picture Researcher Jo Walton

First published in Great Britain in 2001
by Dorling Kindersley Limited,
9 Henrietta Street, London WC2E 8PS

2 4 6 8 10 9 7 5 3 1

A CIP catalogue record for this book is available from the British
Library

ISBN 0 7513 1411 0

Colour reproduction in Italy by GRB Editrice
Printed and bound in Mondadori in Verona, Italy

see our complete catalogue at
www.dk.com

CONTENTS

INTRODUCTION

When starting out in business, people rank independence as their primary motivation. Fewer than one in six have making money as their foremost reason, although few would list losing money as a key goal. Whatever your motives, launching a small business or expanding an existing one successfully is not a simple task. Good ideas, hard work, enthusiasm, skills, and knowledge about your product and how to make it, although essential, are not enough. Barely 40 per cent of small firms survive intact to see their fifth birthday.

Most of these failures occur within the first few years, and poor or no financial management is the most cited reason for a small firm getting into difficulties. Owners and managers often need help in acquiring business skills in such areas as bookkeeping and accounting. Most failing businesses simply do not know their financial position. The order book can be full when the cash runs out.

Owners and managers also need to know what sorts of finance are available and how to put themselves in the best possible position to raise it. Surprisingly, there is no shortage of funds. Problems lie, rather, in the business proposition itself, or, more often, in the way in which the proposition is made to the financier. This calls for a business plan, a statement of business purpose, with the consequences spelled out in financial terms. For most people this calls for new knowledge.

Managing Your Finances provides you with this knowledge. Aimed at those who want to either start up a business or review their prospects, it shows you how to keep accurate financial records and how to translate plans and projections into cash. It outlines how to estimate how much cash your business needs and how much you can expect "outsiders" to put in. It also explains the use of ratios in analyzing the profitability of your business and the effect on it of various factors.

By following the wide range of advice and techniques offered in this book, you will ensure that your business is properly financed and controlled from the outset.

Estimating finances

A well-prepared business plan is the foundation upon which the financial success of your business will depend. In preparing the business plan, you will have to forecast the amount of cash you are likely to need, when you will need it, and for how long. In making projections, you have to be ready for likely pitfalls and prepared for the unexpected events that may create problems with your cash flow.

PREPARING YOUR BUSINESS PLAN

A well-prepared business plan is the foundation upon which the financial success of your business depends. It will also help you to decide how much money is needed, by when, and for what purposes. A business plan is a selling document that conveys the excitement and promise of your business to any potential backer or stakeholder. That audience can include outsiders, such as the bank, venture capitalists, or even current and prospective new employees who need to be confident that there is a future in the business for them.

Perhaps the most important step in managing the finances of any new venture or expanding an existing one is the construction of a business plan. The plan should be prepared and written by you in conjunction with any other people who are vital to its implementation. Such a plan must include your goals for the enterprise, both short and long term, as well as a description of the products or services you will offer, and the market opportunities you have anticipated for them. Finally, it should include an explanation of the resources, financial and other, that you are able to employ to achieve your goals in the face of competition.

No start-up or growing business should be without a current business plan that has been reviewed within the past six months. The planning horizon should be at least three years, because it takes this long to implement anything of strategic merit. The first year of the plan will form the framework for the operating budget. This is the profit and loss style description of how you will execute your business strategy. (For more information on profit and loss, see pp. 84–9.)

Why Have a Business Plan?

A business plan will be a useful tool both for you, as owner of the business, and for any outsiders who are interested in your business, such as prospective employees and potential financial backers. Its benefits justify the work

CASE STUDY: The Benefits of Thorough Planning

MARTIN JENKINS planned to start a restaurant in central London. He had worked as a chef in a small hotel for five years and from this experience he had gained a sound knowledge of most aspects of the business. One area in which he was less experienced was financial planning. Acknowledging his ignorance, he read up on the subject and taught himself how to prepare a business plan. While gathering data for the cash flow forecast in his business plan, this potential entrepreneur made the discovery that if he delayed purchasing some of the necessary equipment, and leased others, he could halve his initial funding requirements. This had a profound effect on his overall financial strategy and meant that far less of his capital was tied up at the outset.

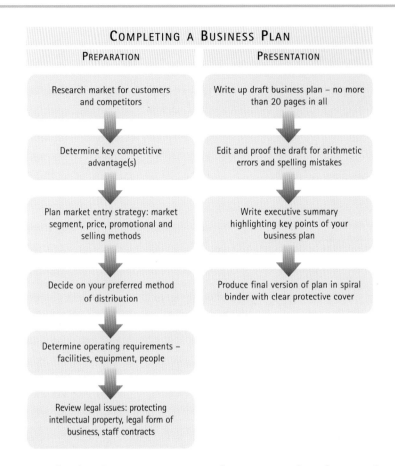

Completing a Business Plan

PREPARATION	PRESENTATION
Research market for customers and competitors	Write up draft business plan – no more than 20 pages in all
Determine key competitive advantage(s)	Edit and proof the draft for arithmetic errors and spelling mistakes
Plan market entry strategy: market segment, price, promotional and selling methods	Write executive summary highlighting key points of your business plan
Decide on your preferred method of distribution	Produce final version of plan in spiral binder with clear protective cover
Determine operating requirements – facilities, equipment, people	
Review legal issues: protecting intellectual property, legal form of business, staff contracts	

needed to prepare the plan. Constructing a business plan has four immediate benefits:
■ It tests the validity of your ideas.
■ It gives you the confidence to proceed.
■ It provides an overview of your financial requirements.
■ It gives you valuable planning experience.

TESTING YOUR IDEAS
The systematic approach required in creating a business plan means you make your mistakes on paper, rather than in the marketplace.

INCREASING YOUR CONFIDENCE
Once completed, a business plan will make you feel more confident in your ability to set up and operate your planned venture. It may even compensate for any lack of capital and experience, provided of course that you have other factors in your favour, such as a sound idea and a sizeable market opportunity for your proposed product or service.

GIVING AN OVERVIEW OF YOUR FINANCIAL REQUIREMENTS
Your business plan will show how much money is needed, what it is needed for, and when and for how long it is required.

Undercapitalization and early cash-flow problems are two important reasons why new business activities fail, so if you have a soundly prepared business plan you can reduce these

TIME SAVER

Prepare a list of all essential expenses needed for your business. Tell your accountant about them while putting your business plan together. If you discuss these only after you have prepared your plan, you may end up having to revise all your figures substantially.

risks of failure. You can also safely experiment, on paper, with a range of viable strategies, and so concentrate on options that make the most efficient use of scarce financial resources.

It would be an overstatement to say that your business plan is the passport to sources of finance. It will, however, help you to display your grasp of the financial dynamics of your business to the full, and to communicate your ideas to others in a way that will be easier for them to understand and to appreciate the reasoning behind your ideas. These outside parties could be bankers, potential investors, partners, or advisory agencies. Once they know what you are trying to do, they will be better able to help and advise you.

Use your business plan to prepare yourself for the rigours and dangers of the marketplace

PROVIDING PLANNING EXPERIENCE

Preparing a business plan will give you an insight into the financial planning process. It is this process itself that is important to the long-term financial health of a business, and not simply the plan that comes out of it. Businesses are dynamic, as are the commercial and competitive environments in which they operate, and no one expects every event as recorded on a business plan to occur exactly as predicted. But the understanding and knowledge you will gain as you go through the process of constructing your plan will prepare your business for any changes that it may face, and so enable it to adjust quickly.

AVOIDING A HIGH-RISK START-UP

Despite these many valuable benefits, thousands of would-be entrepreneurs still attempt to start without a business plan. The most common among these are businesses that appear to need little or no capital at the outset, or whose founders have funds of their own; in both cases it is believed unnecessary to expose the project to harsh financial appraisal.

The former hypothesis is usually based on the easily exploded myth that customers will all pay cash on the nail and that suppliers will wait for months to be paid. In the mean time, the proprietor has the use of these funds to finance the business. Such model customers and suppliers are, unfortunately, thinner on the ground than optimistic entrepreneurs think. In any event, two important market rules still apply: either the product or service on offer fails to sell like hot cakes, and mountains of unpaid stocks build up in the warehouse, all of which eventually have to be financed, or it does sell like hot cakes, as a result of which more financially robust entrepreneurs are attracted into the market. Without the staying power that adequate financing provides, these new competitors will rapidly kill off the business. In the second scenario, those would-be entrepreneurs with funds of their own or, worse still, borrowed from friends and relatives, tend to think that the time spent in preparing a business plan could be more usefully spent looking for premises, buying a new car, or installing a computer. In short, anything that inhibits them from immediate action is viewed as time-wasting.

Most people's initial perception of their business venture is flawed in some major respect, so jumping in at the deep end is risky, and unnecessarily so. Flaws can often be discovered cheaply during the preparation of a business plan; they are always discovered in the marketplace, invariably at a much higher and often fatal cost.

Aiming Your Plan at Potential Financiers

All successful businesses need external finance at some stage in their development, and if you are to succeed in raising those funds it is important to examine what financiers expect from you.

It is often said that there is no shortage of money for new and growing businesses, the only scarce commodities being good ideas and people with the ability to exploit them. From the potential entrepreneur's position, this is often hard to believe. Out of every 1,000 business plans received by venture capital providers, only 100 or so are examined in any detail, less than ten are pursued to the negotiating stage, and only one of those is finally invested in.

To a great extent, the decision whether to proceed beyond an initial reading of the plan will depend on the quality of the financial arguments and the revenue, or sales, model used to support the investment proposal. The business plan is the ticket of admission, giving the entrepreneur their first and often only chance to impress any prospective sources of finance with the quality of their proposal.

It follows from this that to have any chance at all of getting financial support, your business plan should pay high regard to the likely requirements of potential financiers. There are two main potential sources of finance: banks and venture capitalists. They each have different requirements.

WHAT THE BANKS LOOK FOR

Bankers, and indeed any other sources of debt capital, are looking for asset security to back their loan and the near certainty of getting their money back. Essentially, banks are in the business of converting illiquid assets, such as property or stock, into liquid assets, such as cash or overdraft facilities. They will also charge an interest rate that reflects current market conditions and their view of the level of risk of the proposal. Depending on the nature of the business in question and the purpose to which the money is being used, bankers will take a two- to five-year view.

Bankers will usually expect a business to start repaying both the loan and the interest on a monthly or quarterly basis as soon as the loan has been granted, although in some cases a capital holiday of up to two years can be negotiated, during which time no repayments are made. In the early stages of any loan, the interest charges make up the lion's share of payments, in the same way as mortgage repayments, and you must allow for this in your cash flow projections.

Bankers hope that a business will succeed in order that they can lend more money in the future and provide more banking services, such as insurance or tax advice, to a loyal customer. It follows from this appreciation of lenders' needs that banks are much less interested in rapid growth and the consequent capital gain than they are in being assured of a steady stream of earnings almost from the outset of the business trading.

DOS AND DON'TS OF BORROWING MONEY

✓ Do borrow as much as your plan says you need.

✓ Do talk to several lenders before deciding from whom to borrow.

✓ Do explain the risks of your business as well as the rewards.

✓ Do make sure the loan term is long enough for you to reach break-even.

✗ Don't borrow from anyone who can't afford it.

✗ Don't raise money until you need it and so incur unnecessary charges.

✗ Don't conceal information about your credit or business record from a prospective lender.

✗ Don't ignore government-supported borrowing schemes; they can be better value.

Deciding Whether to Invest
Venture capitalists are looking for winners to back. If your idea appeals to them, they will look at your business plan in detail. If it is impressive in its content and presentation, you may persuade them to invest in your business.

What the Venture Capitalists Look For

Most new or fast-growing businesses generally do not make immediate profits, so money for such enterprises must come from elsewhere. Risk or equity capital – the capital of a business that comes from the issue of shares – as other types of funds are called, comes from venture capital houses, as well as being put in by founders, their families, and friends.

Because the inherent risks of investing in new and young ventures are greater than those of investing in established companies, venture capital fund managers have to offer their investors the chance of larger overall returns. To do that, fund managers not only have to keep failures to a minimum, they also have to pick some big winners – ventures with annual compound growth rates above 35 per cent – to offset the inevitable mediocre performers. (Bearing in mind the massive growth in internet access, it is hardly surprising that the dot.com sector has sucked in so much equity finance.) Typically, a fund manager would expect any ten investments to comprise one star, seven also-rans, and two flops. However, despite this outcome, venture capital fund managers are looking only for winners, so, unless you are projecting high growth in the short to medium term, the chances of getting venture capital are slim.

■ **Venture Capitalists as Shareholders**
Not only are venture capitalists looking for winners, they are also looking for a shareholding in your business. The size of the shareholding will vary with each business.

If the venture capital firm sees that you have a great business idea, a first-class team, and a product/service that is ready to roll, they would be looking for up to a third of the shares in your business as their reward for putting up the money. That third could be further reduced if the management are putting (or have put) in some of their own money, or if a bank is lending. If the idea is

---

Time Saver

Prepare your business plan before approaching venture capitalists. Send them your two-page executive summary, then phone them to find out if they want to see the full plan. This will save wasted meetings with venture capitalists who turn out to be unprepared to back you.

not fully developed, or your team is weak – in which case they may want to put in a non-executive director and work with you to strengthen the team – they may aim for more than a third of your business to compensate for the increased risk.

It all comes down to how much you need the money, how risky the venture is, how much money could be made from your business, and your skills as a negotiator.

Fast-growing companies typically have no cash available to pay dividends and, in the case of many dot.coms, may not have made any profits in any case, so investors can profit only by selling their holdings. With this in mind, the venture capitalists need to have an exit route in view at the outset, such as a stock exchange or a potential corporate buyer.

■ **SHORT-TERM INVESTMENT**
Unlike many entrepreneurs (and some lending bankers), who see their ventures as lifelong commitments to success and growth, venture capitalists have a relatively short-term horizon. Typically, they look to liquidate small company investments within two to six years, allowing them to pay out individual investors and to have funds available for tomorrow's winners. So your financial plan needs to accommodate this timescale.

BALANCING THE SOURCES

To be successful, your business must be targeted at the needs of these two sources of finance, and in particular at the balance between the two. Lending bankers ideally look for a ratio of 1:1, which means that half the business's finances are borrowed and half comes from risk capital. Banks have been known to go to a ratio of 4:1, but rarely willingly or at the outset of their involvement. Venture capital providers will almost always encourage entrepreneurs to take on new debt capital to match the level of equity, or share, funding.

If you are planning to raise money from friends and relatives either as debt or equity, then their needs must also be taken account of in your business plan.

BELIEVABLE GROWTH FORECASTS

Right at the heart of every investment or lending proposition is the need to demonstrate that the business will deliver a satisfactory financial result. The business plan needs to show, in summary form, the key results to be achieved. This should cover sales, cash flow, profits, margins, and investment returns for a sufficient period to give confidence.

Entrepreneurs are naturally ebullient when explaining the future prospects for their businesses. They frequently believe that the sky is the limit when it comes to growth and that the lack of money is the only thing that stands between them and their almost certain success.

It is true that if you are looking for venture capital, then the providers are also looking for rapid growth. However, it is as well to remember that financiers are dealing with thousands of investment proposals each year, and already have money tied up in hundreds of business sectors. It follows that they already have a perception of what the accepted financial results and marketing approaches currently are, for any sector. Any new company's business plan showing projections that are outside the ranges perceived as acceptable within an industry will raise questions in the investor's mind.

Make your growth forecasts believable, supporting them with hard facts wherever possible. If your forecasts are on the low side, then approach the more cautious lending bankers, rather than venture capitalists. The former often see a modest forecast as a virtue, lending credibility to the business proposal as a whole, rather than being impressed by ambitious goals.

Take into account the interests of its potential readers when writing your financial plan

The Presentation of a Business Plan

Having decided on the content of your business plan, you now need to consider how to present the material in order to make it into a professional and impressive document that will convince backers to support your idea.

DECIDING ON THE PACKAGING

Every product is enhanced by appropriate packaging, and a business plan is no exception. Most experts prefer a simple spiral binding with a clear plastic cover front and back. This makes it easy for the reader to move from section to section, and it ensures that the document will survive the frequent handling that every successful business plan is likely to get. A letter-quality printer, using a size 12 typeface, double spacing, and wide margins, will result in a pleasing and easy-to-read plan.

There is no such thing as a universal business-plan format. That being said, experience has taught us that certain styles have been more successful than others. Following these guidelines will result in an effective business plan that covers most requirements. Not every subheading will be relevant, but the general format is robust and is equally suitable for new businesses of any size.

COVER AND TITLE PAGE

First, the cover should show the name of your business, its address, phone and fax numbers, e-mail address, and web site (if you have one), and the date on which this version of the plan was prepared. It should confirm that this is the business's current view on its position and financing needs.

Second, the title page, immediately behind the front cover, should repeat the above information and also give the founder's name, address, and phone number. A home phone number can be helpful, particularly for investors, who often work irregular hours.

THE EXECUTIVE SUMMARY

Ideally one page, but certainly no longer than two, the executive summary follows the title page. Writing this is the most difficult task, but it is the single most important part of the business plan. Done well, it can favourably dispose the reader from the outset. Done badly, or not at all, then the plan may not get beyond the mail room. The executive summary can be written only after the business plan has been completed, because it summarizes all the contents of the plan.

THE TABLE OF CONTENTS

This page follows the executive summary and is the "map" that will guide readers through the business proposal. If that map is obscure, muddled, or even missing, then you are likely to end up with lost or irritated readers who are in no mind to back your proposal.

Each main section should be listed, numbered, and given a page number. Elements within each section should also be numbered; for example, Section 1 would contain elements 1.1, 1.2, and so forth.

THE BODY OF THE PLAN

The contents of the business plan should include the following main sections, each with its own heading:

▓ **THE BUSINESS AND ITS MANAGEMENT** Outline a brief history of the business and its performance to date and give details on key staff, current mission, capital structure, legal entity, and professional advisers.

▓ **PRODUCTS AND SERVICES** Give a description of products and services, their applications, competitive advantage, and proprietary position. Include details on the state of readiness of new products and services and development cost estimates.

▓ **MARKETING** Provide a brief overview of the market by major segment, showing size and growth. Explain the current and proposed marketing strategy for each major segment, covering price, promotion, distribution

BUSINESS PLAN: SIMPLY PERFECT

SUMMARY

BUSINESS DESCRIPTION:	New retail shop (ladies fashions for the over 50s).
LOCATION:	Small provincial town.
PROPRIETOR:	Joan Smith (trading as a sole trader).
STAFF:	The proprietor only.
MARKET:	The main market is ladies, over 50, living in the town (population 66,500). The nearest shops catering for this market are in the city, 28 miles distant.
PREMISES:	About 500 sq ft in a good location.
PROPOSED SHOP NAME:	"Simply Perfect"
TURNOVER:	First-year estimate: approximately £48,500. Second-year estimate: approximately £60,000.
FINANCING:	Depending upon which shop is rented, capital of some £17,000 is required, of which the proprietor can raise £10,000, leaving a balance of £7,000 to be found. A three-year bank loan of £4,000 would be sufficient, together with an overdraft facility of £3,000 to allow for initial stock purchases.
TIMESCALE:	The plan is to start trading by 1 May, in time for the summer season, though stock will be ordered earlier.

3

EXECUTIVE SUMMARY
This gives the essential details of your proposed business operations and forms a vital part of your business plan.

A description of the products or services, together with details on any rights or patents and details on competitive advantage

The reasons why customers need this product or service, together with some indication of market size and growth

The current position of the business, including a summary of past trading results (for existing businesses)

How much money is needed to fund the growth and how and when the provider will benefit

A summary of forecasts of sales and profits, together with short- and longer-term aims and the strategies to be employed

channels, selling methods, location requirements, and the need for acquisitions, mergers, or joint ventures, if any.

■ **MANAGEMENT AND STAFFING** Give details on current key staff and on any recruitment needs to achieve the planned goals. Include information on staff retention strategies, reward systems, and training plans.

■ **OPERATIONS** Describe how your products are made, how your services are provided, how quality standards are assured, and how your output can be stepped up or down to meet the varying levels of demand implied in the business plan. It is important to demonstrate a degree of flexibility.

■ **FINANCIAL FORECAST AND CONTROLS** Provide a projected profit and loss account (see pp. 84–9), together with a description of the key controls used to monitor and review your performance.

■ **FINANCING REQUIREMENTS** Show the finances needed to achieve the planned goals, together with timings. You should also demonstrate how the business would

ASSESSMENT OF THE CONTENT OF YOUR BUSINESS PLAN

By answering the questions below you will get some idea of how well your business plan is progressing. Score 1, 2, or 3, following the key below, for each of the questions. Mark the options closest to your instincts, and be honest. Then add up your scores and refer to the results at the end of the questionnaire to see how you scored and to check the potential of your plan.

Whatever your score, remember that this type of self-assessment test is broadbrush. It is designed only to give an indication of whether you have the basic attitude, instincts, and capabilities to make a success of launching a home-based business. If your score is low, the chances are that you do not. If it is high, the opposite is true.

1 = Made a start   2 = Some data only   3 = Comprehensive

Title page ☐1 ☐2 ☐3
Name of business, contact details, date of business plan, contents

Executive summary ☐1 ☐2 ☐3
Your details; summary of key strategies; why you are better or different; summary of profit projections; summary of financial needs

The business and its management ☐1 ☐2 ☐3
You and your team's relevant experience; business goals and objectives; legal structure of the business

The marketing strategy ☐1 ☐2 ☐3
Market segment analysis; pricing strategy; promotion plans; product mix and range; e-commerce strategy; location; selling strategy

Management and staffing ☐1 ☐2 ☐3
Staff numbers; roles and responsibilities; recruitment needs

Operations ☐1 ☐2 ☐3
What facilities and equipment are needed; what services will be bought in?

Legal issues ☐1 ☐2 ☐3
What intellectual protection do you have as a barrier to entry; what other legal issues affect your business?

Financial forecasts ☐1 ☐2 ☐3
Summary of financial projections; monthly cash flows; profit-and-loss accounts; balance sheets; break-even analysis

Financing requirements ☐1 ☐2 ☐3
How much money do you need; what is it needed for; how much money can you provide; how much do you need to raise from outside; what security is available?

RESULTS

9 points or less
You still have a lot more information to gather or decisions to make. No serious plan could be drawn up at this stage.

Between 10 and 20 points
You have made progress, but still have a few gaps to fill. Concentrate your efforts on completing your plan.

More than 20 points
Your plan is now complete and ready for final editing.

proceed using only internal funding. The gap between the two levels of production is what the extra money will help to deliver.

■ **APPENDICES** could include a curriculum vitae (CV) for each of the key team members, technical data, patents copyrights and designs, details on professional advisers, audited accounts, consultants' reports, abstracts of market surveys, details of orders on hand, and so on.

ADDRESSING THE READER

Clearly a business plan will be more effective if it is written with the reader in mind. This will involve some research into the particular interests, foibles, and idiosyncrasies of those readers. Of the four likely types of readers, bankers are more interested in hearing about certainties and steady growth, venture capitalists are also interested in dreams of great things to come, potential partners are concerned with whether or not this is a venture they want to share in, and potential employees will want to be convinced that you can offer them interesting and secure employment.

It is a good idea to carry out your research before the final editing of your business plan, so that you can incorporate something of this knowledge into the way it is presented. You may find that slightly different versions of the plan have to be made for different audiences. This makes the reader feel that the proposal has been addressed to them rather than just being a "Dear Sir or Madam" type of missive. The fundamentals of the plan will, however, remain constant whatever the readership.

EDITING YOUR PLAN

The first draft of the business plan may have several authors and it can be written ignoring the niceties of grammar and style. Now would be a good time to talk over the proposal with your legal adviser, to keep you on the straight and narrow, and with a friendly banker or venture capitalist. Their opinions can give you an insider's view as to the strengths and

weaknesses of your proposal at a stage when you still have time to alter it.

When the first draft has been revised, then comes the task of editing. Here grammar, spelling, and a consistent style do matter. The end result must be a crisp, correct, clear, and complete plan, no more than 20 pages long. If you are not a confident writer, you may need help with the editing. Your local librarian or college may be able to help by providing you with suitable contacts.

Making an Oral Presentation

I f any of your chosen financiers find your plan of interest, they will want to meet you to discuss particular aspects, to iron out any elements that are unclear, and to evaluate your skills and character. Anyone backing a business does so primarily because they believe in the management. They know from experience that

TIPS FOR PREPARING A SUCCESSFUL ORAL PRESENTATION

1 Rehearse beforehand, having found out how much time you have.

2 Allow at least as much time for questions as you take in your talk.

3 Use visual aids, and if possible bring and demonstrate your product or service.

4 Explain your strategy in a businesslike manner, demonstrating your grasp of the competitive market forces at work.

5 Listen to comments and criticisms carefully, avoiding a defensive attitude when you respond.

6 Make your replies to questions brief and to the point to allow for as many different questions to be put as possible.

7 Use eye contact, tone of speech, body language, and enthusiasm to create empathy between yourself and listeners.

things rarely go to plan, so your presentation must convince them that the team involved can respond effectively to changing conditions.

Any financier that you are presenting to will have read dozens of similar plans to your own and will be well rehearsed in the art of finding the ones worth backing. They may even have researched something of your business and financial history already. Your oral presentation must convince them that your business is a sound investment.

Maintaining Confidentiality

Finding an investor or a bank to lend to your business may take weeks or months. During that time, potential backers will diligently gather information about the business so that they will not have unpleasant surprises later. The business plan will be only the starting point for their investigations.

OBTAINING LEGAL PROTECTION

If you and the prospective financiers are strangers to one another, you may be reluctant to turn over business information to them until you know that they are serious. To allay these fears, ask for a confidentiality letter or agreement.

A confidentiality letter will suffice in most circumstances, but if substantial amounts of intellectual property are involved you may prefer a more formal confidentiality agreement drafted by a lawyer. Do make sure that the document contains no binding commitment on you. The confidentiality letter should be limited to the potential investor's agreement to treat the information you give them as confidential, and to use it only to investigate lending to, or investing in, your proposed business.

THE SUBJECT OF RESEARCH

Investors may want to learn about your own financial status, job, or business history. They are interested in your financial stability, business knowhow, and reputation for integrity because they will, in effect, be extending credit to you.

DISCUSSING YOUR PLAN
When presenting your business plan to a potential backer, your aim is to convince the listener that you are worth backing. A well-prepared plan and a confident manner will help to achieve this goal.

CONFIDENTIALITY LETTER

This letter provides you with safeguards against an interested party stealing your idea and either developing the concept or selling it to a third party.

This protects the contents of your business plan

WHEREAS

1 The purpose of communication between the Parties to this Agreement is for the Investor/Lender to evaluate the suitability as an investment or lending proposition, the business proposition as set out in the business plan.

2 The information to be communicated in strict confidence between the Parties to this Agreement includes the business plan, demonstrations, commercial and technical information, all forms of intellectual property, and includes material for which patent or similar registration may have been filed.

THEREFORE THE PARTIES HEREBY UNDERTAKE AS FOLLOWS:

FIRST: Each Party hereto agrees to maintain as confidential and not to use any of the information directly or indirectly disclosed by the other Party until or unless such information becomes public knowledge through no fault of the recipient Party, or unless the Parties to the Agreement complete a further Agreement making provision for utilization of information disclosed. Each Party undertakes to prevent the information disclosed from passing to other than those representatives who must be involved for the purpose of this Agreement.

SECOND: In the event that no further Agreement on utilization or publication of information is concluded each Party hereto undertakes to return to the other all confidential items submitted and to furnish certification that no copies or other records of those items have been retained.

THIRD: In the event that either Party requires the assistance of a further party in pursuing the purposes of the Agreement the approval of the other Party to this Agreement shall be secured.

FOURTH: Any information which either Party can prove was in his possession prior to disclosure hereunder and was not acquired from the other Party or his representatives is excepted from this Agreement.

FIFTH: The construction, validity and performance of this Agreement shall be governed in all respects by Law and the Parties hereto submit to the jurisdiction of the Courts.

You can discuss details only with those who have signed the agreement

You should confirm the country whose law the agreement comes under

Principals concerned must sign here for agreement to be valid

SIGNED for	SIGNED for
First Party _____	First Party _____
Position _____	Position _____
For and on behalf of: _____	For and on behalf of: _____
In the presence of: _____	In the presence of: _____

FORECASTING CASH FLOW

The most reliable way to estimate the amount of money a business will require to meet its future needs is to make a cash-flow forecast; that is, determine the pattern and extent of cash payments and receipts by a business over a particular period. The different aspects of a business that need to be taken into account when drawing up an accurate cash-flow forecast are examined and explained here, in order to help you to feel as confident as possible that you have considered every necessary factor.

A profit is made if a business has any money over after paying all the costs associated with making goods, or supplying a service. Typically such costs will fall under two headings: cost of sales and overheads. Cost of sales, or direct costs, includes raw materials if you are making products or the bought-in costs of providing a service. For example, a travel company might have to buy in airline tickets and hotel bedrooms, to "produce" a package holiday. Overheads, or indirect costs, are the cost of premises, telephone, insurance, and so forth.

ADDITIONAL COSTS TO CONSIDER

Even after these costs have been allowed for, however, a business may have other major expenses. For example, if fixed assets such as a computer or a van are required, these have to be allowed for in your cash calculations. As your business grows, it may need more stock and it may attract more customers, who in turn take time to pay their bills. This gap between cash outflow and cash inflow will, in part, be offset by the increasing credit you will be able to take from your suppliers, but inevitably some finance will be required.

SETTING COSTS AGAINST INCOME

For the purpose of deciding how much money you need to start up or expand your business, you have to prepare a cash-flow forecast. This means estimating your likely future costs and your likely income from sales.

TAKING ACCOUNT OF ALL YOUR COSTS TO DETERMINE YOUR NET PROFIT

Cash in from sales

Cash out for: → Cost of sales

Leaves a profit → Overheads

Take more credit from suppliers → New fixed assets

More cash out for: → More stock

Equals net profit → More money owed by more customers

Estimating Fixed Costs

Many costs have to be incurred before sales income can be generated, such as buying a car, office furniture, or a computer, or renting premises. You need to anticipate both the likely

		MINIMIZING FIXED COSTS			
ASSET	DO WE REALLY NEED IT?	DO WE NEED IT NOW?	DO WE REALLY NEED TO BUY IT?	COULD WE FINANCE IT SEPARATELY?	CAPITAL COST (£)
BOARDROOM TABLE	Nice, but not essential	No	No, could use hotel	?	800
COLOUR COPIER	Yes	Yes	No, could use bureau	?	1,400
DELIVERY VAN	Yes	No, not for eight weeks	Yes	Yes, hire purchase	21,000

amount and the timing of the purchase of these. Minimize your fixed costs by asking yourself the following questions about them.

DO WE REALLY NEED THEM?

Business assets often have an element of vanity attached to them. For example, one company founder felt that a boardroom table and eight chairs were essential to his business from the outset. However, this meant paying the rent on a room that could now not be used for any productive purpose, incurring the cost of purchasing the furniture, and wasting a day on choosing and selecting the table and chairs. It was over two years before the company actually employed eight people, so this was really an unnecessary start-up cost.

DO WE NEED TO BUY THEM?

Even if an asset is essential, it may not be necessary to buy it. For example, the founder of the business mentioned above could have held his board meetings at a local hotel for a fraction of the cost, or he could have searched out another entrepreneur, with an underutilized boardroom that he was keen to see being used.

A colour photocopier may be nice to have, but for the relatively few occasions it is needed, using a copying centre would suffice. This may still make sense even if there is a big difference between the cost per copy of using your own machine and the cost per copy at the copying

AN UNNECESSARY ASSET
Buying a colour copier – which will tie up large amounts of cash – may well be a waste of money if you could manage with visits to a local copying centre instead.

centre, because it frees up scarce capital for other vital costs. If you need to produce colour work quite often, then consider leasing a copier. Less capital is tied up, and you should benefit from terms such as free maintenance and possibly the option to buy the machine at a reduced price at the end of the lease period.

DO WE NEED TO BUY THEM NOW?

Timing is a vital element in determining the financing needs of a business. If a particular asset is not needed for several months, then do not buy it now. One owner-manager bought a refrigerated van for his food deliveries while still getting his production facility on stream. The van sat, unused, for three weeks before being misused as a fetch-and-carry vehicle for waste disposal. It was not used to deliver fresh food to customers until eight weeks after its purchase.

ARE THESE THE RIGHT THINGS TO BUY?

Even when you know that an asset is essential to your business, it is not always easy to predict the right one to buy. In the example above, the van was discovered to be the wrong size for the job almost the first time it was used, and it had to be exchanged for a larger van. The business founder's predictions of sales demand were made with prudence and caution, but actual sales per customer turned out to be much better than expected. Unfortunately, much of the gain from extra sales was wasted on the loss in value of the original van.

FACT FILE

Cash is the money assets of a business, both in hand and at the bank. Profit is the excess of sales over costs and expenses during an accounting period. It follows, therefore, that many businesses that run an overdraft, and so technically have no cash, can nevertheless still be profitable.

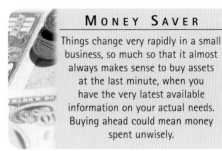

MONEY SAVER

Things change very rapidly in a small business, so much so that it almost always makes sense to buy assets at the last minute, when you have the very latest available information on your actual needs. Buying ahead could mean money spent unwisely.

WHAT IS THE BEST WAY TO BUY?

Rather than buy an essential asset outright, using cash or mainstream finance such as an overdraft or loan facility, it may make sense to finance a particular asset directly. A car, for example, could be financed on hire purchase, freeing up money for less tangible costs such as advertising, which a bank may not be so keen to support. (See pp. 59–60 for more details.)

Estimating Sales Revenue

The sales forecast is perhaps the most important set of numbers to come out of the business planning process. How much stock to hold, how many staff to employ, and how much material to buy are all decisions that hinge on the sales forecast. These sales figures are also used to predict the cash-flow forecast and hence the funding requirements of the business.

These projections are also the key to valuing the business, and so they will determine whether or not bankers will lend and investors invest. Furthermore, they will give some guidance as to how much of an enterprise investors expect in exchange for funding. Naturally enough, potential backers do not accept a new business's sales forecast unchallenged, because in their experience new ventures nearly always miss the target by a wide margin.

While all forecasts may turn out to be wrong, it is important to demonstrate in your business plan that you have thought through all the different factors that could impact on your performance. You should also show how you can deliver satisfactory results even when many of these factors work against you. Backers want security, so they will inevitably be measuring the downside risk, to evaluate the worst case scenario and its likely effects, as well as looking towards an ultimate exit route.

RESEARCH SIMILAR BUSINESSES

Your overall projections will have to be believable. Most lenders and investors will have an extensive experience of similar business proposals. Unlike yourself, they will have the benefit of hindsight, being able to look back several years at other ventures they have backed, and see how they fared in practice as

---

CASE STUDY: Predicting Zero Sales Revenue

MEDSOFT WAS SET UP to sell dedicated computer systems to hospital consultants. The concept grew out of a chance meeting between Richard Kensall, a successful department-store owner and disillusioned computer dealer, and an eager young doctor with a love of computers.

The doctor's problem was that he had too large a volume of patient data to classify and analyze. Some 16,000 consultants had a need to

record details on 35 million patient attendances and 5 million inpatients per annum. A record had to be generated containing all details of each patient. At that time, almost all such records were generated and maintained manually. So, for Medsoft, the market opportunity was substantial and, with some further development, their product range was proven. The only problem was the time taken to get a decision made as to whether to buy or not, and then to get the cash in.

Capital investment decisions such as this follow a long and complex procedure in the hospital service. From finding a consultant who wanted to buy, to finally obtaining approval by the Regional Scientific Officer, could take up to nine months. Even when over all these hurdles, a project could fail if the region had insufficient funds to pay for all the properly approved proposals. Consequently, Medsoft's business plan had to anticipate zero sales revenue for the first nine months at least, and only modest sums until well into the second year. Their resultant cash-flow forecast looked very sick indeed over this period, but in their business plan they were able to argue for this situation occurring. Fortunately, while investigating the decision-making process, they uncovered four types of potential customer who could "buy" within six months. These people were to be the focus of all sales effort for the first six months of Medsoft's life.

COMPREHENSIVE ACCESS
Once installed, Medsoft's dedicated computer system enabled hospital consultants to generate and update both the record details and the attendances of any of their patients at any time.

compared with the initial forecasts of their enthusiastic owners.

You could gather some useful knowledge on similar businesses yourself by researching filed company accounts, trade magazines or by talking with the founders of similar ventures, who will not be your direct competitors.

EVALUATE MARKET SHARE

How big is the market for your product or service? Is it growing or contracting? At what rate, percentage, per annum? What is the economic and competitive position? The answers to these questions can all provide a market share basis for your forecasts. An entry market share of more than a few per cent would be most unusual. For all the hype, after a decade of hard work, the internet booksellers still account for less than 2 per cent of all books sold, and Amazon is just one of a score of major players.

Beware, however, of turning this argument regarding small percentages on its head. Many sales forecasts are made on the premise that "if we capture only 1 per cent of the potential market, we'll be a great success", with the belief that just 1 per cent must be achievable. This argument is then advanced as part of the business plan, so that no time is "wasted" in doing basic market research. After all, the business has to sell to only this tiny percentage of possible buyers! In fact, this is ambitious and unrealistic thinking, which leads to more new business failures than any other single factor.

If the market is so huge that achieving sales to only 1 per cent of it is very profitable, then inevitably there are large and established competitors. For a small firm to try to compete head on in this situation is little short of suicidal. It can be done, but only if sound research has clearly identified a market niche.

No investor will be impressed by clearly unsubstantiated statements, such as "in a market of £1 billion per annum we can easily capture 1 per cent, which is £1 million a year", because they know that achieving this 1 per cent of the market will not be nearly as easy as it sounds.

USE RULES OF THUMB

For some businesses there are useful generalizations, called rules of thumb, that can be used to estimate sales. This is particularly

ON-LINE RESEARCH
Market research takes commitment and a methodical approach. Libraries are a good starting place. In addition to providing access to magazines, reports, and annuals, they also allow you to research using the internet. You can then to choose to view data on an international, national, or individual basis.

CASE STUDY: Steady Build-up of Sales

FOR THE PAST TWO YEARS Anthea Cody has been running a very successful outdoor clothing shop called Exploration Works. Last year she took on an agency from Asian Adventure Holidays, one of the largest and most respected tour operators in the market. With virtually no marketing effort, 200 adventure holidays have been sold in the past six months, netting £40,000 in commissions. Sales of insurance policies and other services have added to this total, and could potentially add more.

When making her sales forecast, Anthea estimated that her enquiry-to-sales conversion rate on the adventure travel holidays sold to date had been 33 per cent, while operating within the outdoor clothing shop. For the purposes of her sales forecast, she made a conservative estimate that only 20 per cent of enquiries would actually result in an adventure holiday being booked.

She expects a steady build-up of clients coming from the clothing shop to talk about holidays. The number of new enquiries generated by promotional activity should also build up during the year, gradually overtaking enquiries from the clothes shop. She expects this trend to continue. Based on the projection below, she is forecasting to sell 660 adventure travel holidays next year at an average price of £2,125 each. Once insurance and other service sales are added in, she expects to generate £160,948 over the year.

SALES FORECAST PROJECTION					
	QUARTER 1	QUARTER 2	QUARTER 3	QUARTER 4	YEAR TOTAL
ENQUIRIES GENERATED THROUGH PROMOTION	200	425	425	750	1,800
ADVENTURE SHOP ENQUIRIES	300	300	450	450	1,500
TOTAL ENQUIRIES	500	725	875	1,200	3,300
HOLIDAYS SOLD	100	145	175	240	660
AVERAGE HOLIDAY'S COST	£2,000	£2,000	£2,250	£2,250	£2,125
COMMISSION RECEIVED (10-11%)	£20,000	£29,000	£43,312	£59,136	£151,448
COMMISSION ON INSURANCE AND OTHER SERVICES RECEIVED (0.5-0.75%)	£1,000	£2,000	£3,000	£3,500	£9,500
TOTAL COMMISSION AND FEES EARNED	£21,000	£31,000	£46,312	£62,636	£160,948

true in retailing, where location studies, traffic counts, and population density are known factors that affect the volume of sales.

OBTAIN DATA FROM CUSTOMERS

How many customers and potential customers do you know who are likely to buy from you, and how much might they buy? Here you can use many types of data on which to base reasonable sales projections.

You can interview a sample of prospective customers, issue a press release or advertisement to gauge response, and exhibit at trade shows to get customer reactions.

TAKE SEASONALITY INTO ACCOUNT

When working out your sales forecast you should also look at seasonal factors that might cause sales to be high or low at certain periods in the year. For example, 80 per cent of toys are sold in just three months of the year, leaving nine very flat trading months. Such seasonality would have a significant effect on your cash-flow projections.

INCORPORATE DESIRED INCOME

Forecasts will also accommodate the realistic aims of the proprietor. Indeed, you could go further and state that the whole purpose of the strategy is to ensure that certain forecasts are achieved. In a mature company with proven products and markets, this is more likely to be the case than with a new business. Nevertheless, an element of "How much do we need to

earn?" must play a part in forecasting your sales, if only to signal when a strategy is simply not worth pursuing.

RELATE SALES FORECAST TO ACTIVITY

However they are arrived at, sales figures will convince no one unless they are tied back to the specific activities that will generate the necessary business.

If, for example, in your business salespeople have to make visits to generate orders, then knowing how many calls need to be made to get one order, and what the average order size could be, are essential pieces of information to include in your sales forecast.

GAIN APPROVAL

If your product or service needs to be on an association's or federation's approved list before it can be bought, then your cash-flow forecast should confirm that you have obtained the relevant approval to trade.

Calculating Working Capital

Once you have completed your sales forecast, you can use it to calculate the amount of raw material and stock you will have to hold (if you are a manufacturing business or in subcontracting, for example) and how much money you will have tied up in customers, if you decide to sell on credit. This may be offset,

---

CASE STUDY: Using Restaurant Rule of Thumb

TIM BROWN, who founded his second restaurant, called Alamo, in Los Angeles, with substantial backing from private investors, used a rule of thumb accepted by many restaurateurs to estimate his likely sales revenue. From the experience gained from setting up and running his first restaurant, he concurred with the accepted rule that once a restaurant has served 25,000 clients it can expect sufficient repeat business to break even.

In the event, during his first eight months of operation Brown served 20,000 customers at Alamo, and so was well on his way to the 25,000 break-even point he required to match his projected sales revenue forecast.

EXHIBITING AT TRADE FAIRS
Exhibiting at trade fairs is an excellent way of viewing and assessing your competitors' merchandise. Trade fairs also provide you with the opportunity to meet potential customers (and competitors) and to get personal reactions to your goods or services.

in part at least, by the amount of credit you take from your suppliers. But the balance, which is known as the working capital, has to be funded by you.

The chart below shows the complete cash-flow cycle, tracing all the movements that occur within working capital. It should provide you with enough information to forecast the cash (and hence the financing requirements) of your business.

Forecasting Cash Requirements

Although a sales forecast can be drawn up on a quarterly basis, your cash-flow forecast should be broken down into months to give more detail. A cash-flow forecast, or pro forma cash-flow statement, for a travel agent on the next two pages shows how this is arrived at.

THE CASH-FLOW CYCLE

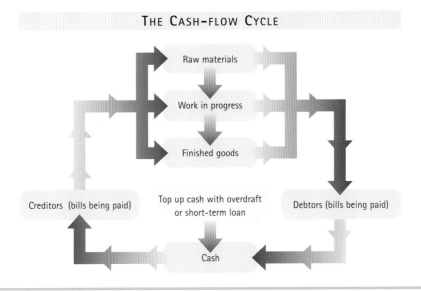

Raw materials

Work in progress

Finished goods

Creditors (bills being paid)

Top up cash with overdraft or short-term loan

Debtors (bills being paid)

Cash

CASH-FLOW ANALYSIS

The business will need additional cash for most of the year, and anything less than £46,000 may be insufficient. In this example, this is the amount of the financing requirement called for in the business plan.

The owner is putting £10,000 of his own money into the business

Although sales are expected in month 1, the owner does not expect to get paid until month 2, or 3 for insurance commissions

The sales income figures come from the sales forecast

Ongoing expenses such as wages and leasing costs are charged monthly

Payments for major fixed assets such as fixtures, fittings, furniture, and web site development come out in month 1

PRO FORMA CASH-FLOW

MONTH	1	2	3
RECEIPTS			
Commission on Travel Sales		6,000	6,500
Commission on Insurance and Other Services			150
Owner's Cash Invested	10,000		
TOTAL RECEIPTS	10,000	6,000	6,650
PAYMENTS			
Rent and Rates	1,500	1,500	1,500
Heat, Light, and Power			875
Telephone System Leasing	166	166	166
Computer Systems and Software Leasing	416	416	416
Marketing and Promotion	1,041	1,041	1,041
Post and Stationery	270	270	270
Telephone			893
Insurance and Legal	3,500		
Wages (Not Owner's)	3,000	3,000	3,000
Consultancy Services (Database and Web Site)	10,000	10,000	
Memberships and Subscriptions	1,500		
Travel and Subsistence	1,250		
Training and Staff Development		2,000	
Fixtures, Fittings, and Furniture	15,000		2,500
Bank Interest and Charges			1,250
TOTAL PAYMENTS	37,643	18,393	11,911
CASH FLOW SURPLUS/DEFICIT (−)	(27,643)	(12,393)	(5,261)
OPENING BANK BALANCE	0	(27,643)	(40,036)
CLOSING BANK BALANCE	(27,643)	(40,036)	(45,297)

Subscriptions are charged once a year

Utilities are paid quarterly

STATEMENT: YEAR ONE

4	5	6	7	8	9	10	11	12	TOTALS
7,500	8,500	9,500	11,000	13,000	14,500	15,812	17,250	19,800	129,362
250	300	300	350	450	450	600	600	700	4,150
5,000			5,000			5,000			25,000
12,750	8,800	9,800	16,350	13,450	14,950	21,412	17,850	20,500	158,512
1,500	1,500	1,500	1,500	1,500	1,500	1,500	1,500	1,500	18,000
		875			875			875	3,500
166	166	166	166	166	166	166	166	174	2,000
416	416	416	416	416	416	416	416	424	5,000
1,041	1,041	1,041	1,041	1,041	1,041	1,041	1,041	1,049	12,500
270	270	270	270	270	270	270	270	280	3,250
		893			893			896	3,575
									3,500
3,000	3,000	3,000	3,000	3,000	3,000	3,000	3,000	3,000	36,000
	5,000								25,000
									1,500
1,000			2,000						4,250
	2,000			2,000					6,000
									17,500
		1,250			1,250			1,250	5,000
7,393	13,393	9,411	8,393	8,393	9,411	6,393	6,393	9,448	146,575
5,357	(4,593)	389	7,957	5,057	5,539	15,019	11,457	11,052	11,937
(45,297)	(39,940)	(44,533)	(44,144)	(36,187)	(31,130)	(25,591)	(10,572)	885	
(39,940)	(44,533)	(44,144)	(36,187)	(31,130)	(25,591)	(10,572)	885	11,937	

Summarizing Financing Needs

You probably have a very good idea of why you need the funds that you are asking for, but unless the reader of your business plan has plenty of time to spare (which is unlikely) and can be bothered to work it out without further explanation, you must clearly state to what use you will put the funds received.

A statement such as the one shown on the right clearly tells the reader of the plan how the funds will be spent.

The £100,000 required for plant and equipment will be be needed several weeks or months before trading can begin, while the £5,000 for the motor vehicle can, in all probability, be left closer to the time at which you will need it. The working capital requirement of £75,000 is needed in varying amounts over the first six months or so of trading. Your funding request should clearly show this "timetable of anticipated funding". An example of this timetable might be as shown in the table opposite.

FINANCE REQUIRED (£)	
TO PURCHASE:	
MOTOR VEHICLE	5,000
PLANT AND EQUIPMENT	100,000
TO PROVIDE:	
WORKING CAPITAL FOR SIX MONTHS	75,000
TOTAL REQUIREMENT	**180,000**
LESS INVESTMENT MADE (BY YOU)	30,000
NET FUNDING REQUIREMENT	**150,000**

MAKING YOUR REQUIREMENTS CLEAR
The bottom line of this summary clearly states that a net investment of £150,000 is required, and the uses to which this money will be put have been outlined above.

The timetable should be carried on for as long as external funding is required, and shows that:
- ■ **AN EQUITY INVESTMENT** of £100,000 is made three months prior to start-up of business and remains in the business for the medium- to long-term future.
- ■ **A BANK OVERDRAFT** facility of £75,000 is required, which is first used during month 3, reaches a peak of £70,000 during month 5,

---

CASE STUDY: Starting from Desired Income

JANE JENKINS set up her business 18 months after finishing a college degree. At first she was not sure what business to start, but she decided to see if she could turn her love of pottery into a money-making business. She began by visiting a number of potteries. "Their vase shapes were revolting, so I drew my own. I found that all my frustration evaporated just like that, and I knew what I wanted to do."

She persuaded some factories to make vases to her own designs, then spent the next few months driving around the country, staying in cheap hotels *en route*. She equipped herself with sponges and colours so that she could apply her designs to her vases in the factories.

"At first people thought I was mad and were sceptical but helpful." However, she soon won her first order, worth £600, from a fashionable London store, and within two months she decided to meet her potential customers by exhibiting at a trade fair.

Jane decided that unless she could earn at least £40,000 per annum in the second year of her new business, she would not want to start up. Her predicted profit margin was 40 per cent, so this "objective" called for a sales forecast of £100,000. She used her market research and the resultant strategies to satisfy herself (and her backers) that this was a realistic goal.

Date	Requirement per Cash-flow Forecast (£'000)	Share Issue (£'000)	Your Cash Introduced (£'000)	Bank Loan (£'000)	HP Loan (£'000)
Pre-commencement of Trading					
Month 1	100	100	30	–	–
Month 2	5	–	–	–	–
Month 3	70		–	45	5.00
Commencement of Trading					
Month 4	20		–	60	4.85
Month 5	10		–	70	4.70
Month 6	–5		–	65	4.55
Month 7	–20		–	45	4.40
Month 8	–21		–	24	4.25
Month 9	–25		–	–	4.10
Month 10	–20		–	–	3.95
Month 11	–10		–	–	3.80
Month 12	–10		–	–	3.65

Table title: TIMETABLE OF ANTICIPATED FUNDING FOR FIRST YEAR

and is cleared by month 9 (i.e. the sixth month of trading). Note that the full £75,000 facility appears not to be needed, but it is always advisable to obtain more than is required to cover any unforeseen circumstances. It is better to borrow too much than to have to go back and ask for more.

■ **A Hire-purchase Loan** of £5,000 is required in month 3, and is repaid over three years.

Expecting the Unexpected

There is little that disturbs a financier more than a firm that has to go back cap in hand for more finance too soon after raising money, especially if the reason should have been seen and allowed for at the outset. So, in making projections, you have to be ready for likely pitfalls and be prepared for the unexpected events that will knock your cash flow off target. Forecasts and projections rarely go to plan, but the most common pitfalls can be anticipated.

You cannot really protect yourself against freak disasters or unforeseen delays, which hit large and small businesses alike. But some events are more likely than others to hit your cash flow, and it is against these that you can guard by careful planning. Not all of the events listed here may be relevant to your business, but some, if not many, will be.

BASED ON A FLAWED PREMISE

There is no doubt that forecasting sales is difficult. The number of things that can and will go awry are many and varied. In the first place, the entire premise on which the forecast is based may be flawed. Estimating the number of people who may come into a restaurant as "passing trade", the number of people who will order from a catalogue mailing, or the proportion of internet site hits that will turn into paying customers depends on performance ratios. For example, a direct mail shot to a well-targeted list could produce anything from a 0.5 to a 3 per cent response. If you build your sales forecast using the higher figure but actually achieve only the lower figure, then your sales income could be barely a sixth of the figure in your cash-flow projection.

Allow for late payers in your cash-flow projections, to avoid unpleasant surprises

SALES BUILD-UP IS SLOWER THAN EXPECTED

Even if your forecasting premise is right, or nearly so, customers may take longer to make up their minds than you expect. Your forecast may include an assumption that people will order within two weeks of receiving your mail-order catalogue. But until you start trading you will not know how accurate that assumption is likely to be. Even if you have been in business for years, buying patterns may change.

CUSTOMERS TAKE LONGER TO PAY THAN EXPECTED

While you set the terms and conditions under which you plan to do business, customers are a law unto themselves. If they can take extra credit, they will. Unless you are in a cash business, you can expect a proportion of your customers to be late payers. If you have good accounting systems, you will keep this to an acceptable figure, but you will never get every bill paid on time. You need to allow for this lag in your cash-flow projections.

BAD DEBTS

Unfortunately, late payers are not the only problem. Some customers will never pay. Thousands of businesses fail each year and individuals go bankrupt, each leaving behind them a trail of unpaid bills. Some steps can be taken to minimize this risk, and we will discuss those later, but the risk cannot be eliminated altogether. You can try to research the rate of non-payment in your sector and allow for it in your plans. As a general rule, the building and restaurant industries have a relatively high incidence of bad debts, while business services have a lower rate.

REPEAT ORDERS TAKE LONGER TO COME IN THAN EXPECTED

It is often hard to know exactly what a customer's demand for your product or service is. Their initial order from you may last them months, weeks, or just days. For strategic reasons, they may want to divide up their business between a number of suppliers. If, for example, they have three suppliers and they order a month's worth at a time, it may be some time before it is your turn for an order. If your customer sales are sluggish or seasonal, then that time frame could extend further still. So even delighted customers may not come back for more for quite some time.

PRICES TOO LOW

The selling price is an important factor in estimating the amount of cash coming into a business and hence the amount of finance needed to operate that business.

Often the only way a new or small business can win certain customers is by matching a competitor's price. This may not be the price in your list, but it is the one at which you have to sell. Also, the mix of products or services you actually sell may be very different from your projection, and this can affect average prices. For example, a restaurant owner will have to forecast what wines his customers will buy. If the house wine is too good, then more customers might go for that rather than the more expensive and profitable wines on the list.

TOO MUCH STOCK

If your sales projections are too high, you will experience the double whammy of having less cash coming in and more going out than shown in your forecast. That is because in all probability you will have bought in supplies to meet demand. Your suppliers offering discounts for bulk purchases may have exacerbated the situation if you took up their offers.

LATE DELIVERIES

If your suppliers deliver late, you may in turn find you have nothing to sell. Such a delay will cause ill will with your customers, and you may have to wait weeks or months for another opportunity to supply them. This problem can be minimized using on-line order tracking systems, but some late deliveries will still occur. Increasing stocks is one way to insure against deficiencies in the supply chain, but that strategy too has an adverse impact on cash flow.

SUPPLIERS WILL NOT GIVE CREDIT

Few suppliers are keen to give small and particularly new businesses any credit. So, before you build in 30, 60, or even 90 days' credit into your financial projections, you need to confirm that normal terms of trade will apply to what a supplier may view as an abnormal customer.

You need to remember that, while taking extended credit may help your cash flow in the short term, it could sour relationships in the long term. So, in circumstances where a product is in short supply, poor payers will be last on the list to get deliveries, and the problems identified above may be further exacerbated.

MISSED OR WRONG COST

If you are starting up, or expanding into new areas of business, it is possible that certain areas of cost are missed out from your business plan. Business insurance and legal expenses are two often-missed items. Even where a cost is not missed altogether, it may be understated. So, for example, if you are including the cost of taking out a patent in your financing plan, it is safer to base the price on those quoted by the Patent Office, rather than just to assume that it will cost the same as it did a friend of yours a few years ago.

FRAUD AND THEFT

Retailers claim that they could knock 5 per cent off everything they sell if they could only eliminate theft, which is an ever-increasing problem. Even more disturbing is theft within the business, as in the case study below, where the fraudster was the company's accountant.

Anticipating Worst-case Scenarios

E ven events that have not been anticipated can be allowed for when estimating financing needs. An analysis using a cash-flow spreadsheet will allow you to identify worst-case scenarios that could knock you off course. From this, you will end up with a realistic estimate of the financing requirements of the business or project. The chart on the right illustrates the effects of some of the possible ways in which financing projections can go awry.

TESTING TO DESTRUCTION

Even events that have not been anticipated can be allowed for when estimating financing needs. A "what if" analysis using a cash-flow spreadsheet will allow you to identify worst-case scenarios that could knock you off course.

Some examples of incidents that could happen are: the expenses that you considered unlikely to happen actually occur; the sales build-up is slower than forecasted; the total sales in the period are lower than expected; suppliers demand payment on delivery; your credit customers take longer to pay up than expected; and operating costs are higher than anticipated. The chart opposite shows the effects of some of the possible ways in which a business's financing projections could go awry.

In the original forecast, this business looks like it may need only £6,300 of capital. But, once "tested to destruction" by having some realism built into the projections, the forecast shows that the business may actually need £31,800 if it is to survive its first few months. This "what if" forecast is usually repeated across a range of possible scenarios to see which set of circumstances could imperil the business. Working with the financial requirement of £6,300 rather than £31,800 would undoubtedly have caused major, if not terminal, problems for this business had the scenario explored actually come to pass.

CASE STUDY: The Effects of Fraud

JANE EDGE DISCOVERED that her founding partner was defrauding her only when she decided to offer shares as incentives to the company's employees. To get the company valued, she needed the audited accounts, which were not ready. Her accountant partner claimed that the auditors were holding up clearing the accounts on a few technicalities. When Jane contacted them, the auditors said that the company was late in producing the accounts and that they had not even seen them! Eventually it was discovered that the partner had siphoned off a quarter of the business's assets for his own purposes.

Needless to say, the partner was fired and sued successfully, though no money was recovered. Unfortunately, the loss of money meant that the employee share option scheme had to be postponed, causing two key employees to leave and set up in business for themselves. The company never fully recovered from this setback.

Expect no credit

Missed cost item

Slower build up and later payment

	THE "WHAT IF" FORECAST					
	ORIGINAL FORECAST			REVISED FORECAST		
	MONTH 1 (£)	MONTH 2 (£)	MONTH 3 (£)	MONTH 1 (£)	MONTH 2 (£)	MONTH 3 (£)
CASH IN						
Sales		10,000	15,000			10,000
Owner's Capital	4,000			4,000		
TOTAL	4,000	10,000	15,000	4,000		10,000
CASH OUT						
Stock/Raw Materials		5,000	7,500	5,000	7,500	10,000
Advertising and Promotion	200	300	500	200	300	500
Insurance				500		
Heat, Light, and Power			300			300
Telephone			1,000			1,000
Professional Services	500			500		
Motor	200	200	200	200	200	200
Travel and Subsistence	500	500	500	500	500	500
Rent and Rates	1,200	1,200	1,200	1,200	1,200	1,200
Wages	1,100	1,100	1,100	1,100	1,100	1,100
Capital Expenditure	0	8,000	3,000	8,000	3,000	
TOTAL	3,700	16,300	15,300	17,200	13,800	14,800
NET CASH FLOW	300	-6,300	-300	-13,200	-13,800	-4,800
CUMULATIVE NET CASH FLOW	300	-6,000	-6,300	-13,200	-27,000	-31,800

The difference between "Cash in" and "Cash out"

The total cash needed by the business

RAISING the money

There are many sources of funds available to small firms. However, not all are equally appropriate to all firms, nor are they available to every type of business. So the legal structure under which you trade can affect the choice of funding sources open to you. Different sources carry very different obligations, responsibilities, and opportunities for a profitable business. The differences have to be understood to allow an informed choice.

ORGANIZING YOUR BUSINESS

There are different legal frameworks for the ownership of a business – sole proprietorship, general partnership, limited partnership, limited company, co-operative, or franchise chain – and not all sources of finance are open to every type of business. Once you know how much money is needed either to start up or to grow, and what that money is needed for, you will be in a better position to make an informed choice from the options.

Each business structure has a range of advantages and disadvantages and each confers different responsibilities, liabilities, and opportunities for creating personal wealth. In general, the more money that is required and the more risky the venture, the more likely it is that a limited company will be the most suitable structure for your new business. However, most successful businesses are very likely to make changes to their ownership structure as they grow and develop.

Only the issues that relate to financial management are considered here, although other factors are affected by legal structure. For example, some people think that trading as a company is more prestigious than, say, a partnership.

Choose sole proprietorship if you want independence and responsibility for your business,

Operating as Sole Proprietor

The vast majority of new businesses are essentially one-man bands. As such, they are free to choose the simplest legal structure. They are known by terms such as "sole trader" or "sole proprietor". This structure has the merit of being relatively formality-free, and there are few rules about the records you have to keep. Your accounts do not have to be audited, and financial information on your business need not be filed.

As a sole trader there is no legal distinction between you and your business. Your business is one of your assets, in the same way as your house or car is. If your business should fail, your creditors have

---

CASE STUDY: Personal Liability – Debt

JAMES IS THE SOLE PROPRIETOR of a small manufacturing business. When business prospects look good, he orders supplies and uses them up. Unfortunately, there is then a sudden drop in demand for his products, so he cannot sell the items he has produced and the supplies continue to pile up in his warehouse.

When the company that sold James the supplies demands payment, he cannot pay the bill.

As sole proprietor, James is personally liable for this business obligation. This means that the creditor can sue him and go after not only his business assets but his other property as well. This can include his house, his car, and his personal bank account.

ADVANTAGES AND DISADVANTAGES OF BUSINESS TYPES

BUSINESS TYPE	ADVANTAGES	DISADVANTAGES
SOLE PROPRIETORSHIP	■ Simple and inexpensive to create and operate ■ Owner reports profit or loss on his or her personal tax return	■ Owner personally liable for business debts ■ No access to external capital ■ Life of business restricted to life of owner ■ Limited potential for value creation
GENERAL PARTNERSHIP	■ Simple and inexpensive to create and operate ■ Owners (partners) report their share of profit or loss on their personal tax returns ■ Some potential for value creation	■ Owners (partners) personally liable for business debts ■ Life of business restricted to life of first partner to die ■ Access to outside capital restricted to partners
LIMITED PARTNERSHIP	■ Limited partners have limited personal liability for business debts as long as they do not participate in management ■ General partners can raise cash without involving outside investors in management of business ■ Wider access to outside capital ■ Some potential for value creation	■ General partners personally liable for business debts ■ More expensive to create than general partnership ■ Life of business restricted to life of first partner to die
LIMITED COMPANY	■ Owners have limited personal liability for business debts ■ Some benefits (pensions etc.) can be deducted as a business expense ■ Owners can split corporate profit among owners and corporation, paying lower overall tax rate ■ Access to full range of external capital ■ Business can live on after founder's death ■ Potential for value creation	■ More expensive to create and run than partnership or sole proprietorship ■ Owners must meet legal requirements for stock registration, account filing and paperwork ■ Separate taxable entity
CO-OPERATIVE	■ Owners have limited personal liability for business debts ■ Owners report their share of corporate profit or loss on their personal tax returns ■ Owners can use corporate loss to offset income from other sources	■ More expensive to create than a sole proprietorship ■ Owners must meet legal requirements for account filing, registration and paperwork ■ Restricted access to outside capital
FRANCHISE CHAIN	■ Access to a stream of capital and income from new franchisees, to fund expansion	■ Limited potential for value creation

a right not only to the assets of the business but also to your personal assets, subject only to the provisions of local bankruptcy rules. These rules often allow you to keep only a few absolutely basic essentials for yourself and your family. You may, however, be able to avoid the worst consequences of bankruptcy by distancing your assets (see p. 152).

Seek professional advice regarding your legal obligations before setting up as a sole trader

The capital to start and run the business must come from you or from loans. As a sole trader you have no access to equity capital, which has the attraction of being risk-free. In return for these drawbacks you can have the pleasure of being your own boss immediately, subject only to declaring your profits on your tax return and, if necessary, applying for a trade licence.

Going into Partnership

A partnership is effectively a collection of sole traders or proprietors. It is a common structure used by people who started out on their own but who want to expand.

There are very few restrictions on setting up in business with another person (or persons) in partnership, and several definite advantages. By pooling resources, you and your partner(s) may have more capital, you will be bringing (hopefully) several sets of skills to the business, and if you are ill the business can still carry on.

The legal regulations governing partnerships in essence assume that competent business people should know what they are doing. The law merely provides a framework of agreement that applies "in the absence of an agreement to the contrary". It follows from this that many partnerships are entered into without legal formalities and sometimes without the parties themselves being aware that they have entered a partnership. Just giving the impression that you are partners may be enough to create an "implied partnership". In the absence of an agreement to the contrary, these rules apply to partnerships:

- All partners will contribute capital equally.
- All partners will share profits and losses equally.
- No partner will have interest paid on their capital.
- No partner will be paid a salary.
- All partners will have an equal say in the management of the business.

It is unlikely that all these provisions will suit you, so you would be well advised to get a partnership agreement drawn up in writing.

FINANCIAL DRAWBACKS

Partnerships have three serious financial drawbacks that merit particular attention.

CASE STUDY: Personal Liability – Personal Injury

ANN IS THE SOLE PROPRIETOR of a flower shop. One day Andrew, one of Ann's employees, is delivering flowers using a truck owned by the business. Andrew strikes and seriously injures a pedestrian. The injured pedestrian sues Andrew, claiming that he drove carelessly and caused the accident. The lawsuit names Ann as a co-defendant. After a trial, the jury returns a majority verdict against Andrew, and therefore against Ann as owner of the business. Ann is personally liable to the injured pedestrian. This means that the pedestrian can go after all of Ann's assets, business and personal, unless she has sufficient insurance cover to meet the claim.

CASE STUDY: Starting with a Partnership

JANE, STEPHANIE, AND TERRY-ANN, all librariansl, planned to open an electronic information searching business with an emphasis on information of special interest to women. They would hold on to their daytime jobs until they could determine if their new business would be successful enough to support all three.

At a planning meeting to discuss buying personal computers and modems, Jane said that she wanted the business to be run as professionally as possible, which to her meant promptly incorporating. The discussion about equipment was put off, and the three women tried to decide how to organize the legal structure of their business. After several frustrating hours, they agreed to continue the discussion later after doing some research into the organizational options.

Before the next meeting, Jane conferred with a small business adviser, who suggested that the women refocus their energy on the computers and modems and getting their business operating, keeping its legal structure as simple as possible. One good way to do this, she suggested, was to form a partnership, using a written partnership agreement. Each partner would contribute equally to buying equipment and would share the workload fairly. Profits would be divided equally.

Later, she advised, if the business succeeded and grew, it might make sense to incorporate and consider other issues, such as a health plan, pensions, and other benefits. But, for now, real professionalism meant getting on with the job, not consuming time and money forming an unneeded corporate entity.

PART OF A TEAM
From the outset, the three partners met regularly and frequently to discuss any issues affecting their business.

First, if your partner makes a business mistake, perhaps by signing a disastrous contract, without your knowledge or consent, every member of the partnership must shoulder the consequences. Under these circumstances, as a partner your personal assets could be taken to pay the creditors, even though the mistake was no fault of your own.

Second, if your partner goes bankrupt in their personal capacity, for whatever reason, their share of the partnership can be seized by their creditors. As a private individual, you are not liable for your partner's private debts, but having to buy them out of the partnership at short notice could put both you and the business in financial jeopardy.

Third, if your partnership breaks up for any reason, those continuing with it will want to recover control of the business, those who remain partners will want to buy the leaver out cheaply, while they want a higher price. The agreement you have on setting up the business should specify the procedure and how to value the leaver's stake; otherwise, resolving the situation will be costly.

LEAVING SETTLEMENT

The traditional route to value the leaver's stake is to ask an independent accountant. This is rarely cost-effective. The valuation costs money and, worst of all, is not definite and consequently there is room for argument.

Another way of valuing the leaver's stake is to establish a formula, for example an agreed eight times the last audited pre-tax profits. This approach is simple but difficult to get right. A fast-growing business will be undervalued by a formula using historic data, unless the multiple is high; by the same token, a high multiple may overvalue the level of hope or goodwill generated by the business, and thus unreasonably profit the leaver.

Under a third option, one partner offers to buy out the others at a price he specifies. If they do not accept his offer, the continuing partners must buy the leaver out at that price. In theory, such a price should be acceptable to all.

Even death may not release you from partnership obligations, and in some circumstances your estate can remain liable. Unless you take public leave of your partnership by notifying your business contacts, and legally bringing your partnership to an end, you will remain liable – with all that that implies – indefinitely.

LIMITED PARTNERSHIPS

One possibility that can reduce the more painful consequences of entering a partnership is to have your involvement registered as a limited partnership. A "limited" partnership is a very different business to a "general" partnership. It is a legal animal that, in certain ircumstances, combines the best attributes of a partnership and a corporation.

A limited partnership works like this. There must be one or more general partners with the same basic rights and responsibilities (including unlimited liability) as in any general partnership, and one or more limited partners

---

CASE STUDY: Creating a Limited Partnership

JUDITH AND TONY have been partners in a small picture-frame shop for two years. Building on their increasing success, they want to expand into a bigger store in a much better location, where they can stock a large selection of fine art prints as well as frames. To raise the extra money, they create a limited partnership, offering a £30,000 investor a 10 per cent interest in the total net profits of the store for the next three years, as well as the return of the invested capital at the end of that period. They sell four limited partnership interests to this value and so raise £120,000, which they use to put their expansion plans into operation. Three years later they return the invested capital to all four investors.

who are usually passive investors. The big difference between a general partner and a limited partner is that the limited partner is not personally liable for the debts of the partnership. The most a limited partner can lose is the amount that he or she:

▉ paid or agreed to pay into the partnership as a capital contribution; or

▉ received from the partnership after it became insolvent.

To keep this limited liability, a limited partner may not participate in the management of the business, except in very few exceptional circumstances. A limited partner who does get actively involved in the management of the business risks losing immunity from personal liability and so having the same legal exposure as a general partner.

The advantage of a limited partnership as a business structure is that it provides a way for the business owners to raise money (from the limited partners) without either having to take in any new partners – who would be active in the business and therefore enlarge the number of people involved in decision making – or having to form a limited company. In addition, a general partnership that has been operating for years can create a limited partnership in order to finance expansion.

Choose limited partnership status if you want to avoid liability for the debts of your partnership

followed suit, and Britain caught up in 1854. Today most countries have a legal structure that incorporates the concept of limited liability.

As the name suggests, in this form of business your liability is limited to the amount you contribute to the business by way of share capital.

A limited company has a legal identity of its own, separate from the people who own or run it. This means that, in the event of failure, creditors' claims are restricted to the assets of the company. The shareholders of the business are not liable as individuals for the business debts beyond the paid-up value of their shares. This applies even if the shareholders are working directors (unless of course the company has been trading fraudulently). In practice, the ability to limit liability is restricted these days because most lenders often insist on personal guarantees from the directors.

Other advantages include the freedom to raise capital by selling shares. Disadvantages of choosing this structure include the legal requirement for the company's accounts to be audited and filed for public inspection.

A limited company can be formed by two shareholders, one of whom must be a director. A company secretary must also be appointed; he or she can be a shareholder, a director, or an

Forming a Limited Company

The concept of limited liability – in which the shareholders in the business are not liable, in the last resort, for the debts of their business – can be traced back to the Romans. It was rarely used, however, because it was granted as a special favour by those in power only to their friends. Some 2,000 years later the idea was revived when, in 1811, New York State brought in a general limited liability law for manufacturing companies. Most American states

FACT FILE

A limited company is a business that is owned by at least two people who may or may not be involved in the day-to-day running of the business. The owners, known as shareholders, have a limited personal liability for the debts incurred by the company, which is itself a separate legal entity. The day-to-day running of a limited company is entrusted to its directors, who may also be shareholders.

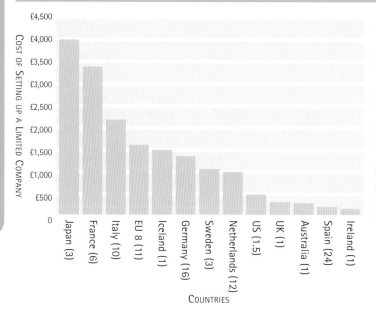

Cost of Setting up a Limited Company

£4,500
£4,000
£3,500
£3,000
£2,500
£2,000
£1,500
£1,000
£500
0

Japan (3)
France (6)
Italy (10)
EU 8 (11)
Iceland (1)
Germany (16)
Sweden (3)
Netherlands (12)
US (1.5)
UK (1)
Australia (1)
Spain (24)
Ireland (1)

Countries

Assessing the Cost

This shows the cost and time to set up a private limited liability company. The time in weeks is shown in brackets. The massive variation in regulations worldwide means that setting up a limited company can cost anything from a few hundred pounds up to £4,000. The time to set up also varies, from one week to four months.

outside person unconnected with the business, such as an accountant or lawyer.

The simplest method of starting a company is to buy one "off the shelf" from a registration agent, who will then adapt it to suit your own purposes. This will involve changing the name, shareholders, and articles of association. It will take a couple of weeks for your agent to register these changes with the relevant authorities. There will, of course, be a fee to pay.

Alternatively, you can form your own limited company from scratch with the name and other details that you have decided upon. You will need to register it with Companies House.

CASE STUDY: Forming a Co-operative

Several years ago Rachel attended a local college to improve her skills in cake baking and decoration. Although her evening classes lasted only a few weeks, she soon found she had an

aptitude for the subject. Her skills were well above average, a fact that was acknowledged by friends and fellow students alike. She often received requests to produce birthday or wedding cakes, usually from friends and relatives.

Although she frequently found herself making one or two cakes a week, Rachel considered this as a hobby rather than a business.

The idea of starting a business came when Rachel met Jane, who had recently moved into the area and was keen to supplement her husband's income. She too was a good pastry cook, and together with her friend Mary was already taking occasional cake orders from friends. The three decided to start up in business together. None of them expected or even wanted to make a fortune from the business. They would be happy to stay small, and their satisfaction would come from being independent and doing something they really enjoyed.

All three had other friends who occasionally helped them out if they got too busy and who at

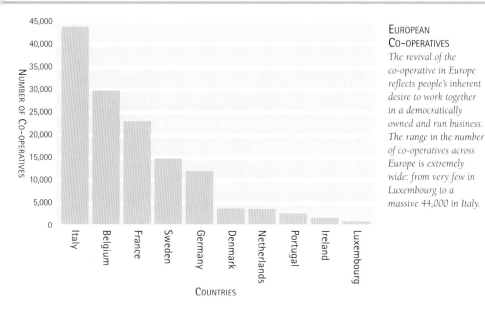

NUMBER OF CO-OPERATIVES

COUNTRIES

Co-operating with Others

A co-operative is an enterprise owned and controlled by the people working in it. Once in danger of becoming extinct, the

some stage might want to get involved on a more permanent basis. After considering other legal forms for their business, they decided that a co-operative was ideally suited to their purpose. Each member has equal control through the principle of "one person one vote", and membership must be open to any friends who satisfy the stipulated qualifications.

Within three months of setting up together as the Commemoration Cakes Co-operative, the business was receiving three or four enquiries a day, with most of those converting into firm orders. Their web site was attracting some large enquiries from the corporate sector, one of which had already resulted in an order for 80 cakes for an annual sales conference.

workers' co-operative is now enjoying something of a revival. There are around 200,000 co-operatives operating in Europe, and many states in the United States have co-op laws to help people who dream of forming a non-hierarchical business of true equals, an organization that is owned and controlled democratically by its members.

A co-operative is certainly not a legal structure designed to give entrepreneurs control of their own destiny and deliver maximum profits, but it does have other advantages, not the least being that you are all equal members with equal rights. If this is to be your chosen legal form, you can pay from £90 to register with the Chief Registrar of Friendly Societies. You must have at least seven members at the outset, although they do not all have to be full-time workers at first.

In the same way as a limited company, a registered co-operative has limited liability for its members (see Forming a Limited Company, p. 45) and must file annual accounts, but there is no charge for this. If a co-operative does not formally register itself, and this is not mandatory, it will be treated in law as a partnership with unlimited liability.

COMMON RULES GOVERNING CO-OPERATIVES

1. Each member of the co-operative has equal control through the principle of "one person one vote".

2. Membership must be open to anyone who satisfies the stipulated qualifications.

3. Profits can be retained in the business or distributed in proportion to members' involvement, for example hours worked.

4. Members must benefit primarily from their participation in the business.

5. Interest on loan or share capital is limited in some specific way, even if the profits are high enough to allow a greater payment.

Taking up Franchising

Another way either to start up or expand a business is via franchising. Buying a franchise falls somewhere in between working for somebody else as an employee and starting a business of your own as an independent entrepreneur. The main appeal is that you can sell a recognized product or service, but you are not in business all by yourself, with no back-up resources to support you. In addition, good franchises offer three financial benefits:

■ **A PROVEN PLAN FOR RUNNING THE BUSINESS**
The franchisor (the company that sells a franchise) will have an operations manual that can serve as a road map to get you

started. This is particularly helpful if you do not have any business experience. They will also have systems in place for book-keeping and financial control.

■ **HELP FROM THE FRANCHISOR** The better franchisors have people available who are experienced in marketing, personnel policies, accounting, and day-to-day operations to whom you can turn if you run into problems. With a well-run franchise organization, being able to call on these resources in effect provides you with expert advisers at an affordable cost.

■ **EXTERNAL FINANCE** A franchise is a proven business model, and so it is much more likely that banks would be prepared to put up funds to finance it.

EXPANDING A BUSINESS

Franchising is also method of expanding a business using other people's energy and capital. Each new franchisee will pay a capital sum to buy into the network, a share of ongoing

SUCCESSFUL FRANCHISE
Fast-food chains lead the way in franchise operations, and McDonald's is probably the most widely recognized of all such establishments.

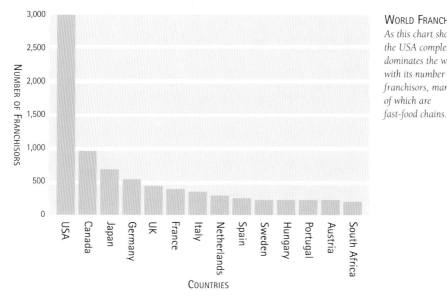

WORLD FRANCHISING
As this chart shows, the USA completely dominates the world with its number of franchisors, many of which are fast-food chains.

NUMBER OF FRANCHISORS

3,000
2,500
2,000
1,500
1,000
500
0

USA, Canada, Japan, Germany, UK, France, Italy, Netherlands, Spain, Sweden, Hungary, Portugal, Austria, South Africa

COUNTRIES

costs, and a fee based on turnover. So, in effect, the franchisors gets a stream of new, risk-free money to finance their expansion. Most of the fast food chains, such as McDonald's and Burger King, are all franchise operations, but the concept extends into many other areas too, including car rental, office and business services, clothing, health care, and property services.

Franchisors should not see selling franchises as a quick route to expanding a business idea. It needs patient and skilled management, plus considerable experience, to iron out all the problems before you can start to persuade franchisees to part with their money. You should run several pilot operations for at least a year to prove the concept and to assess problem areas. A thorough operations manual and audited accounts will be needed. It also helps to get the franchise department of your bank involved so that they can endorse the operation.

CHOOSING A SOURCE OF FINANCE

Different sources of money have different conditions attached. Some financiers require an involvement in the business, others may take take months or even years to arrange the funding. Some are costly but involve the recipient in little risk, while others are inexpensive and quick to arrange, yet impose comprehensive personal liability. The most important thing is to get the right balance between debt and equity.

If you can fund the project from your own resources, there are attractions to doing so. Only in this way do all of the rewards of success flow to you. As soon as you bring in other sources of finance, they slice off some of the reward, be it interest, a share of the value on the sale of the business, or dividends. They may also constrain the business through the use of covenants, borrowing limits, and the placement of financial obligations on the business. By these means they are potentially not only carving off part of your rewards but also capping them by restricting your operation.

Be prepared to invest some of your own assets in your new business

Most firms will, however, require outside finance to realize their full potential, if not at the outset then at some stage in their growth.

Reviewing the Financing Options

There are many sources of funds available to small firms, although not all are equally appropriate to all firms at all times. These different sources of finance carry very different obligations, responsibilities, and opportunities for profitable businesses. The differences have to be understood to allow an informed choice.

Most small firms confine their financial strategy to bank loans, either long term or short term, viewing the other financing methods as either too complex or too risky. In fact, in many respects the reverse is true. Almost every finance source other than banks will, to a greater or lesser extent, share some of the risks of doing business with the recipient of the funds.

The great attraction to borrowing from the bank lies in the speed with which facilities can usually be arranged. Many small businesses operate without a business plan, so most events that require additional funds, such as sudden expansion or contraction, come as a surprise, either welcome or unwelcome. It is to this weakness in financial strategy that banks are ultimately appealing. Since the loan is often taken out in a hurry to solve a crisis, it is hardly surprising that many difficulties arise.

Comparing Lenders and Investors

At one end of the financing spectrum lie shareholders, either individual business angels or corporates, such as venture capital providers. These share all the risks and vagaries of the business alongside the founder and

THE EXPECTATIONS OF LENDERS AND INVESTORS

LENDERS – RISK AVERSE	INVESTORS – RISK TAKERS
Interest paid on outstanding loan	No dividends paid, unless profits warrant it; frequently not even then
Capital repaid either at end of term or sooner if they have concerns	Capital returned with substantial growth by new shareholders
Security given either from assets or from personal guarantees	Security comes from belief in people and their business vision

ASSESSING THE RISK
Lenders, such as banks, are looking for safe ventures that will repay their capital on demand. By contrast, investors, such as venture capitalists or business angels, seek exciting and therefore risky prospects that will generate profits in the long term.

expect an equal share in the rewards if things go well. They are less concerned with a stream of dividends, which is just as well because few small companies ever pay them, and instead hope for a radical increase in the value of their investment. They expect to realize this value from other investors who want to take their places for the next stage in the firm's growth cycle, rather than from any repayment by the founder. Investors in new or small businesses do not look for the security of buildings or other assets to underpin their investment. Instead, they look to the founder vision and the core management team's ability to deliver results.

At the other end of the financing spectrum are the banks, who try very hard to take no risk, but who expect some reward irrespective of performance. They want interest payments on money lent to you, usually from day one. While they too hope that the management of the business is competent, they are more interested in securing a charge against any assets the managers own, either business or private, in the form of a personal guarantee. At the end of the day, and that day can be sooner than the borrower expects, a bank wants all its money back. It would be more prudent to think of banks as people who will help you turn a proportion of an illiquid asset, such as an unmortgaged property or life insurance policy, into a more liquid asset, such as cash, at a heavy cost, rather than as lenders.

KNOWING THE DIFFERENCES

To make the correct decision on which source of financing is appropriate, you need to understand the differences in expectation between lenders, who provide debt, and investors, who provide equity or share capital. This is central to a sound grasp of financial management. In between the extremes of shareholders and the banks lie myriad other financing vehicles, which have a mixture of lending or investing criteria.

A business needs to keep its finances under constant review, choosing the most appropriate mix of funds for the risks it plans to take and the economic climate ahead. The more risky and volatile the road ahead, the more appropriate it will be to take a higher proportion of risk capital. In times of stability and low interest, higher borrowings may be more acceptable to both borrower and lender.

Understanding Bank Loans

Banks are the principal and frequently the only source of finance for nine out of every ten new and small businesses. Bankers are looking for asset security to back their loan and the near certainty of getting their money back. They are not risk takers willing to take a gamble on your success. They will not consider

QUESTIONS TO ASK THE BANK

1 How quickly can you make decisions about lending?

2 Do you visit your clients and get to know their business?

3 What rate of interest will you charge?

4 What factors do you take into consideration in arriving at that rate?

5 What other charges will there be?

6 Under what circumstances would you want personal guarantees?

7 What help and advisory services do you have that could be useful to me?

8 What is unique about your banking services that would make me want to use you rather than any other bank?

9 How long will it be before my present manager moves on?

10 Are there any situations in which you would ask for repayment of a loan to be made early?

risking their money in your business if you are not prepared to risk your own in it. They will also charge an interest rate that reflects both the current market conditions and their view of the risk level of the proposal.

Bankers like to speak of the five Cs of credit analysis, which are the factors they look at when they evaluate a loan request.

■ **CHARACTER** Bankers lend money to borrowers who appear honest and who have a good credit history. Before you apply for a loan, it makes sense to obtain a copy of your credit report and clean up any problems.

■ **CAPACITY** This is a prediction of the borrower's ability to repay the loan. For a new business, bankers look at the business plan. For an existing business, bankers consider the business's financial statements and general industry trends.

■ **COLLATERAL** Bankers generally want a borrower to pledge an asset that can be sold, if necessary, to pay off the loan if the borrower lacks funds.

■ **CAPITAL** Bankers scrutinize a borrower's net worth, which is the amount by which assets exceed debts.

■ **CONDITIONS** Whether bankers give a loan or not can be influenced by the current economic climate as well as by the amount of money required.

When applying to a bank for a loan, be prepared to address the following points.

BANKING CRITERIA

These are a summary of the areas that a bank will consider when deciding to advance funds. They are all negotiable and all under your control. It follows that, the better your case is prepared, the better the terms you can negotiate.

LOAN AMOUNT

The amount of funds a bank will advance are a factor of a number of conditions. First it will look to see how much money the owner and other shareholders have put into the business. Ideally it will want to see those investors put in as much as the bank is being asked for. If the bank's proportion gets too high, there is the danger that the owners end up seeing the business as virtually belonging to the bank. In these circumstances, bankers think the founder may not be motivated to give of their best and indeed may even put their energies elsewhere.

The bank will also look to see what level of profit is being made or is being forecast in the business plan. That is not because it wants to share in the firm's success; it simply wants to satisfy itself that the profit is more than sufficient to cover the interest charges that may be levied on the loan both now and in the future. Lenders, such as banks, are less interested in rapid growth and the consequent capital gain there will be than they are in a

steady stream of earnings – for both the owner and them – almost from the outset.

SECURITY

The bank will also look for security to back the loan. The balance sheet details will show the bank what unencumbered assets there are in the business. Unmortgaged property is a most desirable asset but others include debtors (who surely one day will pay up), stock, and work in progress, which will get sold. Intangible assets, such as patents, copyrights, and other intellectual property, may be the firm's most valuable assets, but they are unlikely to be of much interest to the bank as security for a loan because they are not actually "worth" anything.

CASE STUDY: Intangible Assets

RICHARD HOLDSWORTHY'S company, Holdworth Press, published a regional series of business magazines. He started the business some 15 years earlier, after a successful career as the editor of a national newspaper. He built up the production from just one black and white magazine concerned with local issues to 12 magazines in full colour covering all the important business regions of the country. Each new magazine took four years to build up to a profitable proposition and each required an investment of £250,000. Once established in the marketplace, the magazine could look forward to at least seven years of profitable life ahead.

In his accounts he agreed with his auditors to treat investment in new magazines as an intangible asset. The argument was that, if the property and equipment for printing the magazines could be treated as a capital investment, why not the equally substantial investment in the titles themselves?

In one year Holdsworthy ambitiously planned to launch four new magazines. He took his accounts to the bank, showing an asset base of over £2 million as security for his proposed borrowings. The bank rejected the £1.75 million of intangible assets representing the investment in the magazines, allowing only £250,000 as the secure asset base of the company. The extra funds were eventually provided by a venture capital firm.

If, in the bank's view, the security available in the business is insufficient, it will look outside for personal guarantees. The first people it will turn to are the directors and their families and other business associates. Here the bank will seek to take a charge on any available assets, such as private property, shares in other companies, and so forth.

The main disadvantage of giving personal guarantees if you are running a company is that they negate the key advantage of limited liability, which is to allow entrepreneurs to take risks they might not otherwise take for fear of losing everything. The second disadvantage is that, once given, personal guarantees are extremely difficult to get back. Banks seek to hold on to personal guarantees even when the business assets have grown to be more than sufficient to cover any probable liability. You can see the bank's point of view – it gives cast-iron security – but for a business owner it can be seen as a Sword of Damocles hanging over them and their family for the whole of their working life.

INTEREST CHARGES

Banks usually make two charges (at least) for any funds they advance. First, a set-up charge is made for putting the arrangements in place. Banks often try to make this charge every year, despite the fact that your basic financing arrangements remain unchanged. You should resist this charge where you can. Second, an interest charge, usually on "points above base rate", is made. Anything from 2 to 5 per cent over base is fairly normal for small firms' bank borrowings, although the more risky the business proposition, the higher the rate.

It follows that you should do anything you can to make your proposition seem less risky so that you will be able to negotiate a better rate of interest. A well-prepared business plan usually helps greatly here, as does any evidence

Think carefully before giving a personal guarantee to a bank: it will be very hard to get it back

of how you have honoured financial commitments in the past. Do not assume, however, that the bank you are dealing with will know about or remember your excellent repayment record on other loans such as your mortgage, a hire purchase agreement, or personal overdraft. Tell them.

Types of Bank Funding

Asking a bank for a loan is not as simple as it may sound. There are loans and loans, and one may be far more suitable for your purposes than another. Make sure you know exactly what you want before you approach your bank manager.

OVERDRAFT

The principal form of short-term bank funding is an overdraft, secured by a charge over the assets of the business. Overdrafts were originally designed to cover the timing differences between, say, acquiring raw materials and manufacturing finished goods, which are later sold.

Starting out in a contract cleaning business with a major contract, you need sufficient funds initially to buy the cleaning equipment. This will have been paid for three months into the contract, so there is no point in getting a five-year bank loan to cover this, because within a year you will have cash in the bank and a loan with an early redemption penalty. An overdraft is the most suitable loan here.

If, however, your overdraft does not get out of the red at any stage during the year, then you need to re-examine your financing and consider a fixed-term loan. All too often companies utilize an overdraft rather than a loan to acquire long-term assets, and that overdraft never disappears, eventually constraining the expansion and profitability of the business.

CASE STUDY: The Danger of Relying on an Overdraft

HENRY MERRYWEATHER'S printing company was experiencing some financial difficulties. After 20 years in business, the rules of the game were changing, and changing fast. New technology was the key now, and he had invested £200,000 in the very latest computer hardware and software out of cash flow. The trouble was that the payback from that investment was coming through more slowly than he expected. Teething problems had been expected, but losing his IT manager within weeks of the new equipment arriving was an unexpected and unwelcome setback. To make matters worse, the company was now coming into its traditionally slow period. Every printer was slack now.

At the limit of his £275,000 overdraft facility, Merryweather started holding back payments to suppliers until customers paid up. Eventually this approach became untenable because they ran out of crucial supplies. Something radical had to be done if the company was to weather this storm.

The management produced a plan that would substantially lower the firm's cost base, quickly. It involved redundancies and would, in the short term, require even more money than was now required, but it was the only viable strategy to allow the firm to trade through its present difficulties and secure the bank's position, too.

Merryweather and his team fixed up an appointment with their bank manager. The meeting did not go well. The bank itself was the subject of a takeover bid and was not prepared to extend further borrowing facilities.

Merryweather and his team prepared for a difficult three months until the seasonal upturn came. What they were not prepared for was the bank's new strategy. As soon as customers paid up, the bank immediately cut Merryweather's overdraft facility back by a similar amount. First £25,000, then £50,000, and then another £30,000 was lopped of the overdraft in a matter of days. Within ten days the bank had whittled the overdraft facility down from £250,000 to just £75,000. That remaining sum was covered by personal guarantees, which meant that the bank had effectively eliminated its risk exposure at the expense of ruining the business.

In order to preserve something of the business, Merryweather had to sell out to a competitor. The deal was quickly done on disastrous terms, reducing Merryweather's stake in the business from several million pounds to just £25,000.

BRINGING THE PRESSES TO A HALT
By reducing the printing company's overdraft facility at its most difficult trading time, the bank forced Merryweather to sell out to a competitor on poor terms.

The attraction to overdrafts is that they are very easy to arrange and take little time to set up. That is also their inherent weakness. The key words in the arrangement document are "repayable on demand", which leaves the bank free to make and change the rules as they see fit, with no consideration of your financial position. With other forms of borrowing, as long as you stick to the terms and conditions the loan is yours for the duration. This is not so with overdrafts, as the case above illustrates.

TERM LOANS

If you are starting up a manufacturing business, you will be buying machinery to last probably five years, designing your logo, buying stationery, paying the deposit on leasehold premises, buying a vehicle, and investing funds in winning a long-term contract. The profits on this are expected to flow in over a number of years, so they need to be financed over a similarly long period of time, either through a bank loan or by inviting someone to invest in shares in the company – in other words, a long-term commitment.

Term loans, as these long-term borrowings are generally known, are funds provided by a bank for a number of years. The interest can be either variable, changing with general interest rates, or it can be fixed for a number of years ahead. In some cases, it may be possible to move between having a fixed interest rate and a variable one at certain intervals. It may even be possible to have a moratorium on interest payments for a short period, to give the business some breathing space while it is getting up and running. Provided the conditions of the loan are met in such matters as repayment, interest, and security cover, the money is available for the period of the loan. Its main advantage over an overdraft is that the bank cannot pull the rug from under your feet if their situation (or the local manager) changes.

Consider a term loan rather than an overdraft if you need a loan for more than a year or two

LOAN GUARANTEE SCHEMES

These are operated in the United States, the United Kingdom, and elsewhere. The schemes guarantee loans from banks and other financial institutions for small businesses with viable business proposals that have tried and failed to obtain a conventional loan because of a lack of security. Loans are available for periods between two and ten years on sums between £5,000 and £250,000. The government guarantees 70 to 90 per cent of the loan. In return for this guarantee, the borrower pays a premium of 1 to 2 per cent per year on the outstanding amount of the loan. The commercial aspects of the loan are matters to be agreed between the borrower and the lender.

Different countries have different conditions and these can change from year to year. But the basic concept of governments taking a hand to encourage banks to be a little bolder in their approach to new and small firm lending has been well entrenched for over two decades.

OTHER TYPES OF BANK LENDING

Banks are usually a good starting point for almost any type of debt financing. If you import raw materials, banks can provide you with Letters of Credit. If you have a number of overseas suppliers who prefer settlement in their own currency – for which you will need foreign currency checking facilities or buying forward – banks can make the necessary arrangements. They are also able to provide many of the other cash-flow and asset-backed financing products described below, although they are often not the only or the most appropriate provider.

CREDIT UNIONS

If you do not like the terms on offer from the high-street banks, as the major banks are often known, you could consider forming your own bank. It is not quite as crazy an idea as it sounds. Credit unions formed by groups of small-business people, both in business and aspiring to start up, have been around for

MONEY SAVER

Term loans are the most secure form of bank finance because the funding is guaranteed for a number of years. A cash-flow forecast can predict how much money you will need, when, and for how long. That will allow you to use some overdraft funding and so pay interest only on the money you use.

decades on both sides of the Atlantic. They have been an attractive option for people on low incomes because they provide a cheap and convenient alternative to banks. Some self-employed people, such as taxi drivers, have also found it convenient to form credit unions. They can then apply for loans to meet unexpected capital expenditure for repairs, refurbishments, or technical upgrading.

The popularity of credit unions varies from country to country. In the UK, for example, fewer than one in 300 people belong to one, compared with more than one in three in Canada, Ireland, and Australia. Certainly, few could argue about the attractiveness of an annual interest rate set 3 per cent below that of the high-street lenders, which is what credit unions aim for. Members have to save regularly to qualify for a loan, although there is no minimum deposit and, after ten weeks, members with a good track record can borrow up to five times their savings, though they must continue to save while repaying the loan. There is no set interest rate, but dividends are distributed to members from any surplus, usually at a rate of about 5 per cent a year. This, too, compares favourably with bank interest on deposit accounts.

Borrowing from Family and Friends

Those close to you can often lend you money or invest in your business. This helps you avoid the problem of pleading your case to outsiders and enduring extra paperwork and bureaucratic delays. Help from friends, relatives, and business associates can be especially valuable if you have been through bankruptcy or had other credit problems that would make borrowing from a commercial lender difficult or even impossible.

Many types of businesses, for example organic farms or specialist bookshops, have loyal and devoted followers, people who care as much about the business as the owners do.

DOS AND DON'TS OF RAISING MONEY FROM FAMILY AND FRIENDS

✓ Do agree proper terms.

✓ Do put the agreement in writing and, if it involves a limited partnership, share transaction, or guarantee, have a legal agreement drawn up.

✓ Do make an extra effort to explain the risks of the business and the possible downside implications to their money.

✓ Do make sure when raising money from parents that other siblings are compensated in some way, perhaps via a will.

✓ Do make sure you want to run a family business before raising money from them. It will not be the same as running your own business.

✗ Don't borrow from people on fixed incomes.

✗ Don't borrow from people who cannot afford to lose money.

✗ Don't make the possible rewards sound more attractive than you would to a bank.

✗ Don't offer jobs in your business to anyone providing money unless they are the best person for the job.

✗ Don't change the normal pattern of social contact with family and friends after they have put up the money.

Their decision to lend is driven to some extent by their feelings and is not strictly a business proposition. Their involvement brings a range of extra benefits, costs, and risks that are not a feature of most other types of finance. You must decide if these are acceptable before agreeing to accept the loan.

Some advantages of borrowing money from people you know well are that you may be charged a lower interest rate, may be able to delay paying back money until you are more established, and may be given more flexibility if you get into a jam. But, once the loan terms are agreed to, you have the same legal obligations as you would with, say, a bank or any other source of finance.

In addition, borrowing money from relatives and friends can have a major disadvantage. If your business does poorly and those close to you end up losing the money they lent you or invested in you, that may well damage some good personal relationships. So, in dealing with people close to you, be extra careful not only to establish clearly the terms of the deal and put it in writing but also to make an extra effort to explain the risks and not to accept money from people who cannot afford to lose it. In short, it is your job to make sure that your helpful friend or relative will not suffer a true hardship if you are unable to meet your financial commitments. If your business does run into trouble at some stage, your personal difficulties will only be compounded if you hurt other people too.

Financing Cash Flow by Factoring

Customers often take time to pay their bills. In the meantime, you have to pay the people who work for you and your less patient suppliers. So, the more you grow, the more funds you need. One way of solving this problem is to "factor" your creditworthy customers' bills to a financial institution, receiving some of the funds as your goods leave the door, hence speeding up cash flow and leaving you with more available funds.

HOW FACTORING WORKS

Factoring is generally available only to a business that invoices other business customers, either in their home market or internationally, for its services. It can be made available to new businesses, although it is usually of most value during the early stages of growth. It is an arrangement that allows you to receive up to 80 per cent of the cash due from your customers more quickly than they would normally pay.

CASE STUDY: Financing Growth Using Factoring

GIBBS INTERNATIONAL, a luxury lingerie business founded by Mary Gibbs and her husband, Andrew, grew to having a turnover of £500,000 within three years. Its two-year business plan calls for sales of £5 million. The company already has sales in Europe and the US.

The company's growth has been financed by invoice factoring, which is about as unglamorous as their products are sexy. It does not have the risk associated with venture capital and does not require the sophisticated negotiating skills needed to borrow large amounts of money from a bank. However, invoice factoring, or invoice discounting, where banks lend against the sales and money owed by debtors, has become the company's preferred funding route.

Mary says: "I was reluctant to use invoice finance because I thought people only used it when their business was in trouble." But experience has convinced the Gibbs that invoice finance was right for them. From being strapped for cash, the company now has the money to invest in product development.

The factoring company in effect buys your trade debts and can provide a debtor accounting and administration service. In other words, it takes over the day-to-day work of invoicing and sending out reminders and statements. This can be a particularly helpful service to a small, expanding business. It allows the management to concentrate on developing the business, with the factoring company providing expert guidance on credit control, 100 per cent protection against bad debts, and improved cash flow.

You will, of course, have to pay for the use of the factoring services. Having the cash before your customers pay will cost you a little more than normal overdraft rates. The factoring service will cost between 0.5 and 3.5 per cent of the turnover, depending on the volume of work, the number of debtors, the average invoice amount, and other related factors. You can get up to 80 per cent of the value of your invoice in advance, with the remainder paid when your customer settles up, less the various charges just mentioned.

If you sell direct to the public, sell complex and expensive capital equipment, or expect progress payments on long-term projects, then factoring is not for you. If, however, you are expanding more rapidly than other sources of finance will allow, this may be a useful service, at least while you find your business feet.

TIME SAVER

Cash-flow finance through a factor is available only to businesses selling to other businesses. The sale must leave few areas of potential for disputes, and the customers must themselves be creditworthy. Take out credit references on customers before approaching a factor, because your customers may not meet their credit standards.

Asset-backed Financing

Physical assets, such as cars, vans, computers, office equipment and the like, can usually be financed by leasing them, rather as a house or flat may be rented. Alternatively, they can be bought on hire purchase. Both these methods leave other funds free to cover the less tangible elements in your cash flow.

Leasing is a way of getting the use of vehicles, plant, and equipment without paying the full cost at once. Operating leases are taken out where you will use the equipment for less than its full economic life, for example a car, photocopier, vending machine, or kitchen equipment. The lessor takes the risk of

USING CAPITAL WISELY

Buying a car ties up valuable capital that could be used for something else. Consider either leasing it or buying it on hire purchase for a more efficient way of using your money.

the equipment becoming obsolete, and assumes responsibility for repairs, maintenance, and insurance. You, the lessee, are paying for this service, so it is more expensive than a finance lease, where you lease the equipment for most of its economic life and maintain and insure it yourself. Leases can normally be extended, often for fairly nominal sums, in the latter years.

The obvious attraction of leasing is that no deposit is needed, leaving your working capital free for more profitable use elsewhere. Also, the cost is known from the start, making forward planning more simple. There may even be some tax advantages over other forms of finance. However, there are some possible pitfalls, which only a close examination of the small print on the leasing agreement will reveal.

So, do take professional advice before taking out a lease on any equipment or vehicle.

Hire purchase differs from leasing in that you have the option eventually to become the owner of the asset, after a series of payments.

Unearthing Business Angels

O ne likely first source of equity or risk capital will be a private individual, with their own funds, and perhaps some knowledge of your type of business. In return for a share in the business, such an individual will put in money at their own risk. These angels often have their own agenda and operate through managed networks.

CASE STUDY: Business Angels on the Net

ANGELS.COM IS A NEW NETWORK for business angels operating via the internet. It filters business plans vigorously and then sends the best to prospective angels. This encourages e-mail exchanges between angels and companies seeking finance.

This use of the internet raises some interesting challenges to the traditional angel model. For example, angels are characterized as "invisible" people who value their privacy, yet on the firm's web site there are a series of named would-be investors. Moreover, some of them are not merely wealthy individuals but are presidents, chairmen, and former CEOs. Although they are seeking to invest as individuals, it is clear from their willingness to be named that they are looking to encourage companies that may have need of their extensive industry experience to approach them.

Potential angels must meet strict US Securities and Exchange Commission guidelines as accredited investors, have a net worth of at least $1 million, and show experience in start-ups.

The time and effort needed to close a deal could be considerably reduced by such a service, although the extent to which angels.com can replace face-to-face discussions is debatable. The

business seeks to raise $1 to $4 million – amounts that are too small for traditional venture capital firms.

INVESTING VIA THE INTERNET
Using the internet to send business plans to angels has opened up this formerly "invisible" world of finance. Angels can now receive details of businesses looking for investors and then decide whether they want to back them.

Angel networks operate throughout the world, and in some cases these networks operate on the internet (see case study, below left). In the United Kingdom and the United States there are hundreds of angel networks with tens of thousands of individual business angels who, between them, are prepared to put up several billion pounds each year for investing in new or small businesses.

Business angels are more likely to invest in early-stage investments, where relatively small amounts of money are needed in areas close to their home base. They operate very quickly, often making decisions in a few days based on little hard data after only a few meetings with the person seeking finance. Their confidence in the owner-manager is a vital part of their decision.

Finding Venture Capital

Venture capital providers are investing other people's money, often from pension funds, in businesses. They have a different agenda to that of business angels and are more likely to be interested in investing more money in a business for a larger stake.

HOW VENTURE CAPITAL WORKS

Venture capital is a means of financing the start-up, development, expansion, or purchase of a business. The venture capitalist acquires an agreed proportion of the share capital (equity) of the company in return for providing the requisite funding. Venture capitalist firms often work in conjunction with other providers of finance in putting together a total funding package for a business. Worldwide, several hundred venture capital firms invest in businesses both small and large.

Venture capital is a medium- to long-term investment of not just money but time and effort. The venture capital firm's aim is to enable growth companies to develop into the major businesses of tomorrow.

FACTS YOU NEED TO KNOW ABOUT BUSINESS ANGELS

1 40 per cent suffer partial or complete loss of their investment.

2 50 per cent do not conduct research into prospective investments.

3 55 per cent do not take up personal references, compared with only 6 per cent of venture capital providers in general.

4 90 per cent have worked in a small firm or owned their own business.

5 Business angels meet owners five times on average before investing, compared with venture capital providers who in general require ten meetings.

6 10 per cent of business angel investment is for less than £10,000, and 45 per cent is for over £50,000.

7 Most business angels invest close to home. Up to 50 miles is usual, with 200 miles as the limit.

8 Angels rarely invest abroad. Only 2 per cent have made overseas investments.

9 Angels often flock together. Syndicated deals make up more than a quarter of all deals, where two or more angels band together to invest.

10 Angels are up to five times more likely to invest in start-ups and early-stage investments than venture capital providers in general.

DUE DILIGENCE

Venture capitalists will go through a process known as "due diligence" before investing. This involves a thorough examination of both the business and its owners. Past financial performance, the directors' track records, and the business plan will all come under close scrutiny by accountants and lawyers. Directors are then required to "warrant" that they have provided all the relevant information, under pain of financial penalties. The cost of this

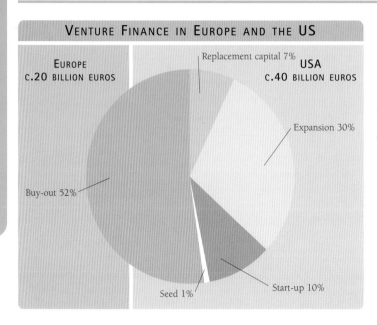

VENTURE FINANCE IN EUROPE AND THE US

EUROPE
C.20 BILLION EUROS

USA
C.40 BILLION EUROS

Replacement capital 7%

Expansion 30%

Buy-out 52%

Seed 1%

Start-up 10%

HOW VENTURE CAPITAL IS USED

Twice as much venture capital is available in the US as in Europe. Just over 10 per cent of that money goes into start-up businesses and seed corn finance for firms before they start to trade. The largest share goes into management buy-outs and those firms seeking to expand.

process must be borne by the firm raising the money, but the consolation factor is that it will be paid out of the money raised.

EXPECTATIONS

In general, venture capitalists would expect their investment to have paid off within seven years, but they are hardened realists. Two in every ten investments they make are total write-offs, and six perform averagely well over the period. So, the one star in every ten investments they make has to cover a lot of also-rans.

Venture capitalists have a target rate of return of 30 per cent plus, to cover this poor success rate.

Raising venture capital is not a cheap option. The arrangement costs will almost always run to six figures. They are not quick to arrange, either. Six months is not unusual, and over a year has been known. Every venture capitalist has a deal done in six weeks in their portfolio, but that truly is the exception.

Venture capital providers will want to exit from their investment at some stage, and their exit route will be planned before they even start

CASE STUDY: Financing Growth Using Venture Capital

DENNIS HUME started his computer business some ten years ago with capital of £40,000. Within five years he had built up a substantial business with a turnover of over £10 million. Hume felt that the business needed more capital to allow it to reach its full potential. It needed development staff, more equipment, and larger premises.

Hume raised £5 million from a venture capital provider to finance growth, and the expansion was so successful that it needed a further £5 million just two years later. By the time the company floated on the stock market a few years later, it was worth over £250 million. Twenty employees were now millionaires and the venture capital firm's stakes were worth £80 million and £45 million respectively.

investing in a business. Their preferred route is via a public offering (see below), but a trade sale is more usual. Either way, they are not in it for the long haul.

Going for an Initial Public Offering (IPO)

There are two possible types of stock markets on which to gain a public listing. A listing on the London Stock Exchange, the New York Stock Exchange, or any other major country's exchange calls for a track record of making substantial profits with decent seven-figure sums being made in the year in which you plan to float, as this process is known. A full listing also calls for a large proportion of the company's shares to be put up for sale at the outset.

THE FLOTATION OPTIONS

The US stock markets look an attractive proposition because they value companies at a much higher rate than their European counterparts, but the flotation costs with the NY Stock Exchange and NASDAQ are very high.

In addition, you would be expected to have 100 shareholders now and be able to prove that a further 100 will come on board as a result of the listing. Having such a large number of shareholders is rarely an appealing idea to entrepreneurs, who expect to see their share price rise in later years and so are loath to sell off so much of the business at what they believe to be a bargain-basement price. There is also the danger of a takeover in the inherent loss of power when so many of the shares are in so many other people's hands.

CHOOSING WHERE TO FLOAT

If an IPO still appeals, however, the US market may be the best place to float. The value placed on new companies on those stock markets is between three and five times that of UK and European markets (see the chart below).

Junior markets, such as London's Alternative Investment Market (AIM) or the Nouveau Marché in Paris, are a much more attractive proposition for business entrepreneurs seeking equity capital. Formed towards the end of the 1990s specifically to provide risk capital for

WHERE TO FLOAT...AND WHY IT MATTERS

MARKET	NUMBER OF STOCKS	FLOTATION COST	ENTRY REQUIREMENTS	MINIMUM MARKET CAPITALIZATION	COMPARABLE PRICE EARNINGS RATIOS (P/Es)
ALTERNATIVE INVESTMANT MARKET	350	£0.5m	Low	None	1
LONDON STOCK EXCHANGE	2,500	£1m+	High	£1m+	1
TECHMARK	200	£0.75m+	High	£50m+	x 3
NEW YORK STOCK EXCHANGE	2,600	£7m	Very high	£12m+	x 2
NASDAQ	5,500	£6m	Very high	£10m+	x 5

new rather than established ventures, these markets have an altogether more relaxed atmosphere than the major stock markets.

The AIM is particularly attractive to any dynamic company of any size, age, or business sector that has rapid growth in mind. The AIM market is the largest junior market in Europe. Over 300 firms are listed and some £2 billion of new equity capital has been raised. The smallest firm on the AIM entered at under £1 million capitalization, and the largest at over £330 million. The formalities are minimal, but the costs of entry are high, and you must have a nominated adviser, such as a major accountancy firm, stockbroker, or banker.

Choose to go public in order to put a stamp of respectability on you and your company

THE BENEFITS OF FLOATING

Going public will enhance the status and credibility of your business and it will enable you to borrow more against the security provided by your new shareholders, should you so wish. Your shares will also provide an attractive way to retain and motivate key staff. If staff are given, or rather are allowed to earn, share options at discounted prices, they too can participate in the capital gains you are making, which gives them an added incentive to make the business a success.

With a public share listing, you can now join in the takeover and asset-stripping game. When your share price is high and things are going well, you can look out for weaker firms to gobble up. All you have to do is offer them more of your shares in return for theirs. You do not even have to find real money.

INTERNET-BASED DIRECT PUBLIC OFFERINGS

(DPOs) are a relatively new US phenomenon that has the potential to change the face of financing for small firms. These involve small companies offering their stock direct to would-be investors over the internet. There are two ways of doing this: one is to use a service; the other is for firms to use their own web sites to go direct to the public. There are already some internet-based listing services for DPOs in the US.

■ **THE ACCESS TO CAPITAL ELECTRONIC NETWORK (ACE-NET)** This DPO was set up in 1997 by the federal Small Business Administration as a public–private

FLOATING AT FRANKFURT
Choosing to float your business on a major stock market brings financial risks and benefits. With so many new shareholders, your authority as owner does become less certain, but you are now in a position to buy up other companies and so expand your profit base.

partnership to lower the legal barriers for small businesses needing financing of up to $5 million. The filing form satisfies federal and many states' securities regulations, with 37 states recognizing it, and it is relatively cheap, at only $450 for an annual listing. The offering document can be completed on-line and can be changed in real time, allowing the entrepreneur the flexibility to modify the offer. Only accredited investors (with over $1 million to spend) are able to invest in this DPO.

▪ **DIRECT STOCK MARKET** Direct Stock Market is a similar, private service that was set up in 1993. A listing on this market costs between $2,000 and $4,000 for a 90-day listing. Firms have to file their own paperwork off-line with the states in which they wish their listing to be registered (unlike the ACE-NET service). It is clear, therefore, that potential investors from Europe cannot participate in companies listed under such schemes. It is also almost certain that regulations mean that these internet services cannot sell securities in non-US firms. However, this does not prevent European entrepreneurs from creating a US company to exploit the fund-raising potential of such services.

▪ **GOING DIRECT** US firms may also decide to go direct and battle their way through various state legislation hoops. The positive side for firms is that this method overcomes barriers of geography and information, and that small investors are unlikely to carry out due diligence or download prospectuses. DPOs allow small investors access to genuine possibilities without paying fees to either a matchmaking service or venture capital firm, and allow much smaller investments (from $500 upwards).

The downside of internet DPOs is that they are time-consuming and high-risk for the business angel (or would-be angel), and it is difficult to distinguish between genuine companies and fraudsters. For the listed business, there are a raft of different state legislations in operation to

TIME SAVER

Consider only grants, awards, or competitions that are of direct relevance to your business goals. The effort involved in being successful can be more costly than the "prize" itself, and the odds of winning are low. If you were going to carry out a particular task, put yourself forward.

protect investors from scams, which can seriously disrupt the offer process. In the US, 83 people have been charged with internet securities fraud, 26 of which concerned entirely fictional deals.

What the difficulties in establishing this sort of service in the US have amply demonstrated is the need for regulation at a federal level rather than at state level, if the service is to be successful. This suggests that, were such a service to be established in the future in Europe for potential European investors, it would be appropriate to regulate it at the European level rather than country level, in order to offer similar sums of money and geographic spread to the US version.

Grants, Awards, and Competitions

Unlike debt, which has to be repaid, or equity, which has to earn a return for the investors, grants and awards are not refundable. So, although they are often hard to get, they can be particularly valuable. Almost every country has incentives to encourage entrepreneurs to invest in particular locations or industries.

GREEN CARDS

The US has an allowance of Green Cards (work and residence permits) for up to several hundred immigrants each year. Each immigrant has to be prepared to put up sufficient funds to start up in a substantial business in the country.

SMART

In the UK, if you are involved in the development of a new technology, then you may be eligible for a Small Firms Merit Award for Research and Technology (SMART). This is open to individuals or businesses employing fewer than 50 people. The grant is in two stages and can be for amounts as high as £100,000 in total. You may also get help with the costs of training staff, gaining quality recognition, or carrying out market research to identify export opportunities.

AUSTRALIAN AWARDS

The Australian Federal Government offers a number of different forms of funding, mainly for small research and development (R&D) ventures. While the names of the different funding programmes have varied with successive governments, the essential nature of what is offered to small businesses in the R&D field generally includes grants, tax concessions, concessional loans, and direct investment.

The latest Australian government committed A$500 million over four years and offers assistance with each of the four types of funding.

BUSINESS COMPETITIONS AND AWARDS

If you enjoy publicity and like a challenge, then you could look out for a business competition to enter. Like government grants, business competitions are ubiquitous and, like national lotteries, they are something of a hit-or-miss affair. But one thing is certain: if you do not enter, you cannot win.

There are more than 100 annual awards in the UK alone aimed at new or small businesses. For the most part these are sponsored by banks, the major accountancy bodies, chambers of commerce, and local or national newspapers, business magazines, and the trade press. Keep a look out in newspapers as well as trade publications for notices advising applicants how to apply.

Government departments may also have their own competitions as a means of promoting their initiatives for exporting, innovation, job creation, and so forth.

The nature and the amount of the awards change from year to year, as do the sponsors. But looking out in the national and local press, or contacting one of the organizations

---

CASE STUDY: Making Initial Exporting Arrangements

BRIAN WILSON commenced trading from a 1,200-square-foot converted baker's shop with only three staff. The objective was to produce ready-grated cheese for the retail and catering market. The initial sales target was three tonnes per week. The business was one of the first in the UK to grate cheese on a commercial scale.

Turnover in the first year was £200,000, with supply to the growing pizza industry accounting for 80 per cent of the sales. Three years after its start-up, with sales continuing to climb steadily, Wilson took the important step of moving the business to its second site, which provided 15,000 square feet of production, warehousing, and office space.

Within ten years the turnover had grown to £5 million. The business had again run out of space, so they followed a strategy of zero growth in turnover while building up profit margins.

Throughout the business's history, Wilson had put considerable effort into securing grants and awards. They picked up six major awards, including the region's coveted Business Excellence Award two years running, as well as being nominated Best Business of the Year. This generated a good deal of favourable publicity, which had a positive effect on staff, customers, and the firm's bank. They also picked up some £50,000 in grant money.

Following the move to still larger premises, the business doubled turnover to £15 million, and when Wilson (aged 46) sold the business it was valued at £12.5 million.

mentioned above, should put you in touch with a competition organizer quickly, as will an internet search.

Money awards constitute 40 per cent of the main competition prizes. For the most part, these cash sums are less than £5,000. However, a few do exceed £10,000 and one UK award is for £50,000. Other awards are for equally valuable goods and services, such as consultancy or accountancy advice, training, and computer hardware and software.

Keeping Your Options Open

Choosing which external source of finance to use is to some extent a matter of personal preference. One of your tasks in managing your firm's financial affairs is to keep good lines of communication open with as many of the sources outlined above as possible. The other task is to consider which is the most appropriate source for your particular requirements at any one time. The main issues you need to consider here are:
■ cost of setting up
■ ownership and control
■ length of time to arrange
■ management time involved
■ flexibility
■ additional expertise
■ security
■ personal liability

Not all of these issues will concern you at any one time. Your decisions will depend on your age, the financial state of your company, and your expectations for the future.

For example, if you are 60, keen to retire to Spain, your company is making superb profits, and you have a strong and experienced management team in place, management time and ownership will not feature high (if at all) among the issues that concern you.

Alternatively, if you are just setting out and are confident that your great new idea will be a

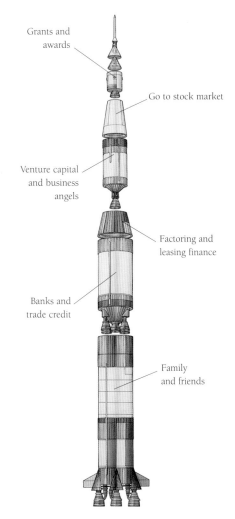

Grants and awards

Go to stock market

Venture capital and business angels

Factoring and leasing finance

Banks and trade credit

Family and friends

LAUNCHING A NEW BUSINESS
Using the analogy of a rocket blasting off, you can see the stages of "fuel" that a new business is likely to take on board as it struggles to get into orbit. Orbit is the point at which the firm has realized its founder's ambitions.

world-beater, then the prospect of selling 51 per cent of the shares to a business angel who offers you the money may not be as appealing as buckling down to write a business plan to raise some bank finance, thereby keeping control of the business in your own hands.

CONSIDERING THE COSTS

Clearly, if a large proportion of the funds you need to expand your business is going to be consumed in actually raising the external finance itself, then your set-up costs for this expansion are going to be very high indeed.

Raising new share capital, especially if the amounts are relatively small (under £500,000), is generally quite expensive. You will have to pay your lawyers and accountants, and those of your capital provider, to prepare the agreements and to conduct the due diligence examination (the business appraisal). It would not be unusual to find that between 10 and 15 per cent of the first £500,000 that you raise will be used up in set-up costs.

If you want sole charge of your business, do not sell shares in it in order to raise external finance

An overdraft or factoring agreement would be relatively cheap to set up, costing usually a couple of per cent or so. Long-term loans, leasing, and hire-purchase agreements could involve some legal costs.

OWNERSHIP AND CONTROL

If you do not want to share the ownership of your business with outsiders, then clearly raising new share capital is not a good idea. Even if you do recognize that owning 100 per cent of a small venture is not as attractive as owning 40 per cent of a business ten times as large, it may not be the right moment to sell off. This is particularly so if, in common with many business founders, long-term capital gain is one of your principal goals. If you can hold

---

CASE STUDY: Keeping in Touch with Financiers

BOLSOVER, A £2-MILLION TURNOVER BUSINESS providing sales and marketing services to the chemical industry, had grown for some time without large amounts of outside money. However, the company's founder, Ian Benton, believed that the next stage of growth would need substantial funds, as strategies shifted from services to products. To this end, he regularly invited venture capitalists to sit in on board meetings or to attend training sessions with his top management team. This, he reckoned, would ensure he got off to a flying start with the money men when his plans were formalized. He also sent copies of business plans to his bank manager even when no changes were envisaged in financing arrangements. This kept the bank up-to-date on what Bolsover was doing and showed that strategy was planned rather than just a series of happy incidents.

Eventually, Ian saw a greater opportunity to turn his business into the only global player in his market. One of the financiers that Ian had been in close contact with for several years was keen to be involved, putting up the £2 million

required in a matter of a few weeks. Ian built his business up and sold it for £50 million eight years after raising the venture capital.

INVOLVING INVESTORS
Keeping prospective investors informed of your business's progress and plans for development can give you a head start when the time comes to ask for finance.

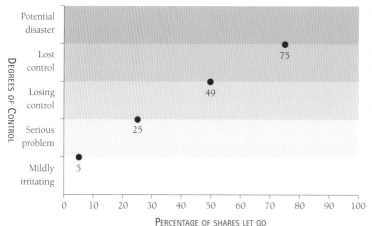

DEGREES OF CONTROL

Selling shares in your business inevitably results in a loss of control on your part. Once over the 75 per cent level, you could find yourself voted out of your own business.

on to your shares until profits are reasonably high, you will realize more gain for every share sold than if you sell out in the early years or while profits are low.

Some capital providers, such as venture capitalists and city institutions, take what is called a hands-on approach. This involves putting a non-executive director on to your board who will have a view on how you should run the business. Generally speaking, though, providers of long-term loans will leave you alone, so long as you service the interest and repay the capital as agreed, in much the same way as your building society does if you pay the mortgage on time.

LOSING CONTROL BY DEGREE

Parting with shares inevitably involves some loss of control. Letting, say, 5 per cent go may be just a mild irritation from time to time. However, once 25 per cent has gone, outsiders could have a fair amount of say in how things are run. Nevertheless, while you have over 51 per cent you are still in control, if only just. Once past the 51 per cent level, things could get a little dangerous. Theoretically, you could be outvoted at any stage.

Things will start to get dangerous for you once you have less than 25 per cent of the business, because then relatively small groups

of shareholders could find it easy to call an Extraordinary General Meeting and, if they so wished, put it to a vote to remove you from the board. You may then have little say in the running of your own business.

MOVING QUICKLY

Overdrafts can be arranged in just days, whereas raising venture capital can take months. It follows that very different amounts of scarce management time will be used, depending on the financing route taken. So, if speed matters, your funding options may be limited.

Venture capital providers have been known to string out negotiations with a finance-seeking business for long enough to see if the forecasts made in the business plan come to pass. After all, venture capital is there to help businesses grow faster, not just to keep them afloat.

TIME SAVER

While some sources of finance are less difficult to obtain than others, all will involve you in some cost and effort. Think your requirements through carefully before approaching finance providers, so you spend time only on sources that you are likely to use.

At the top of the timescale is any form of stock market flotation. Not only can this take a year or so to arrange, but you then have to take your place in the queue of other firms wanting to float. As if that were not enough, the whole thing may have to be called off or postponed if market conditions change suddenly. This change in the market is particularly prevalent in internet flotations, where the market is inclined to great volatility.

MANAGEMENT TIME

Any source of finance that takes a considerable amount of time to arrange can be a problem for a business owner or manager already fully stretched. As we have seen, injecting new equity capital can take anything from six to 15 months, with the directors being required to prepare several versions of the business plan and make dozens of presentations to potential backers. Many companies experience a profit dip in the months following a share issue. This is brought about largely because management energy was drawn away from the day-to-day running of the business.

STAYING FLEXIBLE

As your plans change, the amount of money you actually need may alter during financing negotiations. Some sources of funds, such as leasing, hire-purchase agreements, and long-term loans, dictate the amount that has to be

Assess all the funding options, and their terms and conditions, before deciding which to choose

agreed at the outset. For new share capital there is some fluidity during negotiations, and for overdrafts it is possible to draw down only what is needed at any one time, with the upper limit negotiated. This usually happens each year.

Once you have investigated and used a source of funds, you may want to be able to use that source again as your plans unfold. This will not always be possible, however. Share capital, loans, and hire-purchase/leasing agreements are for a specific sum, and it can be difficult and expensive going back to the same source for more. Venture capitalists may also not be willing to offer more finance. They may already have a full weighting of investments in your business sector and so may not be anxious to invest more, however successful your firm. In this case, further expansion might mean starting all over again with another venture capital firm, which would involve extra and highly unwelcome costs in time and money.

It may pay to make sure that at least some of your financing comes from a source such as factoring (see pp. 58–9). This method, in contrast to the other methods outlined above, gives total flexibility to change the amount of money drawn down, so that you can mirror the amount needed at any one time – both upwards and downwards.

POTENTIAL TO ADD VALUE

With some sources of finance you can get useful expertise as well as money. For example, with factoring you could get expertise in managing your home and overseas credit, which could result in better credit control, fewer bad debts, and less capital tied up in debtors. You will save time, and therefore money, by not having to deal with these aspects of credit control yourself.

With new share capital you may get a non-executive director placed on your board who has industry-relevant experience. While the

CLOSING THE DEAL
The final handshake marks the end of often long negotiations to receive the finance you want at the terms you consider reasonable. Your expansion can now begin.

director's principal task is to ensure that the capital provides interest, you will also get the benefit of his knowledge and expertise.

SECURITY AND CERTAINTY

For most sources of money, once you have agreed terms and you comply with them the future is reasonably predictable – in so far as that money is concerned. The exception to this rule is an overdraft. These are technically, and often actually, repayable on demand, and they are sometimes called in just at the precise moment when you need them most, with potentially disastrous consequences (see p. 54).

PERSONAL LIABILITY

As a general rule, most providers of long-term loans and overdraft facilities will look to the directors to provide additional security if the

business assets are in any way inadequate. This may be in the form of personal guarantees, such as pledging specific assets like your house. Only when you raise new share capital do you escape increasing your personal liability, although you may be asked to provide warranties to assure new investors that everything in the company's past history has been declared.

Hiding information can have costly results, as the following example demonstrates. One business founder was pursued for two years after the cheque for the sale of his business to another company had been banked. The reason was that he had failed to reveal that a wrongful dismissal case was working its way through the courts. The case was lost and the new owners were presented with a £20,000 bill, which they in turn claimed from the business founder under the directors' warranty.

TRACKING
the money

Every business needs reliable financial information both for decision making and accountability. The starting point for gathering such information is having a sound system for keeping the books. After the basic accounting transactions have been recorded, the profit and loss account and balance sheet have to be prepared. You will need to understand how these accounts are constructed and what they tell you about your business's performance.

KEEPING THE BOOKS

Every business needs reliable financial information for both decision making and accountability. Reliable information does not necessarily call for a complex bookkeeping system: simple is often best. If and when the business grows, more sophisticated information will be required. That is when using a computer and some of the relevant software packages may be the best way forward. Even with a computer, errors will occur, however, and a process for detecting and correcting them will have to be evolved.

To survive and prosper in business, you need to know how much cash you have and what your profit or loss on sales is. These facts are needed on at least a monthly, weekly, or occasionally even a daily basis, in order for your business simply to survive, let alone grow. Without these facts, your apparently thriving business could, in fact, be making a loss rather than a profit, and you will certainly never be in complete control of your business when you do not know exactly what is going on financially.

RECORDING FINANCIAL INFORMATION

While bad luck plays a part in some business failures, a lack of reliable financial information plays a part in most. However, all the information needed to manage well is close at hand. Between them, the bills to be paid, invoices raised, petty cash slips, and bank statements are enough to give a true picture of performance. All that needs to be done is for that information to be recorded and organized so that the financial picture becomes clear. The way in which financial information is recorded is known as bookkeeping.

WHO WILL READ THE BOOKS?

It is not only the owner who needs these financial facts. Bankers, shareholders, and tax inspectors will be unsympathetic audiences to anyone without well-documented facts to back them up. If, for example, a tax authority presents a business with a tax demand, the onus then lies with the businessperson, using their records, either to agree or to dispute the

CASE STUDY: The Dangers of Not Keeping Accounts

STARTING UP THEIR BUSINESS consumed all the cash Eleanor and her partner Chris had. So, to save money, Eleanor planned to do their accounts. Unfortunately, they were so successful that she never had time to do the books. They sent out invoices, and when the bank complained that they had exceeded their overdraft limit they would call in a few favours and get some customers to pay up. She paid the bills when she had the money, or if they needed more supplies from someone they owed money to.

They thought that, as they were so busy, they must be making money. At the end of the year, Eleanor realized that she would never get the accounts done, so she took her shoe boxes full of bills to an accountant. As well as presenting them with a four-figure bill for sorting out the mess, the accountant revealed that they had lost money, not made it. To make matters worse, they had passed the threshold for VAT registration and failed to register, so were now in trouble with the VAT authority. With a good accounting system they would have seen where they were going wrong within three months.

sum claimed. If you are unable to explain a bank deposit adequately, the tax authority may treat it as taxable income.

Similarly, a bank manager faced with a request for an increased overdraft facility to help a small business grow needs financial facts to work with. Without them, the bank will generally have to say no to the request, because they have a responsibility to invest other people's money wisely.

Single-entry Bookkeeping

No matter how small your business is or how few the number of transactions that are made, having some note of financial events is better than having none at all. Keeping even the simplest of records, perhaps just as little as writing down the source of the deposit on the slip or in your cheque book, and recording the event in a book or ledger, will make your relations with tax inspectors and bankers go much more smoothly.

Unfortunately, many small businesses let their financial affairs take a back seat. It is easy to see why this can happen. The excitement or pressure of selling and fulfilling orders is more attractive and interesting than doing the books, so any bookkeeping tends to be left until after normal business hours.

If you are doing your books by hand and do not have a lot of transactions, the single-entry method is the easiest acceptable way to choose. Single entry means that you write down each transaction in your records once, preferably on a ledger sheet. This written record will be known as your cash book.

You record the flow of income and expenses through your business by making a running total of money taken in (gross receipts) and money paid out (payments or, as they are sometimes called, disbursements). Receipts and payments should be kept and summarized daily, weekly, or monthly, as the business needs

REASONS FOR KEEPING PROPER RECORDS

1. To know the cash position of your business precisely and accurately.

2. To discover how profitable your business is in reality.

3. To know which of your activities are profitable and which are not.

4. To ensure a timely flow of information for decision making.

5. To give bankers and other sources of finance confidence that your business is being well managed.

6. To allow you accurately to calculate and agree your tax liability.

7. To help you prepare financial forecasts and projections.

8. To make sure you both collect and pay money due correctly.

9. To keep accountancy and audit costs to a minimum.

require. At the end of the year, the 12 monthly summaries are totalled up. You are now ready to deal with your tax form.

For a more detailed account, you need to keep an analyzed cash book, where you break down the receipts and payments. Details and examples of both cash books are given overleaf.

KEEPING MORE DETAILED RECORDS

If you are taking or giving credit, then you will need to keep some more information as well as the cash book, whether analyzed or not.

You will need to keep copies of paid and unpaid sales invoices, paid and unpaid purchases, as well as your bank statements. The bank statements should then be reconciled to your cash book to tie everything together. For example, the bank statement for the simple cash book example (overleaf) should show £808.14 in the account at the end of June.

KEEPING A CASH BOOK

Shown below is an example of a simple cash book. This written record system uses the single-entry bookkeeping method.

■ You can see at a glance the receipts and payments both in total and by main category. This breakdown lets you see, for example, how much is being spent on each major area of your business, and who your most important customers are.

■ In the left-hand four columns, the month's receipts are entered as they occur, together with some basic details and the amount of the sales. At the head of the first column is

A SIMPLE CASH-BOOK SYSTEM							
RECEIPTS				PAYMENTS			
DATE	NAME	DETAILS	AMOUNT (£)	DATE	NAME	DETAILS	AMOUNT (£)
1 JUNE	Balance	Brought forward	450.55	4 JUNE	Gibbs	Stock purchase	310.00
4 JUNE	Anderson	Sales	175.00	8 JUNE	Gibbs	Stock purchase	130.00
6 JUNE	Brown	Sales	45.00	12 JUNE	ABC Telecoms	Telephone charges	52.23
14 JUNE	Smith & Co	Refund on returned stock	137.34	18 JUNE	Colt Rentals	Vehicle hire	87.26
17 JUNE	Jenkins	Sales	190.25	22 JUNE	W Mobiles	Mobile phone	53.24
20 JUNE	Hollis	Sales	425.12	27 JUNE	Gibbs	Stock purchase	36.28
23 JUNE	Jenkins	Sales	56.89				
						Total payments	672.01
				30 JUNE	Balance	Carried down	808.14
		Total receipts	1,480.15				1,480.15
1 JULY	Balance	Brought down	808.14				

The amount of cash now in the business. This will be brought down to the next month

The difference between payments and receipts is carried down to the receipts side of the book

the amount of cash brought forward from the preceding month.
■ On the right, expenses are listed in the same way. The total receipts for the month are £1,480.15 and for expenses £672.01. The difference is the amount of cash now in the business. The business has brought in more cash than it has spent, and so the figure of £808.14 is higher than the amount that was brought forward at the beginning of the month (£450.55).
■ This figure of £808.14 is the amount to be brought forward to the next month. The total of the month's payments and the amount carried down equals the sum of the receipts.

ANALYZING YOUR CASH BOOK

Shown below is an example of the payments side of an analyzed cash book. (The receipts side is similar, but with different categories.)
■ Using the analysis side of the entry, you can now see at a glance how the payments break down: how much has been spent on stock, vehicles, telephone expenses, and any other expenses in any one month. The monthly totals for each category can then be totalled for the year. These are useful pieces of management information, because they tell you exactly what your money is being spent on. In addition, they are essential facts for the completion of your tax return.

AN ANALYZED CASH-BOOK SYSTEM

PAYMENTS				ANALYSIS			
DATE	NAME	DETAILS	AMOUNT (£)	STOCKS	VEHICLES	TELEPHONE	OTHER
4 JUNE	Gibbs	Stock purchase	310.00	310.00			
8 JUNE	Gibbs	Stock purchase	130.00	130.00			
12 JUNE	ABC Telecoms	Telephone charges	55.23			55.23	
18 JUNE	Colt Rentals	Vehicle hire	87.26		87.26		
22 JUNE	W Mobiles	Mobile phone	53.24			53.24	
27 JUNE	Gibbs	Stock purchase	36.28	36.28			
TOTALS			672.01	476.28	87.26		108.47

Totalling down the amount column and across the analysis columns gives the same figure

Land line and mobile phone charges are both listed in the "telephone" column

Double-entry Bookkeeping

I f you operate a partnership, trade as a company, or plan to get big, then you will need a double-entry bookkeeping system. This system requires two entries for each transaction, which provides built-in checks and balances to ensure accuracy. Each transaction requires an entry as a debit and as a credit. This may sound a little complicated, but once you get started it will become second nature. The example from a double-entry ledger opposite will give you an idea of what is involved.

A double-entry system is more complicated and time-consuming if done by hand, as everything has to be recorded twice. Also, if it is done manually, this method requires a formal set of books, namely journals and ledgers. All

KEEPING GOOD RECORDS
A successful business is dependent upon a constant flow of money coming in from customers, which can then be used to pay suppliers. Keeping good records of which payments are due and which have been paid, which bills have been settled and which are pending, means that at any given time you can assess the financial state of your business.

transactions are first entered into a journal and then posted (written) on a ledger sheet; that is, the same amount is written down in two different places. Typical ledger accounts are titled income, expenses, assets, and liabilities (debts).

The types of records to be kept are:
■ day books
■ cash books
■ purchase ledger
■ sales ledger
■ capital or asset ledger
■ nominal or private ledger

DAY BOOKS
Day books, sometimes called journals or books of original entry, are where every transaction is initially recorded in date order. Each day book is used to cater for one kind of transaction, so if there are enough transactions of a particular kind, you open a day book for it. For example, there are always enough cash transactions to warrant a cash day book. If a firm sells on credit, then there will be a sales day book.

CASH BOOKS
Many small businesses trade in both notes and coins and cheques. For bookkeeping purposes these are all called cash, although initially a

A SIMPLE SYSTEM OF BUSINESS RECORDS

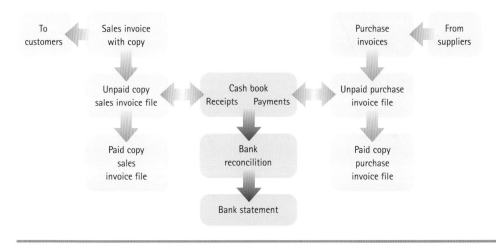

USING DOUBLE-ENTRY LEDGERS

Shown here is an example of a double-entry ledger. The debits in a double-entry ledger must always equal the credits. If they do not, you know there is an error somewhere.

■ In a double-entry system, a payment of rent would result in two separate journal entries: a debit for an expense of £250 and a corresponding credit of £250 – in other words, a double entry.

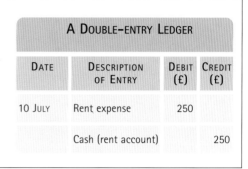

A DOUBLE-ENTRY LEDGER			
DATE	DESCRIPTION OF ENTRY	DEBIT (£)	CREDIT (£)
10 JULY	Rent expense	250	
	Cash (rent account)		250

separate record is kept of each: notes and coins are recorded in the petty cash book, and cheques are entered in the cash book.

The petty cash book is used to record transactions in notes and coins. Money in is recorded on the left-hand page and money out on the right. The money out could include such items as stamps or office coffee. Always keep receipts, even for inexpensive items, because one day you may have to verify these records. Once a week, or daily if the sums involved justify it, total the money in and out to get a cash balance. Check that it agrees with the actual cash in the till or petty cash box.

The cash book records all receipts and payments made by cheque. Once again, money coming in is on the left-hand page and money going out on the right. Every week, add up both pages to arrive at a cash at bank balance. This should be checked against your bank statement at least once a month to ensure that the basic information you are working with is correct.

PURCHASE AND SALES LEDGERS

If your business gives credit to customers, or takes credit from suppliers, you will need a sales and a purchase ledger. Each ledger should ideally have a separate page for every business with which you deal.

■ **PURCHASE LEDGER** On the right-hand side of the purchase ledger are listed the date, description, amount, and cost of each item bought on credit. On the left-hand side, a

record is kept of all payments made to the supplier, with the items for which the payments were made. Each month, by deducting the left-hand total from the right, you can see how much each supplier is owed. Suppliers ought to send you a statement and you can use that to check your own view of the financial situation.

■ **SALES LEDGER** The sales ledger deals with customers in much the same way. One important difference is that credit sales are shown on the left-hand side of the ledger, while customers' payments appear on the right-hand side. This is simply an accounting convention to deal with credits and debits.

It would also be very useful to keep a note of customers' (and suppliers') addresses, telephone numbers, and contacts' names with each entry in the ledgers. This will ensure that you have all the relevant information when it comes to chasing up late payments or dealing with queries.

MONEY SAVER

If you just pile your bills, receipts, and cheque stubs into an old shoe box and take it to an accountant at the end of the year, or when you run out of cash, it will cost a lot more to get your accounts done than if you keep good records.

Capital or Asset Register

Limited companies have to keep a capital register. This records capital items they own, such as land, buildings, equipment, and vehicles, showing the cost at date of purchase. It also records the disposal of any of these items and the cumulative depreciation.

The Nominal or Private Ledger

This ledger is usually kept by your accountant or bookkeeper. It brings together all the information from the primary ledgers, as these other basic records are called. Expenses from the cash books and purchase ledger are posted (entered) to the left-hand side of the nominal ledger. Income from sales (and any other income) is posted to the right. Normally, each type of expense or income has a separate page, which makes subsequent analysis easier.

■ **The Trial Balance** Every month, each page in the nominal ledger is totalled and used to prepare a trial balance. In other words, the sum of all the left-hand totals should end up equalling the sum of all the right-hand totals. This is the basis of double-entry bookkeeping, and this balancing of the sums is what gives you confidence that the figures are correctly recorded. If the sums do not balance, then an error has crept in. Advice on remedying this situation is given on pp. 81 and 82.

Using a Computer for Record Keeping

There are many advantages to using a computer. It reduces the chances of arithmetic errors, saving time in adding and subtracting columns, and makes the calculations in an analyzed cash book that

much easier to do. If you use a computer you can choose between using a computerized system (recommended if you have more than 50 transactions a month) or, if your business is small, a spreadsheet.

Using a Computerized System

If you use a computerized system for keeping your records, double-entry bookkeeping becomes a much simpler affair: each entry needs to be recorded only once; the computer does the rest. Specific plus points are:
■ It is not possible to make any simple arithmetic errors.
■ You will achieve better stock control.
■ You will be able to fill in your tax return quickly and accurately.
■ You will achieve better control of your payments.
■ You will save money on your accountant's fees.
■ **No Arithmetic Errors** As long as the information is entered correctly on the computer, it will be added up correctly. For example, with a computer, the £250 rent expenditure in the example given on p. 79 is

Bookkeeping on a Computer
Double-entry bookkeeping becomes a much simpler operation on a computer. There is also less margin for error, as long as you enter the amounts correctly.

entered as an expense (a debit), and then the computer automatically posts it to the rent account as a credit, thereby providing the double entry. In effect, the computer eliminates the extra step or the need to master the difference between debit and credit yourself.

■ **BETTER STOCK CONTROL** If your business is concerned with stock holding, a computerized system can help you to match stock levels to demand. It could even provide you with profit margin information quickly by product, so that you can discover which products are selling well and are therefore worth promoting and which are less attractive, and so might need to be discontinued.

■ **FASTER TAX RETURNS** Routine tasks, such as filling in your tax return (and VAT in Europe and sales tax in the United States), take minutes to complete if you use a computer rather than days if you do not. In addition, the system can ensure that your returns are accurate and fully reconciled.

■ **CONTROL OF PAYMENTS** With a computerized system, invoices will always be accurate. You can also see at a glance which customers are regularly taking too long to pay their bills. Reminder statements of payments for late payers can be automatically prepared on the computer.

■ **SAVING MONEY** Your year-end accounts preparation and, where appropriate, audit will be greatly streamlined if you use a computer to do your accounts. This will save time and money, particularly on accountant's fees, and allow you to monitor profits and cash flow accurately.

USING A SPREADSHEET
If your business has relatively few transactions each month – say, no more than 20 or 30 items of receipt and payment to record – instead of using a double-entry accounting system you may be able to use a simple spreadsheet. This will provide an accurate, if minimal, record of your payments and receipts. It will not give you the advantages of a double-entry accounting system, but then with this number of records the chances are that you do not need one. Using a spreadsheet will, however, give you the other advantages of using a computer.

CORRECTING ERRORS
While using a computer will eliminate arithmetic errors, this does not mean that your computerized bookkeeping will always be perfect. There are, in fact, quite a few things that can still go wrong.

Aim for accuracy – computers are only as foolproof as the person entering the figures

Most errors show up in the trial balance, when you will see a difference between the sum of credits and debits. The difference between the two is what you need to look for. You need to discover whether that sum has been entered incorrectly or has simply been missed out. By using the "find" facility on the computer for that specific number, you may be able to locate the error.

If the error is very small, say £30 or so, and it has proved difficult to trace, you can put the missing amount into a suspense account. Removing the sum in this way means that you can get on and complete the accounts. Then when you locate the error, you can make the necessary correction. If you deduct the amount in order to make the figures agree, you will have to readjust the books when you do find the error.

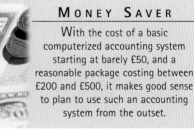

MONEY SAVER
With the cost of a basic computerized accounting system starting at barely £50, and a reasonable package costing between £200 and £500, it makes good sense to plan to use such an accounting system from the outset.

COMMON BOOKKEEPING ERRORS

When the books do not balance it could be down to any one of a number of different errors inadvertently made when doing the books. Check for any of the following to find the source.

■ **ERRORS OF OMISSION** A transaction has been missed out altogether.

■ **ERRORS OF COMMISSION** A transaction has been posted to the wrong account, though to the right side. For example, it has been posted to the "John Brown A/c" instead of the "James Brown A/c".

■ **COMPENSATING ERRORS** Different errors of the same value, made on opposite sides of the ledger. The effect of one is hidden by the equal effect of the other, so that the trial balance still balances. There could even be more than two errors involved, with the total debit errors matching the total credit errors.

■ **ERRORS OF PRINCIPLE** Where a payment item has been posted to a receipt account; for example, if you entered a bill to be paid as money due in from one of your customers.

■ **ERRORS OF ORIGINAL ENTRY** The original entry was wrong. Perhaps the source document, such as an invoice, has been added up wrongly or misread.

■ **ERRORS OF REVERSAL** Both aspects have been posted to the wrong sides: the debit aspect to the credit side, and the credit aspect to the debit side of the books.

■ **OMITTING ONE SIDE OF DUAL POSTING** Errors due to complete omission of one side of the dual posting. (A computerized system would not allow this to happen.)

■ **ERRORS OF SUMMATION** Sometimes known as "casting errors". Columns have been added up wrongly, and the wrong balance carried down. Computerized accounts eliminate this problem.

■ **ERRORS OF TRANSPOSITION** A figure has been accidentally reversed in writing. For example, 32 has been written as 23, or 414 as 441. This error is always a multiple of 9, and if the error is one of transposition it can be spotted fairly easily.

Dealing with Incomplete Records

Sometimes a business gets started without having a bookkeeping system in place, or accurate and timely recording has been neglected for a period. There is no cause for despair here, because the incomplete record process can still help you to produce reliable books from unreliable data.

If you have been so imprudent as to have been trading without records, and a tax demand has come in, all is not completely lost. With the help of your accountant you should be able to produce a profit figure from the information in your incomplete records.

If you kept no records to begin with, resolve to start reliable bookkeeping for the future

To do this, use what records you have got to add up all the assets, such as cash, stock, equipment, money owed by customers, and so forth, at the year end. Do the same for the liabilities, such as money owed to the bank or creditors. Then take the sum of the assets from the sum of the liabilities: the difference is the profit made in the period, and so the amount to be taxed.

This is undoubtedly not the most accurate way to keep track of your finances, and it certainly lacks any detail, but if incomplete records are all that you have, this method has the advantage of allowing you to draw a line under the past financial year. You can then decide to make a fresh start for the future by using a sound and reliable bookkeeping system.

WORKING OUT YOUR PROFIT FROM INCOMPLETE RECORDS

ASSETS		(£)
CASH IN HAND		150
MONEY OWED BY CUSTOMERS		355
FIXED ASSETS (CAR, COMPUTER, ETC.)		1,080
TOTAL		1,585
LESS LIABILITIES	Overdraft	500
	Money owed to suppliers	735
TOTAL		1,235
DIFFERENCE BETWEEN ASSETS AND LIABILITIES		350
TO WHICH ADD DRAWINGS FOR PERIOD		4,000
TAXABLE PROFIT		4,350

OVERALL PICTURE
These accounts lack the detail of a double-entry system and the breakdown of an analyzed cash book, but they are sufficient to produce a figure for the profit made during a certain period.

THE PROFIT AND LOSS ACCOUNT

The purpose of bookkeeping is to provide yourself with the data needed to run your business efficiently. It also helps you to work out how much tax you owe. The way to calculate these matters is to prepare a profit and loss account, which uses the figures for the income of the business, the cost of providing the goods or services being sold, and the cost of running the business to provide a detailed picture of your financial affairs.

In carrying out any business activity, two very different actions go on: producing goods or services at a cost to yourself, then selling these goods or services to your customers.

In order to secure your customers and give them the product or service they want, you will incur necessary costs, such as raw materials, salaries, rents, and so forth. These costs are also known as expenses.

When you sell your goods and services, the money may not come in immediately, but eventually the cash will arrive. This money goes by a variety of names including revenues, income, and sales income.

By taking the expenses away from the income, you end up with the profit (or loss) for the particular period under review.

Creating a Detailed Account

A simple profit and loss account is certainly better than nothing, but it does provide only the skeleton facts about the business's financial standing. You can, however, use the basic bookkeeping information to give a much richer picture of events within the business if you set up the right analysis headings. To develop a basic profit and loss account into a more detailed and informative one is simply a matter of including more information.

BASIC PROFIT AND LOSS ACCOUNT FOR SAFARI EUROPE	
YEAR 1	(£)
TOTAL INCOME	1,416,071
TOTAL EXPENSES	1,389,698
PROFIT	26,373

BASIC ACCOUNT
At its simplest, the profit and loss account has at its head the period covered, followed by the income, from which all the expenses of the business are deducted to arrive at the profit (or loss) made in the period.

The following pages show how you can build up a basic profit and loss account to give a more complete picture of the trading events of a year. The accounts of a fictional company named Safari Europe, which sells package holidays, will be used to show the development of a very basic profit and loss account into a detailed one for any service industry. For a manufacturing, rather than a service, business, this development differs in the way gross profit is calculated (see p. 86).

CALCULATING GROSS PROFIT
Whatever the business activity, you have to buy certain raw materials. These will include anything on which you have to spend money to

produce the goods and services you are selling. So, if you sell cars, the cost of buying in the cars you sell will be one such cost. In Safari Europe's case, the cost of airline tickets and hotel rooms are the raw materials of the package holidays they provide.

What you have left from your sales revenues after deducting the cost of sales, as these costs of production are known, is the gross profit. For Safari Europe, the difference between the income of £1,416,071 and the cost of the goods (holidays and insurance) they have sold is just £160,948. That is the sum with which the management have to run the business, not the much larger headline-making income figure of nearly £1.5 million.

Calculate your gross profit to find out how much money you can spend

THE IMPORTANCE OF GROSS PROFIT

The gross profit is one of the most important figures in the profit and loss account. It represents the only money coming into the business about which you can have much say on how it is spent, because it is not needed actually to produce the goods or services. It will, instead, be used to pay for all the running costs of the business, and any money remaining after all the bills have been settled and all the employees paid may either be taken as earnings by the owner or used to expand the business. It follows, therefore, that those products or services that produce the highest gross profit

(that is, they have the largest difference between cost of sale and selling price) are a business's most valuable asset.

The gross profit, not the much larger income sum, is the figure to use when taking out a loan or making plans for expansion. To use the income figure would probably be disastrous.

INCLUDING BUSINESS EXPENSES

The expenses that are likely to arise in a business need to be itemized in the profit and loss account. These expenses are listed after the gross profit has been calculated. They

GROSS PROFIT CALCULATION FOR SAFARI EUROPE		
YEAR 1		(£)
INCOME	TOURS SOLD	1,402,500
	INSURANCE AND OTHER SERVICES	13,571
	NON-OPERATING REVENUE	0
TOTAL INCOME		1,416,071
LESS COST OF GOODS SOLD	Tours bought	1,251,052
	Insurance and other services	4,071
TOTAL COST OF GOODS SOLD		1,255,123
GROSS PROFIT		160,948

GROSS PROFIT
Safari Europe has two sources of income: one from tours and one from insurance and other related services. They also, of course, have the costs associated with buying in holidays and insurance policies from suppliers.

A MANUFACTURER'S GROSS PROFIT

To calculate the gross profit in a manufacturing business the process is quite different, as the example below shows.

■ In the first instance, the basic accounting for a manufacturing business is the same as for a service business. The difference comes when you take into account the raw materials needed for manufacturing. You will be holding raw materials in stock, but you want to count into the cost of goods sold only the materials that are actually used. You do this by noting the stock at the start of the period, adding in any purchases made, and deducting the closing stock figure.

■ To arrive at the gross profit, you also need to build in the indirect labour cost in production, in addition to any overheads, such as workshop usage, with its inherent costs of heat, light, and power.

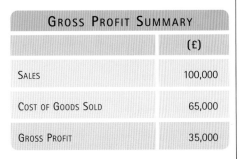

GROSS PROFIT SUMMARY	(£)
SALES	100,000
COST OF GOODS SOLD	65,000
GROSS PROFIT	35,000

EXPANDED GROSS PROFIT CALCULATION		(£)	(£)	(£)
YEAR 1				
SALES				100,000
MANUFACTURING COSTS	Raw materials opening stock	30,000		
	Purchases in period	25,000		
LESS RAW MATERIALS CLOSING STOCK		15,500		
COST OF MATERIALS USED			39,500	
DIRECT LABOUR COST			18,000	
MANUFACTURING OVERHEAD COSTS	Indirect labour	4,000		
	Workshop heat, light, and power	3,500		
TOTAL MANUFACTURING COSTS			7,500	
COST OF GOODS SOLD				65,000
GROSS PROFIT				35,000

GROSS PROFIT SUMMARY
By deducting the cost of goods sold from the sales income, you are left with the gross profit. At this level of accounting, there are few differences between a service business and a manufacturing one.

EXPANDED ACCOUNTS
By giving more detail in the accounts, you can see which figures (the manufacturing overhead costs, labour costs, and the cost of the stock used in the production of the sold items) need to be deducted from the income to give the gross profit figure.

include all costs associated with running the business, such as rent, rates, telephone, marketing, and so forth.

In Safari Europe's case, the business expenses include not only the basic services, such as telephone, electricity, and gas, which will be paid for on a monthly basis, but also annual bills, such as memberships and subscriptions, and irregular events, such as staff training (see table right). There is also a sum for the depreciation of fixtures, which your accountant will help you to calculate (see pp. 98–100). While all these expenses are correctly included, they are not necessarily all allowable for tax purposes in all countries (see pp. 159–65).

The heading "total expenditure" in the table is not quite accurate because, although all the most obvious forms of expenditure have been taken into acount, there are some other expenses associated with running a business. These are treated in a slightly different way, for reasons that will become apparent when you look at the different types of profit.

APPRECIATING THE DIFFERENT TYPES OF PROFIT

The figures on p. 89 are the full profit and loss account for Safari Europe. It is clear from this that profit can be measured in several ways, each one a step on from the last. They are:
■ gross profit
■ operating profit
■ net profit before tax
■ net profit after tax
■ **GROSS PROFIT** This is the profit that remains after all the costs related to making what you sell have been deducted.
■ **OPERATING PROFIT** After you have taken away from the gross profit the expenses, or expenditure, you are left with what is known

ACCOUNT INCLUDING EXPENSES
The gross profit calculation has now been taken to the next stage, where all the costs of actually running the business are taken into account. The gross profit minus the total expenditure is known as the operating profit.

BUSINESS EXPENSES FOR SAFARI EUROPE		
YEAR 1		**(£)**
INCOME	Tours sold	1,402,500
	Insurance and other services	13,571
	Non-operating revenue	0
TOTAL INCOME		**1,416,071**
LESS COST OF GOODS SOLD	Tours bought	1,251,052
	Insurance and other services	4,071
TOTAL COST OF GOODS SOLD		**1,255,123**
GROSS PROFIT		**160,948**
EXPENDITURE	Rent and rates	18,000
	Heat, light, and power	3,500
	Telephone system lease	2,000
	Computer lease	5,000
	Marketing and promotion	12,500
	Postage and stationery	3,250
	Telephone	3,575
	Insurance and legal	3,500
	Wages (not owner's)	36,000
	Consultancy services	25,000
	Membership and subscription	1,500
	Travel and subsistence	4,250
	Training and staff development	6,000
	Depreciation of fixtures	5,500
TOTAL EXPENDITURE		**129,575**

LEVELS OF PROFIT FOR SAFARI EUROPE		
YEAR 1		**(£)**
INCOME	Tours sold	1,402,500
	Insurance and other services	13,571
	Non-operating revenue	0
TOTAL INCOME		1,416,071
LESS COST OF GOODS SOLD	Tours bought	1,251,052
	Insurance and other services	4,071
TOTAL COST OF GOODS SOLD		1,255,123
GROSS PROFIT		160,948
EXPENDITURE	Rent and rates	18,000
	Heat, light, and power	3,500
	Telephone system lease	2,000
	Computer lease	5,000
	Marketing and promotion	12,500
	Postage and stationery	3,250
	Telephone	3,575
	Insurance and legal	3,500
	Wages (not owner's)	36,000
	Consultancy services	25,000
	Membership and subscription	1,500
	Travel and subsistence	4,250
	Training and staff development	6,000
	Depreciation of fixtures	5,500
TOTAL EXPENDITURE		129,575
OPERATING PROFIT		31,373
LESS BANK INTEREST AND CHARGES		5,000
NET PROFIT BEFORE TAX		26,373
TAX		5,474
NET PROFIT AFTER TAX		20,899

THE FINAL ACCOUNT
The accounts have now been taken to their last stage, where the operating profit has had interest charges and tax deducted from it, to produce the final figure of the net profit after tax.

as the operating profit. When it comes to valuing the business, it is the operating profit that is generally used as the multiplying factor in the "xxx times earnings" valuation.

▓ **NET PROFIT BEFORE TAX** Next, any financing costs must be deducted. The reasoning here is that the business manager can have little influence over the way in which the business is financed (no borrowings means no interest expenses, for example; high borrowings mean high expenses) or over the interest rates, which are regulated at a macro-economic level. In Safari Europe's case, once you have taken away the financing costs (£5,000 in interest charges), you are left with a net profit before tax of £26,373.

▓ **NET PROFIT AFTER TAX** Finally, tax is deducted to leave the net profit after tax. This is the sum that belongs to the owners of the business. In the case of a limited company, this is the sum from which dividends are paid.

The Projected Profit and Loss Account

A profit and loss account for the first year of trading can be used as a basis for creating a projected account for the future. Here Safari Europe's accounts have been estimated for the following two trading years on the basis of the first year's accounts.

A projected profit and loss account forms a vital part of your business plan when you are seeking finance for expansion. A new business seeking finance will have to project all three years.

LOOKING INTO THE FUTURE
The accounts for the first year of trading can be used as a means to estimate the figures for the next two years. A total profit of just over £500,000 is foreseen by Safari Europe by the end of Year 3.

THREE-YEAR PROFIT AND LOSS ACCOUNT FOR SAFARI EUROPE
(INCLUDING PROJECTED FIGURES FOR YEARS 2 AND 3)

		YEAR 1 (£)	% OF SALES	YEAR 2 (£)	% OF SALES	YEAR 3 (£)	% OF SALES
INCOME	Tours sold	1,402,500		3,085,500		4,502,025	
	Insurance and other services	13,571		29,856		43,563	
	Non-operating revenue	0	0	0	0	0	0
TOTAL INCOME		1,416,071	100	3,115,356	100	4,545,588	100
LESS COST OF GOODS SOLD	Tours bought	1,251,052		2,732,557	1,251,052	3,941,594	
	Insurance and other services	4,071		8,956		13,068	
TOTAL COST OF GOODS SOLD		1,255,123	89	2,741,513	88	3,954,662	87
GROSS PROFIT		160,948	11	373,843	12	590,926	13
EXPENDITURE	Rent and rates	18,000		18,000	18,000	24,000	
	Heat, light and power	3,500		3,500		4,000	
	Telephone system lease	2,000		2,000		2,000	
	Computer lease	5,000		5,000		5,000	
	Marketing and promotion	12,500		18,000		25,000	
	Postage and stationery	3,250		5,000		7,500	
	Telephone	3,575		4,750		6,500	
	Insurance and legal	3,500		5,500		10,000	
	Wages (not owner's)	36,000		40,500		58,000	
	Consultancy services	25,000		10,000		10,000	
	Membership and subscription	1,500		2,500		5,000	
	Travel and subsistence	4,250		10,500		18,500	
	Training and staff development	6,000		10,000		21,000	
	Depreciation of fixtures	5,500		5,500		5,500	
TOTAL EXPENDITURE		129,575	10	140,750	5	202,000	5
OPERATING PROFIT		31,373		233,093		388,926	
LESS BANK INTEREST AND CHARGES		5,000		5,000		5,000	
NET PROFIT BEFORE TAX		26,373	2	228,093	7	383,926	8
Tax		5,474		45,619		87,276	
NET PROFIT AFTER TAX		20,899	1	182,474	6	296,650	7
CUMULATIVE PROFIT/LOSS		20,899		203,373		500,023	

THE BALANCE SHEET

To sum up the current financial position of your business you need to draw up a balance sheet. The balance sheet is the primary reporting document of the business. It contains evidence of all the financial events over the entire life of the business, showing where money has come from and what has been done with that money. Logically, the two sums must balance. A balance sheet is also a useful tool for ordering your personal financial affairs. This chapter demonstrates how to compile both types of balance sheet.

When important financial issues are at stake it is always helpful to draw up a balance sheet, whether the subject of concern is personal or business. Before deciding whether to move house or buy a new car you need to size up your financial situation. This could be formalized into a personal balance sheet.

The Personal Balance Sheet

The first step in the process of drawing up a personal balance sheet is to summarize your basic financial position. To demonstrate the entire process, consider the finances of Amanda Smith. A basic summary of her current financial situation is shown in the table on the right. To understand her true position, the information needs to be reorganized and more detail added.

DEFINING LIABILITIES AND ASSETS

In money matters everything divides neatly into two: things you have and things you owe, with the latter usually exceeding the former. Using this concept and slightly different words, the same basic financial information could be presented in the manner of the table shown at the top of page 91. On the right-hand side is a

list of Amanda's assets: what she has done with the money she has had. On the left is listed where she got the money from to pay for these assets: the liabilities and claims against her.

Things get a little more complicated at the bottom of the left-hand column. She has acquired £159,035 worth of assets and so must have provided an identical sum from one source or another to pay for these assets. She owes only £45,650 to other people, so it is likely that Amanda must have put in the balance over the past years. In other words, she has put her past salary towards buying the assets, to which was added an increase in her house value.

AMANDA SMITH'S BASIC FINANCIAL POSITION	
	· (£)
CASH	50
HOUSE	150,000
MORTGAGE	45,000
MONEY OWED BY SISTER	135
OVERDRAFT	100
CAR	7,000
CREDIT CARDS	50
JEWELLERY/PAINTINGS	350
HIRE PURCHASE (ON VARIOUS GOODS)	500
FURNITURE	1,500

BASIC ACCOUNTS
This very limited information reveals the basics of Amanda's financial situation, such as the value of her house and what loans she has.

LONG- AND SHORT-TERM POSITIONS

This presentation still does not tell the whole story. Even though she appears to have a fairly dazzling £159,035 of assets, Amanda knows that she is short of cash for day-to-day living. She would like to be able to see at a glance both long- and short-term aspects of her current financial position. To do this, the information needs to be restructured in the manner of the table shown at the foot of this page.

Amanda's short-term financial position is dominated by the money that her sister owes

LIABILITIES AND ASSETS
Adding more detail gives a fuller account of Amanda's financial position. Her liabilities and claims (that is, where she got her money) equal her assets (that is, what she has done with her money).

AMANDA SMITH'S LIABILITIES AND ASSETS			
LIABILITIES & CLAIMS	**(£)**	**ASSETS**	**(£)**
OVERDRAFT	100	CASH	50
MORTGAGE	45,000	HOUSE	150,000
HIRE PURCHASE	500	CAR	7,000
CREDIT CARDS	50	JEWELLERY/PAINTINGS	350
TOTAL CLAIMS BY OTHER PEOPLE	45,650	MONEY OWED BY SISTER	135
		FURNITURE	1,500
MY CAPITAL	113,385		
TOTAL OF MY AND OTHER PEOPLE'S MONEY	159,035	MY ASSETS	159,035

LONG AND SHORT TERM
Breaking down her liabilities and assets into long term (fixed) and short term (current) makes Amanda's financial situation clearer. The bottom line tells her that she owes £150 and has assets of £185

AMANDA SMITH'S LONG- AND SHORT-TERM POSITIONS			
LIABILITIES (LONG-TERM)	**(£)**	**ASSETS (LONG-TERM)**	**(£)**
MY CAPITAL	113,385	HOUSE	150,000
MORTGAGE	45,000	CAR	7,000
HIRE PURCHASE	500	FURNITURE	1,500
		JEWELLERY/PAINTINGS	350
TOTAL	158,885	TOTAL	158,850
LIABILITIES (SHORT-TERM)	**(£)**	**ASSETS (SHORT-TERM)**	**(£)**
OVERDRAFT	100	MONEY OWED BY SISTER	135
CREDIT CARDS	50	CASH	50
TOTAL	150	TOTAL	185

her. If that is safe, then all current liabilities can be met. If it is unsafe, and so unlikely to be repaid quickly, the position is not so good. "Current" is used in financing language to mean something that is going to be realized or consumed within one year. So current liabilities are those that have to be paid within a year, and current assets will turn into cash within a year.

THE NET POSITION

Only one more adjustment to the information is needed to turn Amanda's short- and long-term position into a balance sheet (see table right). Having broken down her liabilities and assets into long- and short-term categories, it is now vital to ensure that both these financial positions are readily visible to the examiner. In other words, Amanda's day-to-day assets and liabilities need to be clearly highlighted.

What Amanda needs to see is the net position. "Net" means a position after the relevant liability has been taken away. So Amanda's net current assets are how much she currently owes subtracted from how much she has. The resulting sum is also referred to as working capital.

You will note that underneath the heading of "fixed assets" in the balance sheet to the right the term "book value" has been used. This means the cost of any fixed assets less the amount of depreciation charged up to that date. (For more on depreciation see pp. 98–100.)

By redrafting the financial position, you can see the whole picture more clearly. Starting with the items that have a long life or will be around for several years, you can deduce that £158,885 is tied up in fixed assets (her house, car, furniture, jewellery, and paintings). Turning next to items with a relatively short life, you can see that a further £35 is tied up in net current assets (that is, current assets minus current liabilities).

All these have been financed by £113,385 of Amanda's capital and £45,500, which has been provided by a mortgage and a hire purchase company, which are Amanda's long-term liabilities. The sum of these two figures also comes to £158,885, and so her balance sheet can be seen to balance correctly.

AMANDA SMITH'S BALANCE SHEET – THE NET POSITION

ASSETS AND LIABILITIES		(£)
FIXED ASSETS	House	150,000
	Car	7,000
	Furniture	1,500
	Jewellery/paintings	350
BOOK VALUE		158,850
CURRENT ASSETS	Money owed by sister	135
	Cash	50
TOTAL CURRENT ASSETS		185
LESS CURRENT LIABILITIES	Overdraft	100
	Credit cards	50
TOTAL CURRENT LIABILITIES		150
NET CURRENT ASSETS		35
NET TOTAL ASSETS		158,885
FINANCED BY	My capital	113,385
	Mortgage	45,000
	Hire purchase	500
TOTAL		158,885

THE NET POSITION

Amanda's balance sheet is now displayed in a vertical format for clarity. You can see that her total assets of £158,885 balance her capital and long-term liabilities.

BALANCE SHEET FORMAT

The balance sheets shown here are displayed in a vertical format rather than the horizontal form used for the two preceding charts. The vertical format is the convention for a balance sheet in the UK, whereas the US uses the horizontal form.

The Business Balance Sheet

The information collected so far is all that is needed for a balance sheet depicting Amanda's personal affairs. To convert this personal balance sheet into one that could be used in a UK business, however, requires a few small adjustments (see table right). The long-term borrowings – in this case the mortgage and hire purchase charges – are now renamed as "creditors, amounts falling due in over one year". They are deducted from the total assets to show the net total assets being employed by her business.

The bottom of the business balance sheet shows how Amanda has supported these assets; in this case, by her own funds. She could also have invested the profit made in earlier years back into the business (see Understanding Reserves, p. 95).

A final change that has been made is to assume that her house is now a business premises owned by her company. (This assumption has wider implications, but none that is relevant to the balance sheet.)

Categorizing Business Assets

Accountants describe assets as valuable resources, owned by a business, that were acquired at a measurable money cost. Assets can be categorized in three ways:
■ cash assets
■ possessed assets
■ owned assets

BUSINESS BALANCE SHEET

Adapting Amanda's personal balance sheet into a business one involves renaming her long-term liabilities and making the assumption that her home is now used as a business premises and so is owned by her company.

AMANDA SMITH'S BUSINESS BALANCE SHEET			
ASSETS AND LIABILITIES		(£)	(£)
FIXED ASSETS	Premises	150,000	
	Car	7,000	
	Furniture	1,500	
	Jewellery/ paintings	350	
BOOK VALUE			158,850
CURRENT ASSETS	Money owed by sister	135	
	Cash	50	
TOTAL CURRENT ASSETS		185	
LESS CURRENT LIABILITIES	Overdraft	100	
	Credit cards	50	
TOTAL CURRENT LIABILITIES		150	
NET CURRENT ASSETS			35
TOTAL ASSETS			158,885
LESS	Creditors, amounts falling due in over one year		45,500
NET TOTAL ASSETS			113,385
FINANCED BY	My capital	113,385	
TOTAL OWNER'S FUNDS			113,385

CASH ASSETS

To be valuable, the resource must be cash, or of some use in generating current or future profits. For example, a debtor (someone who owes a business money for goods or services provided) usually pays up. When the debtor does pay the debt, the repayment becomes cash and so meets this test. If there is no hope of getting payment of a debt in the foreseeable future, then you can hardly view the sum as an asset of any kind.

POSSESSED ASSETS

Ownership, in its legal sense, can be seen as different from possession or control. The accounting use of the word is similar but not identical. In a business, possession and control are not enough to make a resource an asset. For example, a leased machine may be possessed and controlled by a business but be owned by the leasing company. So, not only is it not an asset, it is a regular expense. However, had the same piece of machinery been bought outright, then it would be treated as an asset of the business. No one but the accountant could detect the difference.

OWNED ASSETS

Most business resources are bought for what is termed by accountants as a measurable money cost. Often, this test is all too painfully obvious. If you pay cash for something, or promise to pay at a later date, it is clearly an asset. Any goods manufactured by your business involved money being paid in wages, materials, etc. during that process, and so these too are assets. There may be problems in deciding exactly

FACT FILE

The asset goodwill is one important grey area of particular interest to those buying or selling a small business. It constitutes the value placed upon the reputation (for example, the brand name) of the business.

what money figure to put down, but there is no problem in seeing that money has been spent.

RANKING ASSETS

There is a useful convention that recommends listing assets in the balance sheet in their order of permanence; that is, starting out with the most difficult to turn into cash and working down to cash itself. Using this convention in current assets, stock and inventories are bought in and would appear before debtors, because goods have to be sold to customers, who then pay up, eventually releasing the cash back into the business.

This structure is very practical when you are looking at someone else's balance sheet for information, or comparing balance sheets. It can also help you to recognize obvious information gaps quickly.

Accounting for Liabilities

These are the claims by people outside the business that one day will have to be met. Liabilities include items that can be easily identified and measured, such as loans and money due to suppliers, as well as those that are less easy to quantify. Accountants have their own rules on how figures are to be arrived at for these grey areas, but they do not pretend to give anything more than an approximation. Common business liabilities are:

■ tax
■ accruals
■ deferred income
■ overdrafts
■ loans
■ hire purchase
■ money owed to suppliers

Every measuring device, including financial controls, has inherent inaccuracies. To make things more complicated, not all financial events are equally easy to measure. Seek advice from your accountant about liabilities.

AMANDA'S RESERVES
The revenue reserve (£50,000) and the capital reserve (£38,385), together with the capital introduced (£25,000) represent all the money invested by Amanda in this venture.

AMANDA SMITH'S RESERVES		
FINANCED BY	(£)	(£)
CAPITAL INTRODUCED		25,000
RESERVES Revenue reserve	50,000	
Capital reserve	38,385	88,385

DEALING WITH BAD DEBTS

Some liabilities can be less easy to identify and even harder to put a figure on, bad debts being a prime example. The difference between the average order placed by your biggest and smallest accounts will provide some idea of the spread that could encompass a bad debt figure. Also, there is no certainty that only one bad debt will occur in each year. In practice, you will probably settle for last year's bad debt figure, with an uplift to reflect any growth in sales.

Understanding Reserves

In the final version of Amanda Smith's business balance sheet on p. 93 her capital was shown as being the sole support for the liabilities of the business. The implication was that she had put this whole sum in at once. In practice, this is much more likely to have happened over time, and in a variety of ways.

Perhaps she started out in business, as that is how we must now look at her affairs, with a sum of, say, £25,000. Since then she has made a net profit after tax of £50,000, which she has reinvested into her business to finance growth. In addition, the business premises that she bought a few years ago for £111,615 has just been revalued at £150,000, providing a paper gain of £38,385. The bottom portion of her business balance sheet could now be recast as shown in the table above.

REVENUE RESERVES

The profit of £50,000 ploughed back into the business is called a revenue reserve, which means that the money actually exists and could be used to buy stock or more assets, for example. A revenue reserve is usually created when a business makes a profit and all or a portion of that profit is left in the business and not paid out in dividends.

CAPITAL RESERVES

The increase in value of the business premises, on the other hand, is a paper increase, which means that the £38,385 increase in capital reserves that it represents could not be used to buy anything, because it will not be in money form until the business premises are sold. However, that paper reserve could be used to underpin a loan from the bank, so turning a paper profit into a cash resource.

ACCOUNTING RULES

Finance has a language of its own. Some of the terms, while sounding like familiar everyday English, can have quite different meanings when used in accountancy. In addition, some rules can appear alien to common sense and become obvious only when you remember that the aim of the accounting reports is stewardship rather than value. Stewardship means accounting for where money came from and what was done with it. This chapter covers the most important rules of the financial game.

A particularly prudent sales manager once said that an order was not an order until the customer's cheque had cleared; the customer had consumed the product and had not died as a result; and, finally, he or she had shown every indication of wanting to buy the product again. By contrast, most of us know quite a different kind of salesperson who, usually as a result of vast optimism (or overconfidence), expects to achieve the most unlikely volume of sales in conditions of anything but certainty.

In finance you should, and indeed ought to, count your chickens before they hatch

Realizing Income from Customers

Common sense suggests that you should wait until customers pay up before calculating your sales figure. After all, anything could happen: they may reject the product, change their mind, or go bust before they pay you. In finance, however, you need to look ahead and to assume that sales will convert into cash. When it comes to bookkeeping and tax returns, income is usually recognized as having been earned when the goods are dispatched, or service rendered, and the invoice sent out. This has nothing to do with when an order is received, or how firm an order is, or how likely a customer is to pay up promptly.

So the sales income figure that is seen at the top of a profit and loss account is the value of the goods dispatched and invoiced to customers during the period in question. It in no way reflects the amount of money actually received during that same period.

THE MATCHING PRINCIPLE

The reasoning behind this lies in what accountants call the matching principle. This states that income and expenditure have to be related to the relevant and same time period. So a profit and loss account is actually measuring economic activity, not cash. It is not that cash is unimportant, it is just that there is another account for measuring it: the cash-flow forecast (see pp. 22–35).

According to the matching principle, if raw materials are purchased and worked on, rent

MONEY SAVER

One element that can consume money for no reward is dealing with returns caused by sending the wrong goods or the wrong quantities. Making sure the right goods in the correct quantities are shipped in the first place is an investment that will result in lower costs and more satisfied customers.

RETURNED GOODS

Allowing for returned goods means that you can provide a more accurate figure for your net sales. Here, £1,000 of goods are expected to be returned each year.

ALLOWING FOR RETURNS		
	(£)	**(£)**
GROSS SALES INCOME	100,000	
RETURNS	1,000	
NET SALES INCOME		99,000

paid, telephone calls made, and so forth, in one month, then alongside those expenses must be matched the income from the sales actually executed in that month.

ALLOWING FOR RETURNS

The matching principle assumes that expenses and income are matched against time. This does not mean, however, that you can ignore the possibilities of bad debts occurring or of products being returned. If such events occur infrequently or at a very low level, then you can allow for these in your financial calculations.

For returns, if you know from experience that they are a certain percentage of sales, then you can allow for that in your calculation by introducing the terms "gross sales income", meaning the figure before returns, and "net sales income", meaning the figure after the allowance has been made.

In the example shown above, the returns are expected to average 1 per cent of sales, and so the rest of the expenses in the profit and loss account are deducted from £99,000 rather than the full £100,000.

ALLOWING FOR BAD DEBTS

For bad debts you can make a similar provision in the accounts, allowing a certain amount each month. In most months there will be no bad debts, but once in a while one will occur and use up all the provision made earlier, so leaving no funds for future occurrences.

If either returns or bad debts are common in an industry, then separate rules will need to be made for dealing with them. Mail-order companies, for example, will handle large quantities of returned goods. Rather than treat these returns as infrequent and unwanted events, they will regard them as an everyday part of their business.

Accruing for the Future

The profit and loss account sets out to match a business's income and expenditure to the appropriate time period. It is only in this way that the profit for the period can be realistically calculated. However, not all these financial events will leave a clear and traceable trail, and this is when you need to introduce the method of accruing. If you do not accrue, your accounts will not reflect your current position.

WHEN TO ACCRUE

The basic transactions, such as sales, purchases, and salaries, will be easy to deal with because the amounts will all be recorded in your books. But suppose, for example, that you are calculating one month's profits when the quarterly telephone bill comes in. The picture might be as follows: sales income for January of £4,000, less telephone bill (last quarter) of £800, giving a profit of £3,200.

This is clearly wrong. In the first place, three months' telephone charges have been matched

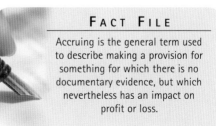

FACT FILE

Accruing is the general term used to describe making a provision for something for which there is no documentary evidence, but which nevertheless has an impact on profit or loss.

THE PRINCIPAL METHODS OF DEPRECIATION USED IN BUSINESS

Described below are three of the most common of many ways of depreciating fixed assets. In choosing which method of depreciation to use – and in practice you may have to use different methods with different types of asset – it is useful to remember what you are trying to do. You are aiming to allocate the cost of buying the asset as it should apply to each year of its working life.

▪ **THE STRAIGHT LINE METHOD** This method assumes that the asset will be consumed (that is, used) evenly throughout its life. In the example below it has been assumed that a computer is being bought for £1,200 and sold at the end of five years for £200. The amount to be written off is therefore £1,000. Using 20 per cent as the depreciation, or write-down, rate, you can work out the book value for each year.

▪ **THE DIMINISHING BALANCE METHOD** This method works in a similar way, but instead of an even depreciation each year you assume that the drop will be less. Some assets, motor vehicles for example, will reduce sharply in their first year and less so later on. So while at the end of year one both these methods of depreciation will result in a £200 fall, in year two the picture starts to change (see below). The straight line method takes a further fall of £200, while the diminishing balance method reduces by 20 per cent (the agreed depreciation rate) of £800 (the balance of £1,000 minus the £200 depreciation so far), which equals £160.

▪ **THE SUM OF THE DIGITS METHOD** This is a more commonly used method in the US than in the UK. While the diminishing balance method applies a constant percentage to a declining figure, the sum of the digits method applies a progressively smaller percentage to the initial cost. It involves adding up the individual numbers in the expected lifespan of the asset to arrive at the denominator of a fraction. The numerator is the year number concerned, but in reverse order.

For example, if the computer asset bought for £1,200 had an expected useful life of five years, then the denominator in the sum would be 1 + 2 + 3 + 4 + 5, which equals 15. In year one it would depreciate by $5/15$ times the initial purchase price of £1,200, which equals £400. In year two it would depreciate by a further $4/15$ (which would take it to £480), and so on.

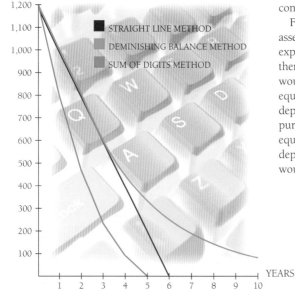

ASSET WORTH (£)

■ STRAIGHT LINE METHOD

■ DEMINISHING BALANCE METHOD

■ SUM OF DIGITS METHOD

YEARS

DEPRECIATION RATES

These three methods – straight line, diminishing balance, and sum of the digits – are used to assess the rate of depreciation of goods and property.

TIME SAVER

Check with your accountant what the generally accepted depreciation rate should be. This will be a range, from which you will have to decide on a specific figure for each type of asset. Keep a record of the rate you have chosen so that you can apply it to any new assets aquired.

against one month's sales. Equally wrong is the fact that the quarterly telephone bill for October to December has been charged against the following January's income.

Unfortunately, bills reflecting the current month are rarely to hand when you are preparing the monthly accounts, so in practice the telephone bill is accrued for. This means that a figure (which may even be absolutely correct if you have a meter) is put in to the profit and loss account as a provision to meet this liability when it becomes due.

Taking Account of Depreciating Assets

Assets are usually entered into the accounts at cost price. In reality, the real worth of an asset will probably change over time. Usually, it decreases in value, but in some cases it will increase. Knowing how an asset is likely to change its value is important when dealing with depreciation.

The worth, or value, of an asset is a subjective estimate on which no two people are likely to agree. This is made even more complex, and artificial, because the assets themselves – property, equipment, computers, and so forth – may not be for sale.

ASSESSING DEPRECIATION
Calculating depreciation values is not an accurate science. Here depreciation of a £10,000 machine has been set at a notional £5,000, leaving a book value of £5,000.

RECORDING COST
In the search for objectivity, the accountants have settled for cost as the figure to record. This inevitably means that a balance sheet does not actually show the current worth or value of a business, but then that is not the intention of a balance sheet.

This recording of the cost of an item does not mean that accountants assume that this figure remains unchanged forever. For example, a machine costing £10,000 with a useful working life of four years may, after two years, have a book value of just £5,000.

ALLOCATING COST OVER TIME
The recording of depreciation is how you show the asset being consumed, or used, over its working life. It is simply a bookkeeping method to allow the allocation of some of the initial cost of an asset to the appropriate time period. This time period will be determined by such factors as how long the likely working life of the asset is.

CALCULATING DEPRECIATION
Depreciation can be calculated using different methods. Three of the most common methods are outlined on p. 98.

Depreciation is not a method of providing for new equipment to replace old. It is simply a bookkeeping event. For example, the machine mentioned above has been bought and paid for. The only real events that have occurred are the machine being paid for (£10,000) and it becoming the property of the company buying

DEPRECIATING ASSETS		
	(£)	**(£)**
FIXED ASSETS	10,000	
CUMULATIVE DEPRECIATION TO DATE	5,000	
BOOK VALUE		5,000

VALUING A GOING CONCERN			
GOING	**(£)**	**GONE**	**(£)**
FIXED ASSETS (AT COST)	100,000	FIXED ASSETS (AT COST)	100,000
LESS DEPRECIATION	20,000	LESS RESALE VALUE	5,000
NET BOOK VALUE	80,000	NET BOOK LOSS	95,000

GOING OR GONE
A going concern with fixed assets worth £100,000 has a net book value of £80,000 (after depreciation has been deducted). If the business were soon to close down, the assets' resale value of just £5,000 would leave a net book loss of £95,000.

it. The depreciation is a notional figure put in for the reasons given. It follows that the book value of the machine of £5,000 after two years is also a notional figure. The machine could be worth next to nothing (as in the case of a computer) or it could even be worth more (as with a vintage vehicle, for example).

Other assets, such as freehold land and buildings, will be revalued occasionally, and stock in trade is entered in the books at cost, or market value, whichever is the lower, in line with the principle of conservatism (see below).

TAX RELIEF

Tax authorities usually do not allow depreciation as a business expense but do allow tax relief on the capital expenditure. This is covered in more detail on pp. 160–62. The proportion of capital purchase allowed by the Inland Revenue to be offset against tax is called the writing-down allowance.

Valuing Going Concerns

A "going concern" is a term that has a ring of confidence about it. It seems to imply that all is well. An accountant has looked the business over and given it the all clear by signing off the year-end accounts with that affirmation. In other words, the accounts have been prepared on the going concern basis. In fact, accounting reports always assume that a business will continue trading indefinitely into the future, unless there is good evidence to the

contrary. This means that the fixed assets of the business are looked at simply as profit generators and not as being available for sale.

Once a business stops trading, you cannot realistically look at the assets in the same way because they are no longer being used in the business to help generate sales and profits. The most objective figure is what they might realize in the marketplace. The same amount of fixed assets have now been given a resale value of just £5,000, resulting in a £95,000 net book loss.

Using Accounting Conventions

The rules described in this chapter provide a useful framework, but they are open to a range of possible interpretations. Over time, however, a generally accepted approach to how the rules are applied has been arrived at. This approach hinges on the use of the following three accountancy conventions:
■ conservatism
■ materiality
■ consistency

CONSERVATISM

Accountants are often viewed as merchants of gloom, always prone to take a pessimistic point of view of the state of your business finances. The fact that a point of view has to be taken at all is the root of the problem. The convention of conservatism means that, given a choice, the accountant takes the figure that will result in a lower end profit. This might mean, for example,

FAST-DEPRECIATING ASSET
In the late 1980s and early 1990s, firms depreciated computer assets over four years. Today few would consider anything over two years as being realistic, and some firms are writing down computer assets to zero at the end of the first year. This reflects a feeling that computers become technologically obsolete in a very short time.

taking the higher of two possible expense figures. This approach is taken on the basis that few people are upset if the profit figure at the end of the day is higher than earlier estimates. The converse is, understandably, rarely true.

MATERIALITY

A strict interpretation of depreciation (see pp. 98–100) would lead to all sorts of trivial paperwork. For example, office sundries such as pencil sharpeners, staplers, and paper clips, all theoretically items of fixed assets, should be depreciated over the course of their working lives. This is obviously a useless exercise with such low-cost items, however, and in practice such items are written off at the time at which they are bought.

Clearly, the level of materiality is not the same for all businesses. A multinational may not keep meticulous records of every item of equipment under £1,000, but this may represent all the equipment a small business has.

View your accountant's approach as conservative rather than pessimistic

CONSISTENCY

Even with the help of these rules and conventions, there is a fair degree of latitude in how you can record and interpret financial information. If you depreciate your assets over two years, you will produce a lower figure for profit than if you chose a longer period.

While it might be appealing to change your depreciation policy to suit your changing needs, you should choose the method that gives the fairest picture of how the company is performing, and stick firmly with that one. The same should apply to all your other accounting policies. This is because it is very difficult for both you and your accountant to keep track of events in a business that is always changing its accounting methods.

This does not mean that you are stuck with one method forever. If trading or financing circumstances change, your policy may have to change, too. Any change in accounting policy, however, should not be taken lightly.

CONTROLLING
the numbers

Rather as the instruments on a car dashboard tell you different things about its performance – speed, engine temperature, fuel level, and so on – a business too has its own set of controls. These are known as ratios. Different ratios can be used to highlight how well a business is doing from every conceivable angle. This chapter examines the key measures that reveal the innermost workings of every business, showing how well or badly they are performing.

WATCHING THE BIG PICTURE

Gathering and recording financial information is all a matter of preparation for analyzing a business's performance. Only when you have all the figures in front of you can you see how well (or how badly) your business is doing. The analytical process requires tools, in this case ratios, and their usefulness and limitations need to be understood before they can be used to good effect.

All analysis of financial information involves comparisons: a business may be more/less profitable, may have more/fewer creditors/debtors, or a higher/lower working capital than last year.

A business is constantly changing, and so the most useful way to measure its activity is through ratios. A ratio is simply one number expressed as a proportion of another. For example, travelling 100 miles may not sound too impressive, until you realize that it was done in one hour. The ratio here is 100 miles per hour. If you knew that the vehicle in question had a top speed of 120 miles per hour, you would have some means of comparing it to other vehicles, at least in respect of their speed.

of work. Some of the information, such as working capital, capital employed, and bank loans, comes from the balance sheet, while the sales (turnover), gross profit, and net profit come from the profit and loss account.

At first glance, Company B looks in better shape than Company A: its sales, gross profit, and net profit are all higher than company A's. But once you begin to apply some ratios, a slightly different picture starts to emerge.

COMPARING GROSS MARGINS

Turning now to the chart above right, you can see that the gross margin, that is, the gross

Analyzing with Ratios

In finance, too, ratios can turn sterile data into valuable information in a wide range of different ways, and this can help you to make crucial choices. The chart on the right presents some basic financial information about two businesses that are in very much the same line

FIRST IMPRESSIONS
Company B's sales figures look most impressive compared to Company A's: its sales, gross profit, and net profit figures are all higher. But a more detailed look at this information reveals that all is not well with Company B.

WHO LOOKS IN THE BEST SHAPE FOR FINANCIAL GROWTH?		
	COMPANY A (£)	COMPANY B (£)
SALES	356,000	545,000
GROSS PROFIT	195,000	255,000
WORKING CAPITAL	27,500	100,025
CAPITAL EMPLOYED	60,000	200,000
BANK LOANS	20,000	150,000
NET PROFIT	30,000	40,000

WHO IS IN THE BEST SHAPE FOR FINANCIAL GROWTH?

	COMPANY A (£)	COMPANY B (£)
SALES	356,000	545,000
GROSS PROFIT	195,000	255,000
WORKING CAPITAL	27,500	100,025
CAPITAL EMPLOYED	60,000	200,000
BANK LOANS	20,000	150,000
NET PROFIT	30,000	40,000

	COMPANY A (%)	COMPANY B (%)
ROCE	50	20
GEARING	33	75
NET PROFIT	8.4	7.3
SALES/CAPITAL EMPLOYED	(£)6	(£)3
GROSS MARGIN	54.7	46.7

profit expressed as a percentage of sales, is nearly 55 per cent for Company A, while Company B's is only nearly 47 per cent. These figures were reached as follows: Company A = 195/356 x 100 = 54.7; Company B = 255/545 x 100 = 46.7. There is a similar disparity in net profit margins.

RETURN ON CAPITAL EMPLOYED (ROCE)

The most serious differences show up, however, when information is brought in from the balance sheet. For example, Company B is using £200,000 of capital, tied up in equipment, inventories, premises, and the like, to make just £40,000 in profit. This represents a 20 per cent

ANALYSIS USING RATIOS

Despite producing a larger profit, Company B is in a worse shape than Company A. Its gross margin and net profit margin are both lower, and its ROCE is only 20 per cent.

return on the capital employed (ROCE). By comparison, Company A's slightly lower profit of £30,000 is being produced using £60,000 of capital. You do not have to be a financial genius to see that this is less than a third of the capital of Company B. So, Company A's ROCE – a ratio that could be considered similar to the interest you might get from a bank on any money deposited – is more than double that of its rival, at 50 per cent.

The more you look, the more successful Company A turns out to be. It has much lower bank borrowings, so it would be safer if the economic climate turned sour, and its sales per pound tied up in capital is double that of Company B. In summary, Company A may sell fewer products and make less profit, but it is much more profitable, makes more efficient use of its resources, and is unlikely ever to be at the mercy of its bankers.

To use a personal illustration, would you rather have £200,000 of your money invested with someone giving you a return of £40,000, or £60,000 invested with someone giving you a return of £30,000? The choice is not a difficult one to make.

The financial ratios used in this example are more fully explained in Going into Detail (see pp. 112–29).

MONEY SAVER

Sophisticated accounting software have "report generator" programs that provide analysis of the ratios. This is like having an accountant advising on any problems in interpreting the ratios. Such software may be more expensive but will save money in the long run by improving the quality of your decisions.

Some Problems with Ratios

There is a natural feeling with financial ratios to think that high figures are good ones and that an upward trend represents the right direction. Unfortunately, there is no general rule on which way is right for financial ratios. In some cases, a high figure is good; in others, a low figure is best. Indeed, there are even circumstances in which ratios of the same value are not as good as each other. These occur when taking into account the following:

■ different financial situations
■ the sizes of different businesses
■ seasonal factors
■ changes in inflation

DIFFERENT FINANCIAL SITUATIONS

Looking at the two working capital statements in the chart below, you can see that the amount of working capital in each example is the same

THE FINANCIAL DIPSTICK

In general, business performance as measured by ratios is best thought of as lying within a range, rather like the oil level that is indicated on the dipstick of a vehicle. So, for example, if liquidity (current ratio) stays between 1.5:1 and 2.5:1, it would be acceptable. Any move outside that range would be a cause for concern, albeit different concerns.

DANGER ZONE

2.5:1

SAFE ZONE

1.5:1

DANGER ZONE

at £16,410, as are the current assets and current liabilities, at £23,100 and £6,690 respectively. It follows that any ratio using these factors would also be the same. For example, the current ratios (current assets divided by current liabilities) in these two examples are

DIFFICULT COMPARISONS

		COMPANY A (£)	COMPANY B (£)
CURRENT ASSETS	Stock	10,000	22,990
	Debtors	13,000	100
	Cash	100	10
TOTAL CURRENT ASSETS		23,100	23,100
LESS CURRENT LIABILITIES	Overdraft	5,000	90
	Creditors	1,690	6,600
TOTAL CURRENT LIABILITIES		6,690	6,690
NET CURRENT ASSETS		16,410	16,410
CURRENT RATIO		3.4:1	3.4:1

BEYOND THE SIMILARITIES

Company A and Company B are identical in their total current assets, total current liabilities, and net current assets, but that does not mean that they are in the same financial shape. Company A's higher number of debtors and lower levels of stock put it in a more favourable position than Company B.

identical at 3.4:1. What must be looked at now are the differences.

For Company A there is a reasonable chance that some cash will come in from debtors, certainly enough to meet the modest creditor position. For Company B, however, there is no possibility of useful amounts of cash coming in from trading, with debtors at only £100; while creditors at the relatively substantial figure of £6,600 pose a real threat to financial stability.

The stock figure for Company B of nearly £23,000 is valuable only if the stock is saleable, and in any event the cash will be a long time coming in. Customers have to be found and sold to, and then there is a wait until they pay up. Both these examples show that although the current ratios are identical, the businesses are by no means in identical situations.

As a general rule, a higher working capital ratio is regarded as a move in the wrong direction. The more money a business has tied up in working capital, the more difficult it is to make a satisfactory ROCE, simply because the larger the denominator, the lower the ROCE.

In some cases, the right direction is more obvious. A high ROCE is usually better than a low one, but even this situation can be a danger signal, warning that higher risks are being taken.

Look at average results for a realistic view; do not be misled by low or high sales figures.

And not all high profit ratios are good: sometimes a higher profit margin can lead to reduced sales volume and so to lower overall profits.

Sizes of Different Businesses

There can also be problems in trying to compare one business's ratios with another. You would not, for example, expect a Mini to be able to cover a mile as quickly as a Jaguar. A new small business can achieve quite startling sales growth ratios in the early months and years. Expanding from £10,000 sales in the first six months to £100,000 in the second would not be unusual, yet to expect a mature business to achieve the same growth would be unrealistic. So some care must be taken to make sure that like is being compared with like.

Allowances must also be made for differing circumstances in the businesses being compared (or, if the circumstances are the same, then the trading/economic environment of the years being compared).

A Mature Business
Growth has to be relevant to the size of the business and the size of the market. For example, if BP grew from sales of £5 billion to £25 billion, it would wipe out every other oil company in the world.

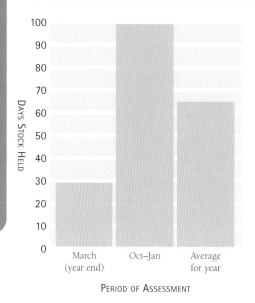

DAYS STOCK HELD

PERIOD OF ASSESSMENT

March (year end) — Oct–Jan — Average for year

SEASONAL VARIATIONS
As this chart shows, taking stock levels at any one time as being indicative of performance would be a mistake. The average figure is the one that gives a true picture.

Using either of these stock figures could give a false picture, but the average of the two might be nearer the mark.

In the example on the left you can see that the year-end stock figure from the accounts is barely a third of the high sales level later in the year. Basing any calculations on either figure would be a mistake. An average of somewhere between the high and low figures would be a more representative figure on which to work.

CHANGES IN INFLATION

Financial ratios all use money as the basis for comparison, and historical money at that. This would not be so bad if all these monies were from the same date in the past, but that is not so. You have to acccept that comparing one year with another may not be very meaningful unless you account for the change in the value of money caused by inflation.

In recent years, inflation has been relatively low in the developed world, ranging between 3 and 6 per cent. But it has not always been low, and if inflation increases again you will have to allow for it in your ratio analysis. Even at 4 per cent inflation, a figure of £1,000 from a four-year-old set of accounts would equate to just £855 today.

You may, for example, have calculated from their accounts that a competitor has been growing at 8 per cent on average over the past four years, without taking inflation into account. If inflation has been running at an average of 4 per cent, however, then the company's real growth has been only 4 per cent. Furthermore, if the economy has also been growing at 4 per cent, then it is possible that the company, far from growing healthily, as you had believed, has in fact been doing no more than drifting along with the current and achieving little growth.

It is also important to check that one business's idea of an account category, say current assets, is the same as yours. The concepts and principles used to prepare accounts do leave some scope for differences, and apparent variations may not, in fact, really exist. The notes to the accounts will help clarify this matter and explain any anomalies you may find. These are to be found at the end of the filed accounts.

SEASONAL FACTORS

Many ratios make use of information in the balance sheet. However, balance sheets are prepared at one particular moment in time and so may not represent the average situation.

For example, seasonal factors can cause a business's sales to be particularly high once or twice a year. A balance sheet prepared just before one of these seasonal upturns might show very high stocks, bought in specially to meet this demand, with accompanying very low cash, as a result of this stock purchase and a slack trading period. Conversely, a look at the balance sheet just after the upturn might show very high cash and rather low stocks.

FACTORS THAT AFFECT ROCE

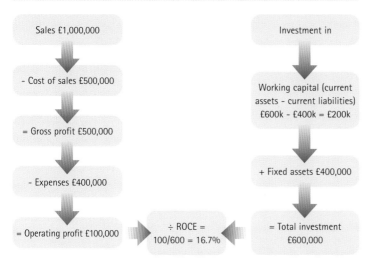

Sales £1,000,000

- Cost of sales £500,000

= Gross profit £500,000

- Expenses £400,000

= Operating profit £100,000

÷ ROCE =
100/600 = 16.7%

Investment in

Working capital (current assets - current liabilities) £600k - £400k = £200k

+ Fixed assets £400,000

= Total investment £600,000

EFFECTS ON ROCE
This combination of a profit and loss account (left column) and a balance sheet (right column) shows the different factors that affect ROCE (centre column). Altering any one of these factors will result in a different perentage.

Deciding on Financial Objectives

Before you can compare a business's performance using ratios, you need to have some idea of what that business wanted to, or should have been able to, achieve. Achieving a 15 per cent increase in sales might sound good, but if 25 per cent has been set as a realistic target, then the lower figure does not impress.

All well-managed businesses share some common objectives in the area of finance, and it is regarding performance in those areas that measurement is required. To make a satisfactory return on the capital or resources employed (ROCE), be it money or people, firms need to keep idle assets (or people) to a minimum. In the long run all businesses have to produce a satisfactory return on the money invested in them, or the money will simply go elsewhere.

FACTORS AFFECTING ROCE
Most, although not all, ratio analysis is about probing the various effects of a range of different actions on ROCE.

A useful generic model to help understand the factors affecting ROCE is shown in the chart above. The left-hand side of the chart is a cut-down profit and loss account and the right-hand side is a slice of the balance sheet, showing how the money is tied up. The numbers included show a return of £100,000 on capital employed of £600,000, which equates to 16.7 per cent.

▪ **INCREASED SALES OR DECREASED COSTS**
Either of these could result in an increase in profit. If the working capital, inventories, and debtors, for example, and the fixed assets (buildings, equipment, etc.) do not rise, then the ROCE will improve. For

TIME SAVER
When deciding on your financial objectives, you should do some research to find out how other businesses similar to your own have performed. You can do this by obtaining copies of their accounts, which usually come with key profit ratios already calculated.

FINANCIAL MATURITY

The maturity of a business is often reflected in its accounting system. A newly set-up business may keep no records at all, but by its second year it should have a basic bookkeeping system up and running. During its third year of trading, the business should be keeping a full set of accounts, and in its fourth year it can use these accounts to plan budgets and analyze ratios.

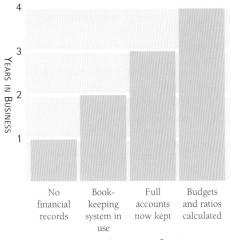

LEVEL OF ACCOUNTING SYSTEM

example, if the profit rises to £120,000, while the capital employed stays at £600,000, the ROCE rises to 20 per cent (120/600 x 100).

■ **A REDUCTION IN INVESTMENT** The same result can be achieved by reducing investment in fixed assets and working capital required to produce a given level of profit. In this example, if you could trim the stock holding down and employ less equipment, so reducing the capital employed from £600,000 to £500,000 (while still getting the same output and profit), the ROCE would once again be 20 per cent (100/500 x 100).

MAINTAINING A SOUND FINANCIAL POSITION

Businesses also want to maintain a sound financial position, achieve a healthy rate of growth, and exhibit signs of financial maturity. Achieving these objectives may require carrying more rather than less stock, for example, as well as having cash in hand for the unexpected. Those actions may appear to make the business look less efficient in the short run, but they will allow it to weather storms and so become more successful.

Some stability in ratios will be seen as a sign of financial maturity by banks and other financial institutions, and will lend some credibility to your projections. This in turn will improve your creditworthiness and make borrowing easier and perhaps less costly.

For example, a business that has consistently collected its money from customers in under 40 days will look more soundly run than one that took 45 days one year, 30 the next,

followed by a return to 45 days. The average is much the same, but in one case it looks as though the business has policies and procedures for collecting money that work, while in the other it looks more as though panic measures were introduced to deal with a cash-flow problem, then promptly dropped when cash became easier.

Applying the Yardsticks

As well as deciding which areas to examine, you need to know what standards to compare performance against. There are four generally accepted yardsticks that you can use. You can compare this year's results with:

■ last year's performance
■ self-imposed targets
■ a competitor's performance
■ industry-wide performances (benchmarking)

COMPARING THIS YEAR WITH LAST YEAR

Firstly, you might want to see how well you are doing this year compared with last, comparing performance against a historical standard. This is the way in which growth in sales or profits is often measured. There are, however, several limitations to this sort of comparison.

If accounting methods change from year to year, perhaps in the way depreciation is dealt with, then you are not comparing like with like. Also, the monies in one year are not the same as the monies in another, simply because inflation has changed them. An even more fundamental weakness with using historical comparisons alone is that your business may be quite different over time. Customers, products, staff, and equipment all change, so comparing one year with another may show up a difference without telling you much about why it occurred.

For example, if sales and profits of a business last year were £100,000 and £20,000 respectively, and this year they are £200,000 and £40,000, at first glance you would think that the business had done twice as well. But if you knew that all of that increase came from a special one-off order of a product that had been bought in from outside, so that the business acted only as a middleman, you might not be so impressed.

COMPARING THIS YEAR WITH A TARGET SET

A second type of comparison would be more revealing in these circumstances. Here you compare performance against the standards set for yourself. For example, you may want to double sales or add 25 per cent to profits, enter a new market, or launch new products and services. These objectives are set out in a budget that says, in effect, that you plan to spend this amount of money to achieve that particular result in this time period. Comparisons can then be made between actual results and the budget (see pp. 130–35).

COMPARING THIS YEAR WITH A COMPETITOR'S RESULTS

You may also want to see how well you are doing compared with someone else's business, perhaps a local competitor or someone in a similar line of business elsewhere. This may provide useful pointers to where improvements can be made or to new business opportunities. For this type of analysis you need external information. Fortunately, there is a wealth of readily available financial data on companies and industries to be found at Companies House, or its equivalent, and from credit-rating agencies.

USING BENCHMARKING

A fourth yardstick you can use is benchmarking. Some business sectors, such as the hypothetical example given in the chart below, submit information in an anonymous form to a central body. Then information, often in the form of ratios, is distributed so that people can see how well their business is doing compared with the best or average of their peers.

In the example below, if your delivery reliability was less than 85 per cent and your employees were absent for more than 5 per cent of the time, then your performance is worse than average and well short of the best.

PEER COMPARISONS
Benchmark ratios allow you to compare your performance with that of the best in your industry. A below average performance should act as a warning signal that all is not well with your business.

BENCHMARKING SMALL ENGINEERING FIRMS		AVERAGE	TOP 25%	TOP 10%
DELIVERY RELIABILITY		87%	98%	100%
TRAINING ON THE JOB	Existing employees	5 days	8 days	10 days
	New employees	12 days	20 days	28 days
ABSENTEEISM		3.2%	2%	1%

GOING INTO DETAIL

Rather as the various instruments on a vehicle dashboard tell you different things about its performance, such as speed, engine temperature, fuel level, and so on, so various ratios are used to reveal the different aspects of how a business is performing. Understanding how to interpret these ratios is a necessary first step before you can decide on areas for improvement in your business. The ratios will also tell you essential information about competitors, customers, and suppliers, and how successfully, or otherwise, their businesses are performing. In this chapter the key measures are examined that reveal the innermost workings of every business, including your own, showing how well or badly they are performing and how safe or risky they are.

For your own business you should have all the information readily to hand, as long as you have kept your bookkeeping up-to-date and prepared balance sheets and profit and loss accounts. Businesses that are limited companies have to file their accounts, which are then in the public domain and so available to all.

Financial ratios (many of which are expressed as percentages – a type of ratio in which everything is based against 100) can be clustered under a number of headings, each of which probes a different aspect of a business's performance. The areas covered in this chapter are the following:
■ profitability
■ liquidity
■ solvency
■ growth
■ value
■ safety

A set of sample accounts for an imaginary company named Fast Food Limited is shown on pp. 113–14. Analyses of these accounts are used throughout the chapter to illustrate the use of financial ratios. These are much simplified accounts, and not everything you would expect to see in a set of accounts has been included, but they provide enough information to illustrate the key ratios.

Measuring Profitability

The usual ratios to measure profitability or the efficient use of resources comprise:
■ gross margin percentage
■ operating margin pecentage
■ net margin percentage
■ Return on Capital Employed (ROCE)
■ Return on Shareholders' Investment (ROSI)
■ profits per employee

GROSS MARGIN PERCENTAGE

To arrive at this figure, you need to deduct the cost of sales from the sales revenue, and then express the result as a percentage of sales. The higher the percentage, the greater the value added to the goods and services produced.

$$\text{Gross margin} = \frac{\text{Gross profit} \times 100}{\text{Sales}}$$

In this case, the gross margin percentage for Fast Food in year 1 is:

$$\text{Gross margin} = \frac{50,000 \times 100}{100,000} = 50\%$$

For year 2 the gross margin percentage for Fast Food has moved down slightly to 48 per cent.

THE PROFIT AND LOSS ACCOUNT FOR FAST FOOD LIMITED FOR PAST TWO YEARS

		YEAR 1 (£)	%	YEAR 2 (£)	%
SALES		100,000	100	130,000	100
COST OF SALES	Materials	30,000	30	43,000	33
	Labour	20,000	20	25,000	19
COST OF GOODS SOLD		50,000		68,000	
GROSS PROFIT		50,000	50	62,000	48
EXPENSES	Rent, rates, etc.	18,000		20,000	
	Wages	12,000		13,000	
	Advertising	3,000		3,000	
	Depreciation			2,000	
TOTAL EXPENSES		33,000		38,000	
OPERATING OR TRADING PROFIT		17,000	17	24,000	18.5
DEDUCT INTEREST ON: BORROWINGS		2,150		2,050	
NET PROFIT BEFORE TAX		14,850	14.8	21,950	16.8
TAX PAID AT 20%		2,970		4,390	
NET PROFIT AFTER TAX		11,880	11.88	17,560	13.5
NUMBER OF EMPLOYEES		2		4	

FAST FOOD'S PROFIT AND LOSS ACCOUNT
The information provided here on sales, expenses, and borrowings enables Fast Food's accountant to calculate their net profit after tax. This is the money that can be used to pay dividends to shareholders or can be invested in the business.

Some possible causes for this downward shift include: lower selling prices, higher material or labour costs, wastage, and theft. In addition, a change in the types of products or services being sold can be a cause for such a downward movement.

OPERATING MARGIN PERCENTAGE

In this case you deduct not only the cost of sales but also expenses (other than financing charges, such as interest, and taxation).

This is a measure of how well the management is running the business. It is

BALANCE SHEET FOR FAST FOOD LIMITED FOR PAST TWO YEARS		YEAR 1	YEAR 2
NET ASSETS EMPLOYED		£	£
FIXED ASSETS	Furniture and fixtures	12,500	30,110
	Less depreciation		2,000
BOOK VALUE			28,110
CURRENT ASSETS	Stock	10,000	12,000
	Debtors	13,000	13,000
	Cash	100	500
TOTAL CURRENT ASSETS		23,100	25,500
LESS CURRENT LIABILITIES	Overdraft	5,000	6,000
	Creditors	1,690	5,500
TOTAL CURRENT LIABILITIES		6,690	11,500
NET CURRENT ASSETS		16,410	14,000
TOTAL ASSETS		28,910	42,110
LESS CREDITORS OVER ONE YEAR	Long-term bank loan	10,000	10,000
NET TOTAL ASSETS		18,910	32,110
FINANCED BY	Shareholders' funds	10,000	18,940
	Profit retained (reserves)	8,910	13,170
TOTAL SHAREHOLDERS' FUNDS		18,910	32,110

FAST FOOD'S BALANCE SHEET
Deducting all Fast Food's liabilities from its fixed and current assets produces the figure for its total assets. This figure also represents the amount of capital the owner has invested in the business.

usually assumed that financing decisions are taken by the business owner rather than the manager (although obviously in a small business the owner and manager are usually one and the same). It is also assumed that interest and taxation rates are set by the government of the day, thus taking decisions concerning these matters out of management control and accountability.

$$\text{Operating margin} = \frac{\text{Operating profit}}{\text{Sales}} \times 100$$

In this case, the operating profit percentage for Fast Food in year 1 is:

$$\text{Operating margin} = \frac{17,000}{100,000} \times 100 = 17\%$$

In year 2 this percentage is up slightly to 18.5 per cent, which is for the most part the result of total expenses being only £5,000 higher (£38,000 compared to £33,000) while sales were £30,000 higher.

NET MARGIN PERCENTAGE

This is the bottom line figure. It can be shown either before tax (EBIT – earnings before interest and tax) or after tax. In its after tax form, which is used here, it represents the sum available to be either distributed as dividends or retained by the business owner to invest in the future of the business.

$$\text{Net margin} = \frac{\text{Net profit}}{\text{Sales}} \times 100$$

In this example, the calculation for Fast Food in year 1 is:

$$\text{Net margin} = \frac{11,880}{100,000} \times 100 = 11.88\%$$

This would generally be considered a respectable figure, the range being between 5 and 25 per cent for most businesses.

In year 2 it is up to 13.5 per cent, which is largely brought about by the same reasons that led to the increase in operating profit. The fact that the cost of borrowing did not go up,

because the growth was financed by retained profits, also helped to achieve this increase in the net margin percentage.

RETURN ON CAPITAL EMPLOYED (ROCE)

This is the primary measure of performance for most businesses. If, for example, £10,000 invested in a bank earned you £500 interest in a year, then the return on your capital employed would be 5 per cent (£500 ÷ £10,000 × 100 = 5%).

In a business, this ratio is calculated by expressing the operating profit (that is, profit before interest and tax) as a percentage of the total capital employed – both in fixed assets and in working capital (called net current assets in the balance sheet).

$$\text{ROCE} = \frac{\text{Operating profit}}{\text{Fixed assets} + \text{Working capital}} \times 10$$

Note that the bottom part of the equation (the fixed assets + working capital) will equal the return on the shareholders' funds plus the long-term loans, that is, the "financed by" bit towards the bottom of the balance sheet.

In year 1 at Fast Food the ROCE is:

$$\text{ROCE} = \frac{17,000}{12,500 + 16,410} \times 100 = 59\%$$

In year 2 it is much the same, at 57 per cent. Both figures represent excellent results.

RETURN ON SHAREHOLDERS' INVESTMENT (ROSI)

The shareholders are usually most interested in the net return on their investment. So here you are concerned with the profit left after interest has been paid on any loans and after the taxman has had his slice. The shareholders have invested not only their initial stake but also any profits left in the business.

$$\text{ROSI} = \frac{\text{Net profit after tax and interest}}{\text{Total shareholders' fund}} \times 100$$

In this example, in year 1 the calculation of the

ROSI for Fast Food is:

$$ROSI = \frac{11,880}{18,910} \times 100 = 63$$

For small firms in general this ratio can be anywhere between a few percentage points and upwards of 35 per cent. Results such as those in this example are excellent.

PROFIT PER EMPLOYEE

If, as in most cases, your principal "assets" are people rather than capital assets, such as machines, then you will need to monitor what value your employees are contributing.

$$\text{Profit per employee} = \frac{\text{Net profit (after interest, but before tax)}}{\text{Number of employees}}$$

In Fast Food's case, the ratio for year 1 is:

$$\text{Profit per employee} = \frac{14,850}{2} = £7,425$$

The figure drops sharply during the following year to £5,487 profit per head. This is not very unusual because small businesses tend to move forward in a jerky fashion. For a firm employing 30 people, taking on two more members of staff would be a relatively small step that would not affect their finances too much. But for Fast Food such a move would represent a doubling of their workforce and therefore a huge increase in their fixed costs.

It can be useful to calculate the sales per employee too, to give you a feel for activity levels. As you can see from the table on the right, things at Fast Food are slowing down, with profits per employee dropping from £7,425 to £5,487.

You could then go on and benchmark Fast Food against others in the industry (see p. 111 for information on benchmarking). The table on p. 117 compares the average performance of

(see p. 111 ... The table on p. 117)

MEASURING PERFORMANCE
By bringing together all the different ratios calculated so far, a profitability chart can be drawn up. You can now see at a glance how Fast Food is performing.

all small firms in the UK, by sector, with that of Fast Food for sales per employee and ROCE. such comparisons can be helpful to a business.

Were Fast Food your business operating in the retail market, you would see opportunities for improvement in terms of sales per employee. The ROCE performance, however, is above average. The message here is that perhaps the capital investment in good new equipment is paying off, but you need to get a better result from your people. Incentive schemes, with rewards worth striving for, could be a way of achieving this.

Measuring Liquidity

L iquidity is a measure of a firm's ability to meet its current financial obligations as and when they fall due. But keeping sufficient finance, or working capital, available to meet these obligations is not necessarily the sound idea it would appear to be. The higher the level of working capital, the higher the overall

FAST FOOD'S PROFITABILITY AT A GLANCE	YEAR 1	YEAR 2
GROSS MARGIN	50%	48%
OPERATING MARGIN	17%	18.5%
NET MARGIN	11.88%	13.51%
RETURN ON CAPITAL EMPLOYED (ROCE)	59%	57%
RETURN ON SHAREHOLDERS' INVESTMENT (ROSI)	63%	55%
PROFIT PER EMPLOYEE	£7,425	£5,487

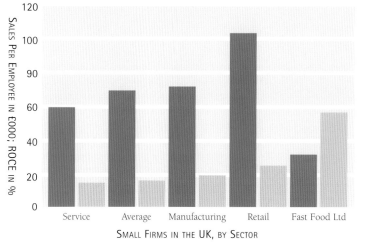

BENCHMARKING FAST FOOD
Comparing Fast Food's sales per employee and ROCE with figures for small businesses across the UK is a very informative exercise. While their ROCE is well above average, their sales-per-employee figure leaves much to be desired.

▓ SALES PER EMPLOYEE
£000

▒ ROCE %

SALES PER EMPLOYEE IN £000; ROCE IN %

SMALL FIRMS IN THE UK, BY SECTOR

(Service, Average, Manufacturing, Retail, Fast Food Ltd)

amount of capital that is being used. That, in turn, means that profits have to be that much higher to make the same (or better) return on the capital employed.

The following measures all help to assess liquidity, or the lack of it:
▓ current ratio
▓ quick ratio
▓ credit control ratios
▓ ageing debtors
▓ average collection period
▓ average payment period
▓ stock (inventory) control
▓ circulation of working capital
All of these measures are analyzed below, with reference to Fast Food's performance, so that you can understand how they are calculated and what their relevance is.

CURRENT RATIO

To identify the current ratio, you need to do the following calculation:

$$\text{Current ratio} = \frac{\text{Current assets}}{\text{Current liabilities}}$$

In the accounts for Fast Food, the first year's picture on the balance sheet shows £23,100 current assets to £6,690 current liabilities.

Therefore, for Fast Food, the calculation is:

$$\text{Current ratio} = \frac{23,100}{6,690} = 3.4$$

This shows current liabilities to be covered 3.4 times, and the ratio is usually expressed in the form 3.4:1. In the second year this has come down to 2.2:1 (25,500 ÷ 11,500 = 2.2).

At first glance, this last figure may look worse than the first year's position. Certainly, current liabilities have grown faster than current assets, but up to a point this is in fact a desirable state of affairs, because it means that the business is having to find less money to finance its working capital.

There is really only one rule that you need to remember about the level of a current ratio: it should be as close to 1:1 as the safe conduct of the business will allow.

This will not be the same for every type of business, however. A shop buying in finished goods on credit and selling them for cash could run safely at 1.3:1. A manufacturer, with raw materials to store and customers to finance, may need over 2:1. This is because the period between paying cash out for raw materials and receiving cash in from customers is longer in a manufacturing business than in a retail business.

Quick Ratio

In this ratio, only assets that can be realized quickly, such as debtors and cash in hand, are related to current liabilities. Note that the term "debtors" refers to the amount owed by debtors.

$$\text{Quick ratio} = \frac{\text{Debtors} + \text{Cash}}{\text{Current liabilities}}$$

In the Fast Food example, looking at year 1 only, you would exclude the £10,000 stock because, before it could be realized, you would need to find customers to sell it to, and then collect in the cash. All this might take several months. Fast Food's ratio would therefore be:

$$\text{Quick ratio} = \frac{13,100}{6,690} = 1.9$$

In the second year this has dropped to 1.2:1 (13,500 ÷ 11,500). A quick ratio of 0.8:1 would be acceptable for most businesses.

Credit Control Ratios

Any small business selling on credit knows just how quickly cash flow can become a problem. This is particularly true if the customers are big companies, despite the wave of legislation in many countries to encourage prompt payment.

Surprisingly enough, bad debts (those that are never paid) are rarely as serious a problem as slow payers. Many companies think nothing of taking three months' credit, and it is important to remember that, even if your terms are 30 days, it will often be nearer 45 days, or possibly longer, before you are actually paid.

TIME SAVER

A simple way to keep track of liquidity is to total the amount of money you are owed by customers and compare that with the money you owe to suppliers. If the numbers are broadly similar, you are likely to be able to pay bills as they fall due. The higher the favourable margin, the better.

This to some extent depends on how frequently invoices are sent out. Assuming they do not go out each day, and, perhaps more importantly, that your customer batches bills for payment monthly, then that is how things will work out. Help is at hand, though, with the following two control methods.

Ageing Your Debtors

The first method of monitoring debts is to prepare a schedule of all your debtors ranked by age of debt. The table shown above right gives some idea of how this might be done. This method has the merit of focusing attention clearly on specific problem accounts. Once you have got the system going, it will pay dividends.

Average Collection Period

The second technique for monitoring debtors is using the ratio of average collection period. This ratio is calculated by expressing a business's debtors as a proportion of its credit sales, and then relating that figure to the days of the trading period in the period in question.

$$\text{Average collection period} = \frac{\text{Debtors} \times 365}{\text{Sales}}$$

Let us suppose that all Fast Food's sales are on credit and the periods in question are both 365-day years (that is, no leap years). In year 1, the ratio would be:

$$\text{Average collection period} = \frac{13,000 \times 365}{100,000} = 47$$

In year 2, the collection period is 36 days (13,000 ÷ 130,000 x 365 = 36). In this second year, therefore, Fast Food are collecting their cash from debtors 11 days sooner than in year 1. Their total debtors are the same, but the relative amount is lower in year 2. Fast Food's sales have grown by 30 per cent to £130,000, and their debtors have remained at £13,000.

This is a good control ratio, which has the merit of being easily translatable into a figure anyone can understand, showing how much it is costing a business to give credit to customers.

FAST FOOD'S DEBTORS' SCHEDULE - END OF YEAR 1

DEBTOR	2 MONTHS OR LESS (£)	3 MONTHS (£)	4 MONTHS (£)	OVER 4 MONTHS (£)	TOTAL (£)
SMITH & CO	1,000				
BROWN & SON	1,000				
BARNES		3,000			
ELLIOTS		2,500			
RUTLINS			500		
LARKIN & CO			2,500		
BRIGHT INC				2,500	
TOTAL	2,000	5,500	3,000	2,500	13,000

RANKING DEBTORS BY AGE
Listing all your debtors by the credit terms you have agreed with each debtor will enable you to keep track of the money owed to you.

If, for example, Fast Food is paying 10 per cent for an overdraft, then giving £13,000 credit for 36 days will cost £128.22 (10 per cent x £13,000 x 36 ÷ 365 = £128.22).

AVERAGE PAYMENT PERIOD
Of course, the credit world is not all one-sided. Once a small business has established itself, it too will be taking credit. You can usually rely

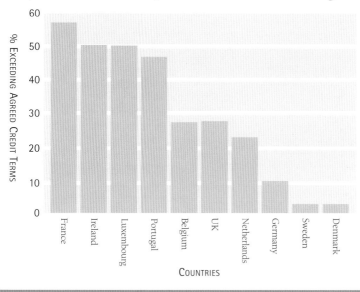

VARIATIONS IN PAYMENT TIMES
This chart shows the percentage of companies exceeding agreed credit terms in selected European countries. If you are selling into overseas markets, the practice on punctual payments can vary widely.

on your suppliers to keep you informed of your indebtedness, but only on an individual basis. To get the overall picture, it would be prudent to calculate how many days' credit, on average, are being taken from suppliers, using a very similar sum to average collection period. Note that the term "creditors" in the ratio means the amount of money you owe to creditors.

$$\text{Average payment period} = \frac{\text{Creditors} \times 365}{\text{Materials}}$$

For Fast Food, in year 1, the ratio would be:

$$\text{Average payment period} = \frac{1,690 \times 365}{30,000} = 21 \text{ days}$$

In year 2, this ratio would be 47 days ($5,500 \div 43,000 \times 365 = 47$). The difference in these ratios probably reflects Fast Food's greater creditworthiness in year 2 (the amount for purchases assumes that all materials were purchased in the period in question). The longer the credit period you can take from your suppliers, the better, provided that you still meet their terms of trade.

There are two other useful techniques to help the business manager keep track of these events: relating credit given to credit taken and ageing your creditors.

Relating Credit Given to Credit Taken

One technique is simply to relate days' credit given to days' credit taken. If they balance out, then you are about even in the credit game.

In year 1, Fast Food gave 47 days' credit to their customers and took only 21 days from their suppliers, so they were a loser. In the second year they got ahead, giving only 36 days while taking 47.

Ageing your Creditors

The other technique is to age your creditors in exactly the same way as the debtors (see p. 118). In this way it is possible to see at a glance which suppliers have been owed what sums of money, and for how long.

Stock (Inventory) Control

A manufacturing, subcontracting, or assembling business, such as a picture framer, will have to buy in raw materials and work on them to produce finished goods. They will have to keep track of three sorts of stock: raw materials, work in progress, and finished goods. A business such as a builder may hold no stock at all, buying materials only as and when needed for each job. A retailing business, such as a shop, will probably be concerned only with buying in finished goods on credit and selling them for cash. If you assume that all of Fast Food's stock is in finished goods, then the control ratio you can use is as follows:

$$\text{Days' finished goods stock} = \frac{\text{Finished goods stock} \times \text{days in period}}{\text{Cost of sales}}$$

Note that the cost of sales is used because it accurately reflects the amount of stock, whereas the sales figure includes other items, such as the profit margin. If you are looking at the accounts of an external company, it is probable that the only figure available for your calculations will be that for sales. In this case, it can be used as an approximation.

For Fast Food in year 1, this ratio is:

$$\text{Days' finished goods stock} = \frac{10,000}{50,000} \times 365 = 73 \text{ days}$$

In year 2, the ratio is 64 days ($12,000 \div 68,000 \times 365 = 64$).

It is difficult to make rules about stock levels. A business has to carry enough stock to meet demand, and a retail business must have it on display or to hand. However, if Fast Food's supplier can always deliver within 14 days, it would be unnecessary to carry 73 days' stock.

The same basic equation can be applied to both raw material and work-in-progress stock, but to calculate raw materials stock you should substitute raw materials consumed ("materials" on the profit and loss account) in the equation for cost of sales.

Once again, the strength of this ratio is that a business can quickly and easily calculate how much it is costing them to carry a given level of stock, in just the same way as customer credit costs are calculated.

Another way to look at stock control is to see how often your stock is turned over each year.

$$\text{Stock turnover} = \frac{\text{Cost of sales}}{\text{Stock}}$$

So, for Fast Food this ratio would be:

$$\text{Stock turnover} = \frac{50,000}{10,000} = 5$$

CIRCULATION OF WORKING CAPITAL

While the current ratio calculated previously gives an overall feel for a business's ability to pay its creditors, this is of less interest to the manager of a business, who is more concerned with how well the money tied up in working capital is being used.

From Fast Food's balance sheet for the last two years (see p. 114) you can see that net current assets – another name for working capital – have fallen from £16,410 to £14,000. This fall is not too dramatic in itself, but now look at these figures in relation to the level of business activity in each year and you will see them in a different light.

The ratio for calculating the circulation of working capital is:

$$\text{Circulation of working capital} = \frac{\text{Sales}}{\text{Working capital}}$$

For year 1 for Fast Food this is:

$$\text{Circulation of working capital} = \frac{100,000}{16,410} = 6\text{x (times)}$$

In other words, each £1 of Fast Food's working capital produces £6 of sales. For year 2, the ratio is now 9 times, or £9 (£130,000 ÷ £14,000 = 9).

You can see from this calculation that not only has Fast Food got less money tied up in working capital in its second year of trading than in its first, but also that it has used its working capital more efficiently. In other words, it has circulated its working capital faster. Each £1 of working capital now produces £9 of sales, as opposed to only £6 in the first year, and because each £1 of sales makes profit, it follows that the faster the working capital is turned around, the higher the profit level will be.

The chart at the top of p. 122 illustrates what happens to a business's profits when its working capital circulation is increased step by step from a basic one times up to an impressive ten times.

CONTROLLING STOCK
Any retailing business must ensure that it carries enough stock to keep the shelves filled to meet demand at all times. An efficient stock control system is essential to maintain the right levels.

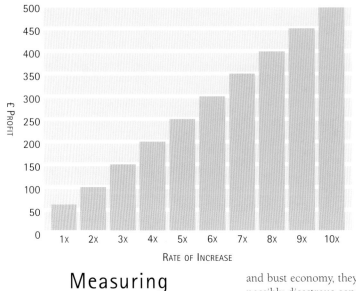

INCREASING WORKING CAPITAL CIRCULATION
This chart shows the effect on profits of increasing the rate of circulation of working capital in a business that makes £50 gross profit per £100 sales.

£ PROFIT

RATE OF INCREASE

Measuring Solvency

J ust as liquidity is concerned with the short-term position, "solvency" is the term used to describe a business's long-term financial position. Trading while insolvent is a serious matter, and any business found guilty of doing this could have the protection of limited liability stripped away.

The long-term financial position consists of looking at two things: the proportion of a business's funds that is borrowed, as opposed to being put up by the shareholders, and how well the business is able to meet any interest costs associated with such borrowing.

GEARING

The more borrowed money a business uses, as opposed to that put in by the shareholders (through initial capital injection or by reinvesting profits in the business), the more highly geared the business is.

Highly geared businesses can be vulnerable either when sales dip sharply, as in a recession, or when interest rates rocket, as in a boom. If one follows the other, as can happen in a boom

and bust economy, they may be hit twice, with possibly disastrous consequences.

$$\text{Gearing} = \frac{\text{Debt (Long-term borrowings)} \times 100}{\text{Debt + Shareholders' funds}}$$

(Debt is listed under less creditors over one year.)

For Fast Food, the ratio for year 1 is:

$$\text{Gearing} = \frac{10,000}{(10,000 + 18,910)} \times 100 = 35\%$$

This means that 35 per cent of the money used in the business was borrowed in the first year. In the second year, that drops to 24 per cent (10,000 ÷ [10,000 + 32,110] x 100 = 24).

Small firms' gearing levels on average range from 60 down to 30 per cent. But many small firms are probably seriously overgeared, especially so as they go into the first stages of growth. This puts them in a vulnerable position.

INTEREST COVER

While gearing is important, it is equally important to look at a company's ability to service the interest on that borrowing. If you were fortunate enough to inherit £250,000, you could buy a substantial country house for £500,000 million and only be 50 per cent

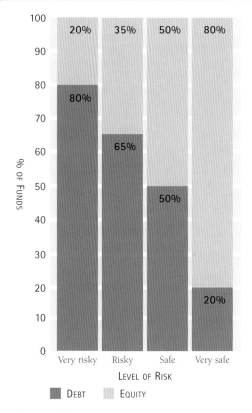

100

| 20% | 35% | 50% | 80% |

90

80

80%

70

% OF FUNDS

60

65%

50

50%

40

30

20

20%

10

0

| Very risky | Risky | Safe | Very safe |

LEVEL OF RISK

▨ DEBT   ▨ EQUITY

FINANCIAL RISK
Overgeared businesses run at high risk because the proportion of their funds that are borrowed is very high. A safer position is reached once debt and equity are balanced, and any further decrease in debt adds to the safety of the business.

geared. What may be difficult is to find the £2,000 per month required to pay the interest on the loan for the remaining £250,000.

$$\text{Interest cover} = \frac{\text{Operating profit}}{\text{Interest on long-term debt}}$$

So, Fast Food's interest cover for year 1 is:

$$\text{Interest cover} = \frac{17,000}{2,150} = 8x$$

In year 2, it increases to nearly 12 times (24,000 ÷ 2,050).

Anything upwards of four times interest cover would be viewed as respectable; below three times might be worrying.

Measuring Growth

The most common measures of growth are sales turnover and the number of employees (popular yardsticks with owners and governments, respectively), but neither is of much use unless profit is taken into account. Many businesses rapidly aspire to growing turnover with little regard to profitability. Healthy growth, however, requires both sales turnover and profits being grown in proportion.

There are five styles of growth that small businesses gravitate towards. Only two have particular merit, two are potentially dangerous, and one seems to make being in business for yourself something of a pointless exercise.

CHAMPIONS
This is a term that would describe companies who grow their profits and turnover by at least 25 per cent each year. This would be fewer than 6 per cent of firms at the last count. This growth strategy gives you a strong position in the market, with a growing sales presence and the profit to develop new products and services without needing to borrow.

Fast Food is an example of a champion. Profits are growing at 41 per cent, while sales are growing at 30 per cent.

PROFIT ENHANCERS
These companies concentrate on growing profits alone. This equally small proportion of the small business population can become vulnerable, because they are building on a fairly static customer base.

GRAZERS
These businesses move forward steadily at a pace that reflects their markets in general, rather like

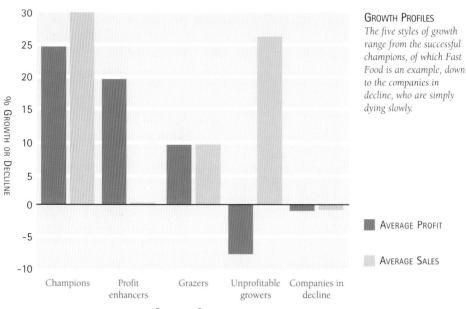

■ AVERAGE PROFIT

░ AVERAGE SALES

a boat being swept along with the tide. The danger here is that although the boat is on an even keel in calm conditions, the tide may turn, bringing with it dangerous conditions.

UNPROFITABLE GROWERS

These are firms whose sales move forward sharply, while their profits are either fairly static or even going down. This is a particularly dangerous course to follow. With sales growth come all sorts of additional costs for producing, distributing, and selling the goods – for example, more stock, more equipment, more

staff – which all have to be supported from a static revenue base. Just one bad debt or quality problem causing delays in payments is enough to sink such a business.

COMPANIES IN DECLINE

These companies are going backwards by both measures. Their market positions are getting weaker, with a smaller sales base, and they are not making enough profit to do anything new.

It may be instructive to position your business and that of any competitors on the growth chart above to see how you compare.

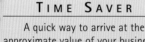

TIME SAVER

A quick way to arrive at the approximate value of your business is to research how much comparable businesses have been sold for. By making an allowance for any difference in size, you can work out how much your business would have been worth to that buyer.

Measuring Value

You may not be thinking about selling your business yet, because your business is perhaps your most valuable asset, but you may want to assess its value from time to time.

If you are thinking of selling, you have a number of options. You may sell to the

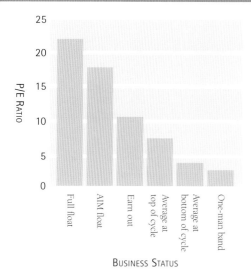

BUSINESS STATUS

(P/E Ratio chart with values from left to right: Full float ≈22, AIM float ≈18, Earn out ≈10.5, Average at top of cycle ≈7.5, Average at bottom of cycle ≈4, One-man band ≈2.5. Y-axis: P/E Ratio 0–25)

EFFECTS OF BUSINESS STATUS ON P/E RATIO

The price/earnings(P/E) ratio will be affected by whether your business has been floated and whether it is a one-man band. A publicly quoted company will have a ratio up to a third higher than a private company, and a sole trader has the lowest P/E ratio of just 4.

The P/E ratio is the number of times its annual profits at which a business is valued.
If you look up a company's performance in the financial press, you will see a P/E ratio calculated in the following way:

$$\text{P/E ratio} = \frac{\text{Market price per share}}{\text{Earnings per share}}$$

To arrive at this ratio, you must first calculate the earnings per share by dividing the net profit by the number of share issues. For example, if a company had made £80,000 net profit and had issued 100,000 shares, the earnings per share would be 80p. If the share price of the business in question was £10 and the share price was 80p, then the P/E ratio is 12.5. This is another way of saying that the company is worth 12½ years' profits.

If you look up another company, in the internet sector for example, you might find a quite different multiple in force; 203 years' earnings is an all-time record in this sector.

If your business is in the food sector, and average P/E ratios there are 12, then that is where outsiders will start when they think about valuing your business. To reach a final figure, any valuer would also need to take the following into account:

▓ any discount for a business not yet floated
▓ unnecessary running costs
▓ the economic cycle

management, pass it on to family members, or sell to another business. But whatever route you take will involve placing a value on the business. There are two options for valuing a business: assessing the value of the assets on the open market or calculating the price/earnings ratio.

VALUE OF ASSETS

One way to measure value is to work out what the various assets of the business would be worth on the open market. So, vehicles, premises, equipment, and any other assets could be professionally valued. From that sum you would take any outstanding liabilities to creditors, bank borrowings, tax authorities, and redundancy payments due. This assessment might make sense if the business were actually going to stop trading, but it is unlikely to produce the best value.

PRICE/EARNINGS RATIO

Part, perhaps even all, that a small business has to sell, in the final resort, is its capacity to make profit. At any rate that is where the debate about value will start. The ratio most commonly used here to calculate the capacity for profit is price/earnings (P/E).

DISCOUNT FOR A BUSINESS NOT ON THE STOCK MARKET

The first seriously negative event is the discount that will be applied because your business is not on the stock market. Private businesses are generally viewed as being worth at least a third less than a publicly quoted firm.

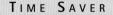

TIME SAVER

Talk to someone in your industry who has recently sold up and who was satisfied with the advice they got and the end result. Get the names of their advisers and speak to them. This will save time by allowing you to focus on the key issues from the outset, having learned from someone else's experience.

This is because shares in a public company are much more liquid. There are more shares, and more buyers and sellers, for quoted than for unquoted businesses' shares. So Fast Food could find itself being valued in this way:

$$\text{P/E ratio} = \frac{12.00}{1.50} = 8$$

If the private company is a one-man band, or is seen as such, that ratio might be halved to a P/E of 4. The reasoning here is that the customers are probably loyal to the business owner and may not come over to any new owner. There is no certainty that the business will have a profitable life without the owner.

UNNECESSARY RUNNING COSTS

On the positive side, any expense seen as being unnecessary to running the business will be added back into profits before the sum is done. So if you have got three family members on the payroll who are performing no useful purpose, or who are taking out more than a new owner would have to pay to have the business run, then that sum would go back to swell the profits.

Operating profit is the figure used in this ratio, alongside the P/E ratio of 4 or 8 (see p. 125). Depending on how good you are at persuading a potential buyer that Fast Food is not a one-man band, and that the boss is currently overpaid, it could be worth anything

from £96,000 (4 x £24,000) up to, say, £296,000 (8 x [£24,000 + £13,000 wages]). Perceptions are at least as important as figures when it comes to valuations.

ECONOMIC CYCLE

One last factor that affects private business valuations is the economic cycle. At the bottom of the cycle (a downturn), small private firms sell on average on multiples of between six and eight. At the top of the cycle (a boom), the same firm may sell for between 10 and 12.

All these figures are illustrative only. Every business sale and every circumstance has unique elements to it that can greatly affect the final outcome, and therefore the valuation.

Measuring Safety

A particular volume of sales is required to cover the overheads and the cost of any materials and labour involved in your product or service. The point at which these different areas balance is known as break-even. Once a business passes the break-even point – in other words, when sales are greater than the overheads, materials, and labour costs – profits start to be made.

Your new business needs to become profitable relatively quickly, or it will run out of money

Any business operating at, or close to, break-even, exposes itself to unnecessary risks, because there is simply no room for error. A small drop in sales could be disastrous.

Obviously the more output, be that hours to sell, spare seats in a restaurant, or extra capacity in a factory, that you have available beyond the break-even volume, the better. The relationship between total sales capacity and the break-even point is called the margin of safety, which is usually expressed as a percentage. The business needs to be kept at a safe percentage margin of safety.

BREAK-EVEN POINT

The break-even analysis is an important tool to be used both in preparing a business plan and in the day-to-day running of a business. Understanding the danger of high fixed costs and the different characteristics of fixed and variable costs are important steps towards calculating the break-even point for your business.

THE DANGER OF HIGH FIXED COSTS

While some businesses have difficulty raising start-up capital, paradoxically one of the main reasons why small businesses fail in the early stages is that too much of the start-up capital is used to buy fixed assets.

Some equipment is clearly essential at the start, but other purchases could be postponed. This may mean that desirable and labour-saving devices have to be borrowed or hired for a specific period. This is obviously not as convenient as having them to hand all the time, but if, for example, colour photocopiers, laptop computers, and even delivery vehicles are brought into the business at the outset, they become part of the fixed costs.

The higher the fixed cost plateau, the longer it usually takes to reach break-even and then profitability. Becoming profitable quickly is essential for the survival of any business.

THE CHARACTERISTICS OF COSTS

Difficulties in calculating break-even usually begin when people become confused by the different characteristics of costs.

Some costs do not change, however much you sell; these are known as fixed costs. If you are running a shop, the rent and rates are fairly constant figures, independent of the sales volume.

The cost of the products sold from the shop, however, is completely dependent on volume: the more you sell, the more it costs to buy stock. These are known as variable costs, or costs of production. Assumptions about sales will have to be made before you can add these to the fixed costs and so arrive at total costs.

CALCULATING BREAK-EVEN

The method of calculating break-even is:

$$\text{Break-even point} = \frac{\text{Fixed costs}}{\text{Contribution}}$$

The term "contribution" refers to the amount of money left over from the sales value after costs of production have been deducted. In Fast

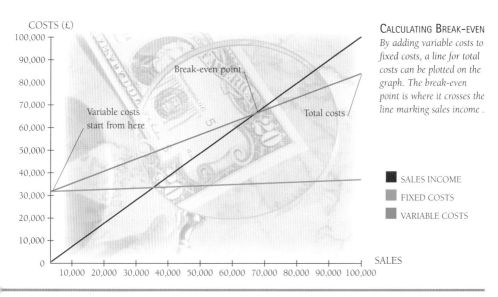

COSTS (£)

Break-even point

Variable costs start from here

Total costs

CALCULATING BREAK-EVEN
By adding variable costs to fixed costs, a line for total costs can be plotted on the graph. The break-even point is where it crosses the line marking sales income .

■ SALES INCOME

▓ FIXED COSTS

▓ VARIABLE COSTS

SALES

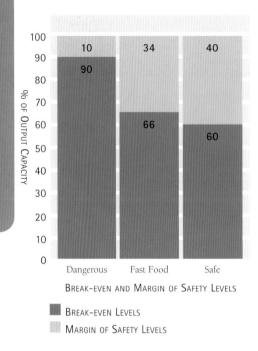

BREAK-EVEN AND MARGIN OF SAFETY LEVELS

■ BREAK-EVEN LEVELS

▨ MARGIN OF SAFETY LEVELS

PLAYING SAFE

Fast Food's break-even point of £66,000 gives them a just about acceptable margin of safety of 34 per cent. Any improvement on that would make the business a safer one. Had their break-even point been £90,000, they would have had a dangerously low 10 per cent margin of safety.

for Fast Food are £50,000 to achieve £100,000 sales, so the line must climb by £50,000 from the £33,000 starting point by the time it reaches £100,000 worth of sales. The total costs are therefore £83,000.

The sales income line starts from zero. If you sell nothing, you get no income, but if you sell everything, you get £100,000.

Now you can see that the break-even point – the point at which the sales income line crosses the total costs line – is £66,000. So when Fast Food achieve £66,000-worth of sales they have broken even. When they get beyond this level of sales, they are in profit.

MARGIN OF SAFETY

The output available after break-even has been reached is known as the margin of safety. It is usually expressed as a percentage. The higher the percentage, the greater the margin. A low margin leaves little room for profitable trading.

Fast Food have £34,000 (£100,000 minus £66,000) out of a total capacity of £100,000 left after break-even. This equates to a 34 per cent margin of safety, which is on the borders of acceptability (see chart above).

Suppose, however, that the break-even point for Fast Food was £90,000, not £66,000. If the limit of their output was still £100,000, then they would have only £10,000 of sales capacity left on which to make the year's profit. This represents a dangerously low 10 per cent margin of safety.

Food's case, this would be 50p in the pound or 0.5 pounds (£100,000 sales minus £50,000 costs of production, or variable costs):

Break-even point = $\dfrac{33,000}{0.5}$ = £66,000

BREAK-EVEN POINT FOR FAST FOOD

By recalculating Fast Food's break-even point step by step, you can see how this simple calculation is done. To make the calculations as comprehensible as possible, they have been displayed in graph format (see p. 127). In this case the assumption has been made that the theoretical limit of sales in year 1 is £100,000.

First the line for fixed costs is put in on the graph. In this case these are the £33,000-worth of expenses. These costs do not vary whether £1- or £100,000-worth of goods is sold.

The next line put in is for variable costs. In Fast Food's case they are the £50,000 cost of goods sold. The variable cost line starts from the fixed cost line (at £33,000) to give the total costs. The variable costs of material and labour

MAKING AN ACTION PLAN

Calculate key ratios for your business, both for the current year and for last year (if you were trading). See how much better or worse your performance is year on year. Now get those ratios for your main competitor and see how much better or worse your performance is by comparison. Finally, identify the areas that need improving and decide on an action plan.

KEY RATIO SUMMARY AND PERFORMANCE IMPROVEMENT ACTION PLAN

	LAST YEAR	THIS YEAR	% BETTER OR WORSE PERFORMANCE	MAIN COMPETITORS	% BETTER OR WORSE THAN OUR PERFORMANCE	ACTION TO BE TAKEN
PROFITABILITY						
GROSS MARGIN PERCENTAGE						
NET MARGIN PERCENTAGE						
PROFIT PER EMPLOYEE						
RETURN ON CAPITAL EMPLOYED						
LIQUIDITY						
CURRENT RATIO						
QUICK RATIO						
AVERAGE COLLECTION PERIOD						
AVERAGE PAYMENT PERIOD						
SOLVENCY						
GEARING						
INTEREST COVER						
GROWTH						
SALES GROWTH PERCENTAGE						
PROFIT GROWTH PERCENTAGE						
SAFETY						
BREAK-EVEN POINT						
MARGIN OF SAFETY PERCENTAGE						
OTHER KEY RATIOS FOR YOUR BUSINESS						

SETTING OUT YOUR BUDGET

As we have seen, the gold standard for measuring our achievement is how close we are to meeting or exceeding the objectives we have set for our own performance. A budget makes you think ahead, set objectives, allocate responsibility for key tasks, and get commitment from management. It sets the goals you intend to achieve, and by comparing your progress with your budget you will know when action is needed to keep the business on course. The budget brings a measure of predictability into an uncertain world.

While the business plan sets the strategic direction and purpose of the business, it is the budget that fleshes out exactly how each year of that plan will be implemented.

The budget sets out, line by line, in much the same format as the profit and loss account, the major sources of income and expenditure for the period of the budget. The year is broken down into weeks or months, depending on the dynamics of your business.

WHEN TO BUDGET

The best way to budget is to look one year ahead and review the whole budget each quarter. At that review, add a further quarter on to the end, so that you always have a one-year budget horizon. This is known as a rolling quarterly budget.

It may seem like hard work at first, but the sooner budgeting becomes a business routine, the more accurate your forecasts will become. This not only makes the whole planning process more easy and reliable, but it can have the knock-on effect of making your business more creditworthy and valuable. Any business that consistently meets or exceeds its targets will have its profit targets accepted more readily than one that doesn't.

If, at the end of a quarter, you are 25 per cent off budget, take heart from the fact that this means that you have been 75 per cent successful.

CASE STUDY: Budgeting for Growth

ALISTAIR HOLMES visited a craft trade show every year in order to sell his work. After a few years he was approached by a foreign buyer, who placed a significant order. This made Alistair think about exporting, because he felt he was by now sufficiently well established. He had spoken at some length to this buyer and thought there was scope to sell even more of his products in that particular country. Unfortunately, the buyer wanted an exclusive arrangement, so Alistair had to consider other territories.

He wrote to the overseas buyer confirming his terms, and he decided to add that the exclusive arrangement would be for an initial two years. The agreement depended on the buyer's company placing enough regular orders for an agreed minimum quantity, and paying on time. Alistair felt confident enough to increase his production budget for the forthcoming year. He also decided to make his most experienced sales person responsible for liaising with the new customer. He set him a target 10 per cent higher than the minimum order quantity.

HOW TO BUDGET

When setting out and using a budget there are a number of guidelines it is prudent to follow. They can be summarized thus:

■ **SET REALISTIC BUT STRETCHING GOALS** The budget must be based on realistic but challenging goals. Those goals are arrived at by both a top-down aspiration and a bottom-up forecast of what seems both possible and likely. So, for example, if sales have been growing at 10 per cent a year for the past couple of years, that seems a possible and likely outcome for next year, and one that your sales force might go for. However, your business plan may involve trying to grow at a faster rate than in the past, in which case a goal of 15 per cent could be seen as challenging but realistic.

■ **ASK THE RIGHT PEOPLE** The budget should be prepared by those responsible for delivering the results. So the salespeople should prepare the sales budget and the production people should prepare the production budget. You need to manage the communication process so that everyone knows and is happy with what the other party is planning.

■ **GET AGREEMENT** Agreement to the budget should be explicit. During the budgeting process, several versions of a particular budget will be discussed. For example, you may want to achieve a sales figure of £2

REASONS FOR BUDGETING

1 Ensures you make financial projections and plans, and keep them up-to-date.

2 Provides you with a standard against which to measure your performance.

3 Highlights areas of your business that need attention or improving.

4 Allows you to delegate responsibility for certain aspects of revenue generation and cost control.

5 Makes it more likely that you will never run out of cash.

million, while your sales team's initial forecast is for £1.75 million. After some debate, £1.9 million may be the figure accepted. Once agreed, a virtual contract exists, declaring a commitment to achieve on one hand (the sales team) and a commitment both to resource and to be satisfied with the team's best efforts on the other (you). It makes sense for this commitment to be in writing.

■ **COMPLETE IN TIME** The budget needs to be finalized at least a month before the start of the year, and not weeks or months into the year. The reason for this is that the sooner people know their goals, the sooner they can start to achieve them.

■ **REVIEW REGULARLY** The budget should be reviewed fundamentally at intervals during the year, in order to make sure that all the basic assumptions that underpin it still hold good. For example, the market itself may be growing much faster than you expected, so rendering your goals too easy a target. Conversely, hard times in the market may mean that you have to reduce your targets.

■ **COLLATE PROMPTLY** You need timely and accurate information to make the process worthwhile. Figures should be ready for review within seven to ten working days of the month end.

FACT FILE

Overtrading describes a business that is expanding beyond its financial resources. As sales expand, the money tied up in stocks and customers' credit grows rapidly. Presssure also comes from suppliers who want payment for the ever-increasing supply of raw materials. The natural escape valve for pressures on working capital is an overdraft (or a substantial increase in the current one).

SIMPLE BUDGET LAYOUT				
	MONTH		YEAR TO DATE	
	ACTUAL (£)	BUDGET (£)	ACTUAL CUMULATIVE (£)	BUDGET CUMULATIVE (£)
SALES	8,288	7,500	24,960	23,250
DIRECT COST OF SALES — Materials	2,475	2,250	7,527	6,825
Labour	2,063	1,950	6,248	5,925
Direct overheads	675	650	2,071	1,950
TOTAL SALES	5,213	4,850	15,846	14,700
GROSS MARGIN	3,075	2,650	9,114	8,550
EXPENSES — Factory	1,140	1,100	3,527	3,375
Selling	375	400	1,201	1,170
Technical	308	300	963	915
Accounting	245	240	757	735
Administrative	335	345	1,080	1,050
TOTAL EXPENSES	2,403	2,385	7,528	7,245
CONTRIBUTION TO ANNUAL PROFIT	672	265	1,586	1,305

BUDGET LAYOUT

This example of a simple budget shows figures for one month as well as cumulative figures for the year to date. You can see that sales of £8,288 have exceeded their budget of £7,500. This increase in sales results in higher than budgeted figures for just about every other aspect of the budget, with the exception of selling and administrative costs.

Monitoring Performance

Performance against budget needs to be carefully monitored as the year proceeds, and corrective action should be taken, where necessary, to keep you on track. This has to be done month by month (or at shorter time intervals if required), showing both the period in question and the cumulative year to date.

Looking at the fixed budget example (see above right) you can see at a glance that the business is behind on sales for this month but

ahead on the year to date. The convention is to put all unfavourable variances in brackets, so a higher than budgeted sales figure does not have brackets, but a higher material costs figure does.

You can also see that, while profit is running ahead of budget, the profit margin is slightly behind (-0.3 per cent). This is in part because other direct costs, such as labour or distribution in this example, are running well ahead of the targets set in the budget.

When monitoring performance against budget, take into account variations in performance and make allowance for increased capital expenditure if sales are higher than expected.

THE FIXED BUDGET

HEADING	MONTH			YEAR TO DATE		
	BUDGET (£000)	ACTUAL (£000)	VARIANCE (£000)	BUDGET (£000)	ACTUAL (£000)	VARIANCE (£000)
SALES	805	753	(52)	6,358	7,314	956
MATERIALS	627	567	60	4,942	5,704	(762)
MATERIAL MARGIN	178	186	8	1,416	1,610	194
DIRECT COSTS	74	79	(5)	595	689	(94)
GROSS PROFIT	104	107	3	820	921	101
PERCENTAGE	12.92%	14.21%	1.29%	12.90%	12.60%	(0.30%)

ANALYZING THE FIXED BUDGET
The fixed budget compares performance with the targets originally set. Sales in this example were £52,000 less than expected for the month, but £956,000 more than expected for the whole year.

VARIATIONS IN PERFORMANCE

The budget is based on a particular set of sales goals, only a few of which are likely to be met exactly in practice. In the example of a fixed budget (see chart above), you can see that £762,000 more material has been used than budgeted. In addition, more goods (£956,000 worth) have been sold, so this is not surprising.

The way to handle these variations in performance is to alter the fixed budget by flexing it. In this way you can show what you would expect to happen to expenses, given the increase in sales that actually occurred. You do this by applying the budget ratios to the actual data. So, for example, materials were planned to be 22.11 per cent of sales in the budget. By applying this same percentage to the actual month's sales, you get a material cost of £587,000 rather than the £627,000 shown in the fixed budget.

When this new figure is entered in the flexed budget (see chart below), you can see that the overspend on the material you would have expected to buy, given the level of sales actually achieved, is in fact only £19,000: a much more comforting figure than £762,000.

ANALYZING THE FLEXED BUDGET
By altering the sales figures from the fixed budget to reflect what actually happened in the preceding month, the relative costs of materials is changed. The variance is reduced from minus £762,000 to minus £19,000.

THE FLEXED BUDGET

HEADING	MONTH			YEAR TO DATE		
	BUDGET (£000)	ACTUAL (£000)	VARIANCE (£000)	BUDGET (£000)	ACTUAL (£000)	VARIANCE (£000)
SALES	753	753	–	7,314	7,314	–
MATERIALS	587	567	20	5,685	5,704	(19)
MATERIAL MARGIN	166	186	20	1,629	1,610	(19)
DIRECT COSTS	69	79	(10)	685	689	(4)
GROSS PROFIT	97	107	10	944	921	(23)
PERCENTAGE	12.92%	14.21%	1.29%	12.90%	12.60%	(0.30%)

The same argument holds for other direct costs, which appear to be running £94,000 over budget for the year. When you take into account the extra sales in the flexed budget, you discover an overspend of only £4,000 on direct costs. While this is still a serious amount, it is a small fraction of the figure that the unflexed, or fixed, budget was suggesting.

The flexed budget therefore allows you to concentrate your actions on dealing with true variances in performance.

TREND AND SEASONALITY

The figures shown for each period of the budget are not the same. For example, a sales budget of £1.2 million would not translate into sales of exactly £100,000 a month. The exact figure for each month would depend on two factors: trend and seasonality.

The projected trend, which may be market-driven, may mean that sales at the start of the period are £80,000 a month and those at the end are £120,000. The average will be £100,000, so making the £1.2 million total.

By virtue of seasonal factors, each month may also be pulled up or down from the trend.

You would expect the sales of heating oil, for example, to peak in the autumn and tail off in the late spring because of variations in the weather (see graph below). Other examples of seasonal fluctuations are increased sales of garden furniture and barbecues in summer and toys and luxury items before Christmas.

ALLOWING FOR CAPITAL EXPENDITURE

The budget will have not only profit and loss implications. If the sales goals are high, there may be a requirement for more money to buy machinery to produce the product. This will have capital implications, because more funds may have to be found to increase the production rate.

There may also be cash-flow implications. Rapidly expanding the sales of manufactured products has the immediate impact of large amounts of cash being used for raw materials and labour and to finance debtors until they pay. For as long as sales growth is accelerating, cash consumption grows. This is not always harmful, but it must be budgeted for in a cash-flow forecast based on the budget.

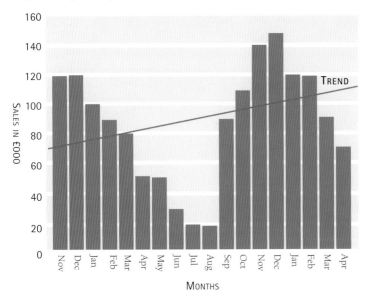

SEASONAL VARIATIONS ON TREND

A company selling heating oil would expect to sell considerably higher quantities during autumn and winter months than during spring and summer. From the combined peaks and troughs, you can calculate average sales. You can also see the general trend of sales, which in this case is moving steadily higher.

BUDGET PROFIT AND LOSS ACCOUNT MODEL

		MONTH			YEAR TO DATE		
		BUDGET (£)	ACTUAL (£)	VARIANCE	BUDGET (£)	ACTUAL (£)	VARIANCE
SALES							
COST OF SALES							
GROSS PROFIT							
LESS EXPENSES	Administration						
	Selling						
	Marketing						
	Distribution						
TOTAL EXPENSES							
OPERATING PROFIT							

SUMMARY OF MAIN REASONS FOR IMPORTANT VARIANCES AND PROPOSED ACTION

1

2

3

Building a Budget Model

Setting a budget requires discussion with key staff in the different departments of a business. As a result of this, several different sets of figures may have to be produced.

A budget model, built using a spreadsheet, is the ideal way to accomplish this. By using a spreadsheet, the effect of changing any figure or figures can be seen on the whole budget automatically and instantly, without any tedious calculations. All that is required is to decide on the relationship between the various elements of the budget.

For example, you may decide that on your balance sheet debtors will be valued at 45 days' sales (in other words, you assume that they will

BUDGET MODEL

A model such as this is a template on to which you can impose figures for any period. Once you have decided on how the different aspects of your budget relate to each other, you can construct a model to set the budget.

take that long to pay their bill), or that on the profit and loss account gross profit should be 50 per cent. Thereafter, changes in sales levels as the budget is formulated will just roll down the model to produce revised profit and loss accounts and balance sheets.

The model will also prove itself extremely useful for carrying out budget updates and revisions throughout the year, thereby keeping you fully up-to-date. If you possess a computerized bookkeeping system, you will find that it includes a budgeting model framework that you can use.

IMPROVING YOUR PERFORMANCE

You may identify areas of poor or declining financial performance while you are monitoring the performance of your business. Do not be overly alarmed – even the best-run companies have areas that do not perform as well as others – but make up your mind to improve these areas as quickly as possible. Involve your colleagues in your decisions so that the business can work together for greater profit and achievement.

If you suspect that your business is not doing as well as it could, then you need to find out which areas are failing. The most fruitful places to look for better results are:
■ prices
■ costs
■ capital employed in the day-to-day running of the business

Small firms are often guilty of getting their prices wrong at first. The misconception that new and small firms can undercut established competitors is usually based on ignorance of either the true costs of a product or service or of the true value of an overhead.

The overhead argument usually runs like this: "They [the competition] are big, own plush offices, and have lots of overpaid marketing executives spending the company's money on expense account lunches. I don't and so I must

Systematically identify areas of improvement by analyzing past performance

be able to undercut them." The errors with this type of argument are, first, that the plush office, far from being an overhead in the derogatory sense of the word, is actually a fast-appreciating asset, perhaps even generating more profit than the company's main products. (Shops, restaurants, and hotels typically fit into this category.) The plush office, especially if accompanied by a prestigious address such as Harley Street, can also contribute to creating an image for the product or service in such a way as to enhance its price.

Second, the marketing executives may well be paid more than you, but if they do not deliver a constant stream of new products and strategies, they will be replaced with people who can.

Clearly, you have to take account of what your competitors charge, but remember that

---

CASE STUDY: The Dangers of Pricing Low

ADRIAN PATTERSON decided that after leaving university he would prefer to start his own business rather than go to work for someone else. He had worked in a bagel shop during the holidays and decided that this was something he would be able to do for himself. He decided that he could undercut his previous employer and so assure himself of a good flow of business from the outset. When his accountant helped him to prepare projections, however, he found that at the price he proposed charging, he would never recover his overheads or break even. Indeed, "overheads" and "break-even" were alien terms to Adrian before he discussed his plans with his accountant.

price is the easiest element of the marketing mix for an established company to vary. They could follow you down the price curve, forcing you into bankruptcy, far more easily than you could capture their customers with a lower price.

Pricing for Profit

While most small firms – 80 per cent according to some reports – set their price with reference to costs, using either a cost- plus formula (for example, materials plus 50 per cent) or a cost multiplier (for example, three times material costs), all customers buy with reference to value, and increasingly (and often via the internet) with competitive pricing. That can leave a lot of scope for managing your prices up. Price is, after all, the element of the marketing mix that is likely to have the greatest impact on your profitability.

In fact, it is often more profitable for a new company to sell fewer items at a higher price while the owner-manager gets

the organization and product offerings sorted out. Once the business is established, they can then increase their range of products and lower their prices. The key is to concentrate on obtaining good margins, often with a range of prices and quality in your products.

THE EFFECTS OF RAISING PRICES

The chart overleaf shows the effect of changing prices on your level of gross profit if the volume of customers remains the same or alters by 5 per cent increments. To take the example of Fast Food, you can see what might have happened had they raised their prices, rather than grown their sales from £100,000 to £130,000. Assume that all this growth came from selling more to more customers.

Had they raised their prices by 5 per cent and lost no customers, they would have made £5,000 more gross profit. As the expenses have all been met, you can assume that all of this profit will drop to the bottom line of the accounts.

If the price rise had resulted in a loss of 5 per cent of their customers, the sum would look like this. Sales would go down

PRICE IS IN THE EYE OF THE BEHOLDER

Many consumers see price as a reliable guide to the quality they can expect to receive. The theory is that the more you pay, the more you get. It follows that, had James Dyson priced his revolutionary vacuum cleaner, with its claims of superior performance, below that of its peers, then some potential customers may have questioned those claims.

In its literature, Dyson cites as the inspiration for the new vacuum cleaner the inferior performance of existing products in the same price band. A product at six times the Dyson price is

the one whose performance Dyson seeks to emulate. The message conveyed is that, although the price is at the high end for general household electrical products, the performance is disproportionately greater than the cheaper models. The runaway success of Dyson's vacuum cleaner, in an already busy market, would tend to endorse this argument.

HOW CHANGING PRICES AFFECT GROSS PROFIT

A price rise of 5% accompanied by no drop in customers would result in a 5% increase in the gross profit. A similar rise accompanied by a 15% fall, however, would result in 3.25% less gross profit.

to £95,000 in volume terms, but the gross margin would rise from 50 to 55 per cent, because the company would be charging more. That would produce a gross profit of £52,250 (£95,000 x 55 per cent). Expenses would remain at £33,000, leaving an operating profit of £19,250. That figure is £2,250 higher than the £17,000 that would have been made on the higher volume of sales made at the original lower price.

Working through the rest of the figures in the same way, you can see that, unless you think that you would lose more than 10 per cent of your business by putting your prices up by 5 per cent, you will not have a problem. In fact, putting up prices by 15 per cent will deliver higher profits even if you lose more than 15 per cent of your business. In Fast Food's case this was 50 per cent. The lower your gross profit, the less business you can afford to lose for any given price rise.

There are other benefits that are not shown. Putting the pressure on price rather than volume means carrying less stock, having fewer bills to chase, using less capital, and wearing out equipment less quickly.

EFFECTS OF RAISING PRICES

CHANGE IN PRICE	CHANGE IN VOLUME OF CUSTOMERS			
	0%	-5%	-10%	-15%
+5%	5%	2.25%	-0.5%	-3.25%
+10%	10%	7%	4%	1%
+15%	15%	11.75%	8.5%	5.25%

Reducing Your Costs

Costs are associated with activity. But, since activity is often misallocated, as the 80/20 rule (or Pareto principle) demonstrates (see chart far right), it follows that the opportunities for cost reduction are almost always greater than you think.

Look at the table below and the two charts above right for examples of the effects on your business of reducing costs.

Write a spreadsheet or build into your acounting software a function that ranks the main items of cost in your business and compares them with a previous period. The costs that are both large and rising are the ones to concentrate your efforts on reducing. The cost of this will be small in comparison to the potential savings.

COST SAVINGS MATTER

	BEFORE		AFTER 2% COST SAVING		EXTRA PERFORMANCE	
	£000	%	£000	%	£000	%
SALES	1,000	100	1,000	100	–	–
COSTS	950	95	930	93	-20	-2
PROFIT	50	5	70	7	+20	+40

REDUCING COSTS

For a business making a 5% net profit, reducing costs by just 2% will raise profits by 40%, from £50,000 to £70,000. They may well have needed to find 10 or even 20% more customers to have the same effect on profit.

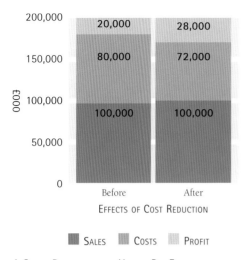

EFFECTS OF COST REDUCTION

▨ SALES ▨ COSTS ▨ PROFIT

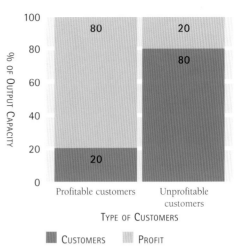

TYPE OF CUSTOMERS

▨ CUSTOMERS ▨ PROFIT

A SMALL REDUCTION CAN HAVE A BIG EFFECT

What makes cost reduction so powerful is the disproportionate effect on profits that even a small reduction in costs can have. By reducing costs by just 10%, this business has raised profits by an impressive 40%.

THE 80/20 RULE

A close examination of your client list will show that 20% of them account for the vast majority of your business and perhaps all of your profit. Yet you spend as much time servicing unprofitable customers as you do profitable ones.

Squeezing Working Capital

Once you have bought your shop, set up your factory, or bought your delivery vehicle, the funds you have used are sunk costs. The items you bought may not be what you now need, but you will have to make do with them, for now at any rate, because the capital is tied up. You do, however, have discretion over your working capital. The more you squeeze that, the less money you have tied up in the business, which means lower borrowing costs.

WAYS TO MAKE BETTER USE OF YOUR WORKING CAPITAL

1 If you sell on credit, set out your terms of trade clearly on your invoices. Customers need to know when you expect to be paid; this has advantages for both of you.

2 Find out when your biggest customers have their monthly cheque run, and make sure your bills reach them in time.

3 Send out statements promptly to chase up late payers, and follow up with a phone call.

4 Always take trade references when giving credit to new customers, and look at their accounts to see how sound they are.

5 Have accurate stock records and monitor slow-moving stock.

6 Have an accurate sales forecasting system so that you can match stock and work-in-progress to likely demand.

7 Take credit from your suppliers up to the maximum time allowed. Try to negotiate extended terms with major suppliers, once you have a good track record.

8 Make any cash you have work harder. Overnight money markets via an internet bank could allow you to get interest on cash, rather than having it sitting in the banking system doing nothing – for you, that is.

9 Work out if it makes sense to pay bills quickly to take advantage of early settlement discounts offered by suppliers (see overleaf).

USING WORKING CAPITAL

The evidence points to small firms being inefficient users of working capital. The smaller they are, the less efficient they are, as these charts show. A very small firm is likely to be paid later by debtors and to have a slower turnover of stock than a medium-sized business. Both of these areas result in lost income.

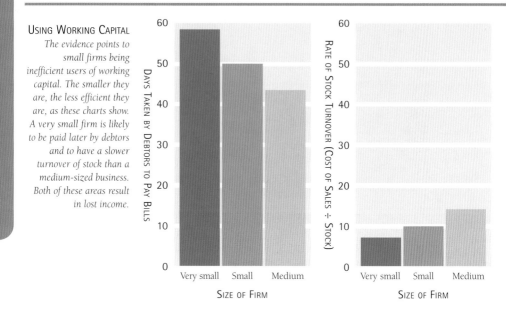

Sometimes suppliers offer high rates of interest for settling up promptly. If you are offered 2.5 per cent to pay up now rather than in two months' time, that is equivalent to an annual rate of interest of 15 per cent (12 ÷ 2 x 2.5 per cent).

■ Bank cheques and cash promptly. This is not only the safest option for cash and cheques, but the sooner you get your money into the banking system, the sooner you are either saving interest costs on loans or earning some interest income.

WORKING CAPITAL DOWN, PROFITABILITY UP

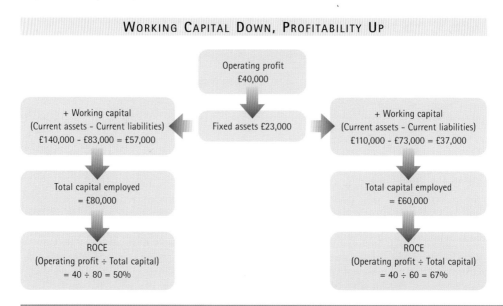

HOW TO EVALUATE A DISCOUNT OFFER

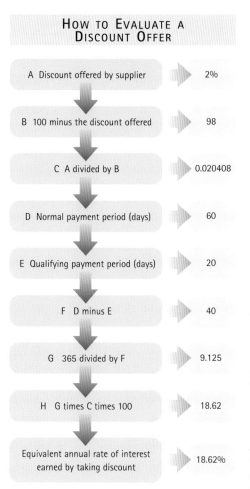

A Discount offered by supplier	2%
B 100 minus the discount offered	98
C A divided by B	0.020408
D Normal payment period (days)	60
E Qualifying payment period (days)	20
F D minus E	40
G 365 divided by F	9.125
H G times C times 100	18.62
Equivalent annual rate of interest earned by taking discount	18.62%

EVALUATING A SUPPLIER'S EARLY PAYMENT DISCOUNT
By following the steps shown here, you can see whether paying your bills early will suit you financially. Here settling your bills 40 days earlier than usual for a year is the equivalent of earning an annual rate of interest on your money of 18.62%.

Changing Gear in Your Business

High gearing describes the situation of a business that has a high proportion of borrowed money. High gearing has considerable attractions to a business that wants to make high returns on the shareholders' capital. (Look back at pp. 115–116 to remind yourself about interest cover and how to calculate the ROSI.)

The table overleaf illustrates the effects of changing the level of gearing on return on investment. The business is assumed to need £60,000 capital to generate £10,000 operating profits. Four different capital structures are considered. They range from all share capital (no gearing) at one end to nearly all loan capital at the other. The loan capital has to be serviced, and it is assumed that an interest of 12 per cent has to be paid. The loan itself can be relatively indefinite, simply being replaced by another one at market interest rates when the first loan expires.

Following the table through, you can see that ROSI grows from 16.6 to 30.7 per cent by virtue of the changed gearing. If the interest on the loan were lower, the ROSI would be even more improved by high gearing, and the higher the interest, the lower the relative improvement in ROSI. So, during times of low interest, businesses tend to increase borrowings rather than raise equity (money from shareholders).

PROBLEMS WITH GEARING

At first sight high gearing looks like a perpetual profit-growth machine. Naturally, business owners would rather have someone else lend them the money for the growth of their business than put it in themselves, if they could increase the return on their investment.

The problem comes if the business does not produce £10,000 operating profits. Very often, in a small business, a drop in sales of 20 per cent means profits are halved. If profits were halved in this example, the business could not meet the interest payments on its loan. That would make the business insolvent, and so not in a sound financial position.

Bankers tend to favour 1:1 gearing as the maximum for a small business, although they have been known to go much higher.

THE EFFECT OF GEARING ON RETURN ON SHAREHOLDERS' INVESTMENT (ROSI)

		NO GEARING (£)	AVERAGE GEARING 1:1 (£)	HIGH GEARING 2:1 (£)	VERY HIGH GEARING 3:1 (£)
CAPITAL STRUCTURE	Share capital	60,000	30,000	20,000	15,000
	Loan capital (at 12%)	–	30,000	40,000	45,000
TOTAL CAPITAL		60,000	60,000	60,000	60,000
PROFITS	Operating profit	10,000	10,000	10,000	10,000
	Less interest on loan	–	3,600	4,800	5,400
NET PROFIT		10,000	6,400	5,200	4,600
RETURN ON SHAREHOLDERS' INVESTMENT		10,000/60,000	6,400/30,000	5,200/20,000	4,600/15,000
EQUALS		16.6%	21.3%	26%	30.7%
TIMES INTEREST EARNED		N/A	10,000/3,600	10,000/4,800	10,000/5,400
EQUALS		N/A	2.8x	2.1x	1.8x

Bringing It All Together

When you improve performance in any of the key areas – pricing for profit, reducing costs, and making efficient use of working capital – you will see some kind of increase in your operating profit. The more individual target areas you can improve, the greater will be the increase in profits for the business. For example, one company reduced the costs of its materials by 5 per cent; increased its stock turnover by 6 per cent; increased its debtor days by 4 per cent; improved its gross margins by 4 per cent; and, finally, reduced its creditors by 7 per cent. As a result, the company saw its operating profit increase by more than 200 per cent.

CHANGING THE LEVEL OF GEARING
In this chart four different financing options show the effects of higher gearing on the return on shareholders' investment. As the net profit drops from £10,000 to £4,600, the ROSI rises from 16.6% to 30.7%.

SETTING YOUR OWN TARGET AREAS

After completing your review of past performance, and identified specific areas where you feel improvements could be made, you should now prepare a profit improvement action plan (see the example opposite). Set targets for your business to achieve in each area and decide how those targets are to be achieved. Then take action. Start first with those targets where the opportunities are large and the work required to get the results is small. Take one area at a time, until you are ready to tackle the most difficult areas.

MY PROFIT IMPROVEMENT PLAN

BUSINESS AREA	ACTIONS	COMPLETION DATE (LATEST DATE BY WHICH IMPROVEMENTS WILL BE MADE)	EXPECTED IMPROVEMENT (£)
PRICES			
RAW MATERIALS			
WASTAGE AND RETURNS			
LABOUR COSTS			
EQUIPMENT COSTS			
PREMISES			
MOTORING AND TRAVEL			
STOCK			
DEBTORS			
CREDITORS			
GEARING			
TOTAL EXPECTED COST REDUCTION			

IMPROVING OVERALL PERFORMANCE

Set improvement targets for each of the key areas in the chart above, then incorporate the tasks needed to achieve them into your next budget review.

USEFUL
information

You will need to understand the
legal aspects of your business to
ensure you operate legally. Your
business will also face a range of
taxes, covering income, capital, value
added, and wages and payroll. This
section provides a basic grounding in
the regulations that are likely to affect
you, and offers guidelines on tax to
ensure that you pay your dues and no
more. The Glossary explains key
business terms, while the Useful
Contacts and Suggested Reading
sections point you towards other
sources of information.

LEGAL MATTERS

The financial aspects of business are less exact than the arithmetic purity of numbers might suggest. In fact, uncertainty and unpredictability are more common features of business financial affairs than you might at first think. After all, add two and two and you ought to get four, but if part of one of those twos is made up by a customer who will not, or cannot, pay, then things are not so clear. In areas of imprecision like this, it is the law that has to be relied on for help and guidance.

The law confers obligations as well as helping people in dispute. Such obligations include filing accounts on time; paying legal charges to banks on assets, both business and personal; accepting the responsibilities of directorship, which are beyond those of a sole trader running much the same enterprise.

To survive in a country ruled by laws, you need an appreciation of the main legal aspects surrounding the financing of your business.

Using the Small Claims Court

Many countries, including the US and the UK, have a procedure for getting legal disputes concerning payment from customers settled quickly and inexpensively.

Names other than "Small Claims Court" are used in certain countries, but the purpose is the same: to provide a speedy and inexpensive resolution of disputes that involve relatively small amounts of money. The advantage of the Small Claims Court is that if you cannot afford a solicitor and you are not entitled to government help with your legal costs, you can still bring your case to the court yourself. Even if you can afford a solicitor, their fees may be more than the amount you are claiming. Needless to say, if you lose the case, or win but do not manage to get your opponent to pay your costs, then you will not be any better off.

The jurisdictional limits (the amount for which you can sue) in these courts are rising fairly quickly. In the US you can sue for $5,000 or sometimes more, and in the UK amounts of money under £5,000 claimed are likely to come under the jurisdiction of the Small Claims Court.

However, if your claim is for personal injury, it will be heard in the Small Claims Court only if the claim for the injury itself is for an amount not exceeding £1,000.

For housing cases involving a landlord's failure to repair the property, the claim will be heard in the Small Claims Court if the cost of repairs or the compensation claimed is not more than £1,000. You are entitled to ask for interest on the amount you are claiming. This is currently 8 per cent per year. If you want to claim interest you must put that on your claim.

A business person can use a Small Claims Court to collect bills, to obtain a judgement for breach of contract, or to seek money for minor property damage claims – for example, suing someone who broke a fence around your property or parking area. The Small Claims Court offers you an opportunity to collect money that would otherwise be lost because the amount is too small to justify suing in a regular court. It is true that it is not always cost-effective for very small cases, and occasionally you will have problems collecting your judgement. But the Small Claims Court should still be part of the financial collection strategies of your business.

Before you start out on the legal route, investigate alternatives. If your case involves a written contract, check to see if the contract requires mediation or arbitration of disputes. If so, this may limit or cut off your right to go to any court, including the Small Claims Court. Second, consider other cost-effective options, such as free or low-cost publicly operated mediation programmes. If you're in a dispute with a customer, or perhaps another business, and you still have hopes of preserving some aspect of the relationship, mediation – even if not provided for in a contract – is often a better alternative than going to court. Any litigation tends to sour people's feelings.

STARTING THE PROCESS

You can make a claim by getting a claim form from your local County Court. On the form, under the Particulars of Claim, you state what your claim is for and why you are claiming; you also include the amount you are claiming and say if you want interest.

In personal injury cases you must also file a medical report giving details about your injury. You will need to send to the court the claim form, plus a copy for the court and a copy for each opponent (if there is more than one).

The court is then responsible for sending copies to your opponent together with a form for defending the claim, a form for admitting the claim, and a form for acknowledging service, which your opponent must complete and send back to the court.

The court will then send you a copy together with a set of instructions on what you should do next, or they may fix a hearing date when you will have to go to court.

Hearings will usually last no more than one day, but most are dealt with in an hour or so. The court can even deal with your case without holding a hearing. They just consider your case "on paper". If the judge decides that your case is suitable to be dealt with without a hearing, the court will tell you and your opponent. The court can also deal with your case by a

"telephone hearing" if you and your opponent agree and as long as you are both legally represented in the court. This will be arranged using a BT conference "call-out" system.

If the court has video conferencing facilities, it may also be possible to hold a hearing by video link.

You do not have to attend the hearing as long as you give seven days' notice before the hearing to the court and your opponent, telling them that you will not be attending.

You can send written evidence to the court, and the court will take your evidence into account when reaching its decision. The court must tell you the reasons for its decision.

GETTING PAID

One of the frustrating things about any legal process is that winning the argument could, in the end, resolve nothing. If the person you are suing has no money, or decides to ignore the judgement against them, then the ball could be back in your court.

If your opponent looks as though they could pay, but won't, you have a number of options.

▨ **ORAL EXAMINATION** is where your opponent is told to come to court to provide the court with details of his or her income, capital, and savings. You can then decide from this information whether they are able to repay the debt.

To apply for an Oral Examination you should get a Request for Oral Examination form from the court, then return the completed form together with a small fee and details of the amount of money that remains unpaid under the judgement.

The court will serve an Order telling your opponent to come to court. Some courts prefer to send an affidavit or questionnaire to the opponent to complete first. When your opponent attends court, he or she will be questioned by either a district judge or an officer of the court. You do not have to be present, but you can give details of any questions you would like asked.

If your opponent refuses to answer any questions or produce documents, you can apply to the court for a Penal Notice demanding that they must do so. If your opponent still fails to obey the Order, they will be in Contempt of Court, and if the Order has a Penal Notice attached, you can apply to the court to commit your opponent to prison for breach of the Order.

If your opponent does not attend court, then a new date has to be fixed to give them the opportunity to attend. Your opponent could ask that you pay their travel expenses for attending court. If they do, you must pay these not less than seven days before the hearing. You must then file a certificate at court to say either that your opponent has not requested any money or that you have paid it. This certificate must be filed with the court four days before the hearing.

It will not have escaped your notice that you have not yet been paid anything and might even have had to pay something by way of expenses for the person you are suing.

▓ **GARNISHEE PROCEEDINGS** may be a simpler option if your opponent is owed money by a third party – a not infrequent defence offered by late payers. You can get an order requiring the third party to pay that money directly to you. Your debt must be at least £50 and the third party must be within England and Wales.

To apply, you must send the court an affidavit to say that the money owed has not been repaid as the court ordered and it is still outstanding. You will need to pay a small fee for a temporary order, which you must serve on the third party. A hearing date will then be fixed when the third party can attend and make objections about the Order.

▓ **WARRANT OF DELIVERY** is a possibility if your opponent has a particular item or goods belonging to you and you want their return. If the Order says that the goods are to be returned, you can apply for a Request for a Warrant of Delivery. No hearing is

necessary; instead the court bailiff will contact your opponent to fix an appointment to remove the goods.

▓ **ATTACHMENT OF EARNINGS** is a direct method that could be a useful route as long as the debt is not less than £50 and your opponent is working. You can apply for an Order that your opponent's employer deduct a certain amount from their wages each week or month to pay the debt. The court will fix a hearing date and serve you and your opponent with details.

Your opponent is entitled to have part of their earnings protected against such deductions. The judge will decide how much this will be and also decide the amount to be deducted and how often.

▓ **GETTING A CHARGING ORDER** is yet another route to ensure payment; this time it applies if your opponent owns property. You can apply to the court to Register a Charge at the Land Registry against your opponent's property to show that you have an interest in the sale proceeds of the property. This forewarns any person intending to buy your opponent's property and will make it more difficult for them to sell. It may just be enough of an irritation to make them pay up and be done with it. If there are other charges, such as a mortgage or bank loan, registered before you on the Land Register, then they will be paid first.

BEING SURE OF YOUR CASE

While the Small Claims Court, or indeed any court, is one way to claim money that is owed to you, it is, as you can see, neither easy nor certain of a positive outcome.

First, you want to be relatively sure of your legal position. You must have a valid legal basis for a lawsuit. Do you have a decent chance of proving in court that the defendant refused to pay a fair and just bill, or broke a contract, or negligently damaged your property? If not, any talk about going to court is just an idle threat that may hurt your credibility.

Filing the Audited Accounts

As a sole trader or partnership, you do not have to get your accounts audited if you do not want to. You may want to consider doing so, however, if the cost is not too steep, because having audited accounts can help in dealings with your tax inspector. It may also help you if you need confirmation of income from your business, for example to obtain a mortgage to buy a house.

If your business is a limited company with sales of over £350,000, you will need to have your accounts audited and copies filed at the relevant government agency. In the UK this agency is Companies House. Limited companies with sales below this amount do not have to comply with this.

FAST FOOD LIMITED
AUDITORS' REPORT
TO THE SHAREHOLDERS OF FAST FOOD LIMITED

I have audited the financial statements on pages 4 to 8 which have been prepared under the historical cost convention and the accounting policies set out on page 6.

RESPECTIVE RESPONSIBILITIES OF DIRECTORS AND AUDITORS
As described on page 2, the company's directors are responsible for the preparation of financial statements. It is my responsibility to form an independent opinion, based on my audit, on those statements and to report my opinion to you.

BASIS OF OPINION
I conducted my audit in accordance with Auditing Standards issued by the Auditing Practices Board. An audit includes examination, on a test basis, of evidence relevant to the amounts and disclosures in the financial statements. It also includes an assessment of the significant estimates and judgements made by the directors in the preparation of the financial statements, and of whether the accounting policies are appropriate to the company's circumstances, consistently applied and adequately disclosed.

I planned and performed my audit so as to obtain all the information and explanations which I considered necessary in order to provide me with sufficient evidence to give reasonable assurance that the financial statements are free from material misstatement, whether caused by fraud or other irregularity or error. In forming my opinion I also evaluated the overall adequacy of the presentation of information in the financial statements.

OPINION
In my opinion the financial statements give a true and fair view of the state of the company's affairs as at 31 July 2001 and of its profit for the year then ended and have been properly prepared in accordance with the provisions of the Companies Act 1985 applicable to small companies.

William Cross
Chartered Accountant
Registered Auditor

17 November 2001
Milton Keynes
Bucks
MK6 3DY

AUDITORS' REPORT
Here is an example of an auditors' report, prepared on behalf of the shareholders of Fast Food Limited. In this case, the auditors have found that the company's accounts are accurate and in good order.

PREPARING ABBREVIATED ACCOUNTS

All companies must prepare full accounts for presentation to the company's shareholders, but small- and medium-sized companies can send abbreviated accounts to the Registrar of Companies. Abbreviated accounts contain very little information that could be of use to a competitor. Nothing is given away on turnover or margins, for example – a luxury denied to larger companies. Small companies' accounts (ones with less than £350,000 turnover, balance sheet totals of less than £1.4 million, and fewer than 50 employees on average, to be precise) delivered to the Registrar must contain:

■ an abbreviated balance sheet
■ selected notes to the accounts, including accounting policies, share capital, particulars of creditors payable in more than five years, and the basis of any foreign currency transactions
■ a special auditor's report (unless exempt)

The rules of disclosure are complex and the above gives only a brief outline of the requirements. If you are unsure about the information that you have to provide, then you should take professional advice. When a company files abbreviated accounts, it must have a special auditor's report confirming that the exemptions have been satisfied, and the directors must make a statement at the foot of the balance sheet saying that they have relied upon the exemptions.

AUDITORS, AND HOW TO MAKE THEIR JOB EASIER

Most companies will be required to appoint an auditor and have their accounts audited. It is the job of the auditor to report to the members (shareholders) of the company as to whether the accounts have been properly prepared, taking notice of the appropriate accounting rules. The auditor must also report as to whether the accounts give a true and fair view of the state of the company's affairs.

In order to arrive at their conclusion, the auditor will carry out an examination of the records on a test basis to ensure that the accounts are not materially incorrect. This does not mean that the auditor will check every detail, but they will look at a representative sample of transactions to get a feel for whether or not the books are being properly kept.

If your bookkeeping records are poorly kept, inaccurate, or missing, expect a hefty bill and a lot of time spent answering questions about long-gone and often trivial financial events.

If you have a computerized system, the year-end audit is made much simpler for you and your accountant. In fact, with some accounting software, you can do much of the work for the accountant before they set foot on your premises.

You can, for example, produce the reports that all auditors will require, such as the trial balance. Some packages have utilities that enable the auditor to run random checks on the transactions and postings, and some have facilities for the pre-production of debtors' confirmation letters. Auditors will normally send those out to debtors to check that the transaction did take place.

In this way, the auditor's life is made much simpler and, hopefully, it will take less time to conduct the audit, your personnel will be free to carry on with their work sooner, there will be a smaller fee for you to pay, and, if you require it, your accountant can get on with some work that will be of rather more benefit to the business. For example, they could recommend how you could tighten up on credit control or stock taking, or get better and more timely management accounts, all of which are infinitely more valuable to the owner-manager than a set of audited accounts.

FILING YOUR ACCOUNTS LATE

If you are trading as a company, then your accounts have to be filed with the appropriate government agency. In the UK that agency is Companies House.

Late filing penalties were introduced in 1992 to encourage directors of limited companies to file their accounts on time because they must,

PENALTIES FOR FILING YOUR ACCOUNTS LATE	
LENGTH OF DELAY MEASURED FROM THE DATE THE ACCOUNTS ARE DUE	PRIVATE COMPANY PENALTY
3 MONTHS OR LESS	£100
3 MONTHS AND 1 DAY TO 6 MONTHS	£250
6 MONTHS AND 1 DAY TO 12 MONTHS	£500
MORE THAN 12 MONTHS	£1,000

as a matter of law, provide this statutory information for the public record.

The amount of the penalty depends on how late the accounts reach the Registrar, as is shown in the table above.

Unless you are filing your company's first accounts, the time normally allowed for delivering accounts to Companies House is 10 months from the end of the relevant accounting period for private companies. If you are filing your company's first accounts and they cover a period of more than 12 months, they must be delivered to the Registrar within 22 months of the date of incorporation for private companies.

Giving Bank Guarantees

When the assets of a business are small, anyone lending it money may seek the added protection of requiring the owner to guarantee the loan personally. For limited companies, this is in effect stripping away some of the protection that companies are supposed to afford the risk-taking owner-manager.

These are eight important things to keep firmly in mind when your bank raises this issue, as at some stage it almost inevitably will.

1 Resist any suggestion that you should provide any guarantees at all. Make it absolutely clear that this is just not an option as far as you are concerned.

2 Your next line of defence should be to offer the new assets themselves as security. Whatever assets you plan to buy with the funds should be comfort enough. If the bank will not accept those assets at the generally accepted discount, then perhaps you are not making a prudent investment. (A generally accepted discount might be 30 per cent of the value of any stock in trade, 50 per cent of debtors, and 80 per cent of freehold property.)

3 If pressed, make any guarantee given as specific as possible. For example, set a maximum value.

4 Try to secure the guarantee against specific assets only. Perhaps you could persuade the bank to limit their claims against you to say one particular property, even though what you actually want the funds for is to finance new stock in trade.

5 Set clear conditions for the guarantee to come to an end, for example when your overdraft or borrowings return to the level they were at before your most recent request for additional funds. If you do not do this, the bank may try to retain the extra comfort of the security of a personal guarantee as part of your permanent banking arrangements. This, in effect, will leave you exposed to this threat forever. It will also take away a negotiating option for any further financing you may need. If the bank already has your personal guarantee, then you have little else to offer them.

6 Make sure that the conditions of the additional financing are clear, as are any events that could allow the bank to exercise their rights. For example, it is likely that any funds advanced by a bank will come with some strings attached. These could include what and how much of that money can be spent on which particular assets. So, if the funds are advance for stock and you use them to buy a new vehicle, however necessary for the business that may be, you will be technically in breach of your loan covenants, as these conditions are known.

7 If you believe that giving a personal guarantee materially changes the nature of the bank's risk, then it may be worth trying for a lower interest rate on the loan. Banks charge interest at a rate above the base rate. A more risky loan to a small firm may be charged out at 4 per cent over the base rate of 8 per cent, i.e. 12 per cent in all. But if your personal assets include a second home worth £150,000 on which there is no mortgage, and the total financing you are looking to secure is, say, £50,000, then any financing with that home as security should be charged at the rate prevailing for a mortgage. That might be 2 per cent over base rate and, if it were, your new borrowing rate would be only 10 per cent rather than the 12 per cent formerly proposed.

8 Remember that everything in business finance is negotiable, and your relationship with a bank is no exception. Banks are in competition too, so if yours is being unreasonably hard, it may be time to move on to a more reasonable one. Obviously, to be able to move on you need to have some advance notice of when the additional funds are needed. Rushing into a new bank and asking for extra finance from next week is hardly likely to inspire the bank manager to have much confidence in your abilities as a strategic thinker. That is where your business plan will come into its own.

Distancing Personal Assets

Only by trading through a limited company, giving no personal guarantees, and never falling foul of the fraudulent or wrongful trading laws, can you be confident that your personal assets are safe. If you are a sole trader, a partner, or have given personal guarantees to support a limited company, then your personal assets are at some risk.

It is possible, if you gave your assets away five years before going bankrupt, to save them from your creditors, but this calls for extraordinary foresight, and even then things can go wrong.

First, the person you "give" the assets to could make off with them. After all, over a third of marriages end in divorce. Second, anyone making a claim against you can ask the court to set aside any gift, however long ago it was made, if they can prove that it was your intention at the time to put those assets beyond their reach. Clearly you can take steps to protect your personal assets from your business liabilities, but it is not a simple matter.

Directors' Responsibilities

Over 1,500 directors are disqualified each year in the UK alone. The reasons for their disqualification range from fraud to the more innocuous wrongful trading, which means carrying on doing business while the business is insolvent. This latter area is more difficult to recognize by a director before the event, but you need to be aware of the danger signs and the available remedies.

In practice, a director's general responsibilities are much the same as those for a sole trader or partner, and indeed they can be better. This is because by forming a company you can separate your own assets from the business assets (in theory, at any rate, unless personal guarantees have been extracted). But this separation is conditional upon responsible business behaviour.

A director also has to cope with some technical, more detailed requirements, for example sending in accounts to Companies House. More onerous than just signing them, a director is expected, and required in law, to understand the significance of the balance sheet and profit and loss account and the key performance ratios.

Some of a director's duties, responsibilities, and potential liabilities are:

- ▦ To act in good faith in the interests of the company. This includes carrying out duties diligently and honestly.
- ▦ Not to carry on the business of the company with intent to defraud creditors or for any fraudulent purpose.
- ▦ Not knowingly to allow the company to trade while insolvent ("wrongful trading"). Directors who do so may have to pay for the debts incurred by the company while it was insolvent.
- ▦ Not to deceive shareholders.
- ▦ To have a regard for the interests of employees in general.
- ▦ To comply with the requirements of the Companies Acts, providing what is needed in accounting records or filing accounts.

How Not to Get Disqualified

The most dangerous of these directors' responsibilities are the ones that could get you disqualified. In summary, the areas to avoid at all cost are:

- ▦ **TRADING WHILE INSOLVENT** This occurs when your liabilities exceed your assets. At this point the shareholders' equity in the business has effectively ceased to exist, and when shareholder equity is negative, directors are personally at risk and owe a duty of care to creditors – not shareholders. If you find yourself even approaching a state of insolvency, you need the prompt advice of an insolvency practitioner. Directors who act properly will not be penalized and will live to fight another day.
- ▦ **WRONGFUL TRADING** This term can apply to a company if, after a company goes into insolvent liquidation, the liquidator believes that the directors (or those acting as such) ought to have concluded earlier that the company had no realistic chance of survival.

In these circumstances, the courts can remove the shelter of limited liabilities and make directors personally liable for the company's debts.

- ▦ **FRAUDULENT TRADING** This is a rather more serious position than wrongful trading. Here the proposition is that the director(s) were knowingly party to fraud on their creditors. The full shelter of limited liability can be removed under these circumstances, and former directors of insolvent companies can be banned from holding office for periods of up to 15 years. Fraud, fraudulent trading, wrongful trading, or a failure to comply with company law – for example, not filing your annual accounts – may all result in disqualification.
- ▦ **BREACHES OF A DISQUALIFICATION ORDER** This can lead to imprisonment and/or fines. Also, you can be made personally liable for the debts and liabilities of any company in which you are involved. You cannot issue your orders through others, having them act as a director in your place, because this will leave them personally liable themselves. A register of disqualified directors is available for fee access on the Companies House web site.

Choosing an Accountant

Keeping your financial affairs in good order is the key to staying legal and winning any disputes. A good accountant inside or outside the firm can keep you on track. A bad accountant is in the ideal position to defraud you, at worst, or derail you through negligence or incompetence. What attributes should you look for and how can you find the right accountant for your business? The key steps to choosing a good accountant are as follows:

- ▦ Check that they are members of one of the recognized accounting bodies.
- ▦ Have a clear idea of what services you

require. You need to consider how complete your bookkeeping records are likely to be and whether you will need the VAT return done, budgets and cash-flow forecasts prepared and updated, as well as an audit.

▨ Clarify the charges scale at the outset. It may well make more sense to spend a bit more on your staff and computer systems to do your bookkeeping internally rather than leaving it all to a much higher-charging qualified accountant.

▨ Follow up personal recommendations from respected business colleagues. There is nothing like hearing from a fellow consumer about a product or service. Pay rather less attention to the recommendations of bankers, government agencies, family, and friends, without totally ignoring their advice. They may have a vested interest.

▨ Find out who else they act for. You do not want them to be so busy that they cannot service your needs properly, nor do you want them to be working for any of your potential competitors.

▨ Find out what back-up they have for both systems and people. The tax authorities will not be sympathetic, whatever the reason for lateness. It would be doubly annoying to be fined for someone else's tardiness.

▨ Take references from the accountant's clients, as well as from the person who recommended the accountant. It could just be good fortune that they get on, or it could be that they are related.

▨ See at least three accountants before making your choice. Check that they deal with companies your size and a bit bigger: you want to be able to grow without having to change accountants too quickly.

▨ Make the appointment for a trial period only. Set a specific task to see how they get on.

▨ Give them the latest accounts of your business and ask them for their comments based on their analysis of the figures. You will quickly see if they have grasped the basics of your financial position.

Closing Down the Business

The lifetime of the average business is relatively short – much shorter, in fact, than the life of the typical business owner. The reasons for its demise range from the relatively benign trade sale to the disastrous bankruptcy. The options are to sell up, close down, or go under. The financial process of a business is not complete until it closes down.

SELLING UP

Getting the best value for your business may involve getting expensive corporate finance advice to maximize the price in the minimum amount of time. Without an auction or controlled auction, you could be short-changed by as much as 50 per cent. Sweetheart deals – a popular strategy for people retiring from a business, where you sell out to someone you know or do business with – are almost always bad deals for the seller.

Having got your price, how can you be sure you will get your money? Warranties, missed earn-outs, and bad tax advice could take 70 per cent of that headline price out of your pocket.

These are the pointers to make sure you get the best result in selling up.

1 Even if your business is not in the greatest of shape, or even it is financially troubled, remember that selling an operating business almost always brings more money than closing it down and selling off the assets. Before you give up and conclude that no one will buy your business, consider that people buy businesses, even ones with financial problems, for all sorts of reasons:

▨ The buyer may have a similar business and can combine the two to operate more efficiently than you can. The buyer may be extremely anxious to take over one or more of your business assets – its location, key employees, or domain name if you are on the internet.

▒ The buyer may have better access to needed financing than you do and therefore be able to stay the course until your good business idea ultimately proves itself.

▒ The buyer may have greater expertise in your business than you do and see a way to turn a profit by changing how the business is run.

▒ The buyer may conclude that it is cheaper to buy your business and turn it around than to start a similar business from scratch.

2 Do not get into a sweetheart deal with a buyer who claims to be able to act quickly if you can just keep the corporate finance people out of the deal. Recently a prospective purchaser offered £7 million for a business and insisted on a lockout deal, with no other purchasers being involved. When the business finally went to auction, they paid up £16 million.

3 Do beauty parades with corporate finance and lawyers. See at least three of each, preferably on the same day. Not only is time of the essence, but you will remember their good and bad points better.

4 Find advisers who are the right size for your deal. There is no point in getting the best guys in town to sell a business worth £250,000 when they are used to dealing with multiple millions. After they have sold you the deal, the partners will vanish and leave you with the office boys. Find a firm that specializes in your size of deal.

5 Everything to do with selling up is negotiable. The corporate finance advisers will want upfront payments and high results-related rewards. You can get everything done on contingency and pay a smaller percentage the more the business is sold for.

6 Nail down everything with the corporate finance people and get your contract with them vetted by your legal advisers; otherwise clauses will slip through. For example, if there is a time clause, you could end up having to sell at a lower price or pay their bill in full when the six months' search time is up.

7 During the due diligence process done by the acquirer, get every skeleton out of every cupboard. If you do not, the warranties will come back to haunt you. You could be pursued years later to compensate for any liability not declared.

8 The corporate finance team bring experience, credibility, and, hopefully, a couple of prospective buyers to the table. Two buyers makes for an auction, and auctions make for better prices.

9 Go through the term sheet (as the offer to buy document is called) very carefully, line by line. The price will be only the headline figure in a fairly complex document. That price may be dependent on customers and key staff remaining with the firm, or it may be dependent on certain projects under development being completed on time and to budgeted cost.

10 Whatever the logic behind the offer price, multiple of sales, price earnings, and so on, it is just a yardstick to make people feel comfortable. Price is just the figure people will pay at a given moment for a given business.

11 Your share of whatever the business sells for will be a lot less if you do not get good tax advice. Owners can end up paying between nothing and 51 per cent tax on any gain. (Note that the gain will be calculated on the price of the share options, which may have been granted at very favourable prices.)

12 The price you agree to sell at will not be paid. The auction process pushes the price up, but the purchaser can win much of that back again using various techniques. For example, they can try to string negotiations out for long enough for other prospective bidders to have lost interest and gone elsewhere. To prevent this you must keep the pressure on during negotiations. Alternatively the purchaser can try to claim that what you are selling is not quite what they thought they were buying. You can limit this danger during due diligence.

13 Be scrupulously honest during due diligence. Once both sides are in general agreement over the terms of the sale, your business will be

reviewed in detail. This will ensure that the buyer gets what they think they are getting.

The ownership of assets, patents, and copyrights will be examined, as will employment contracts, the customer terms and conditions, and so on. The basis of plans and projections will also be reviewed. If you think that your annual audit is an intrusive experience, due diligence is more like invasive surgery.

Just in case the prospective buyer has missed anything, you will be asked to warrant the deal. This basically means that, if any material liability is uncovered after the sale that was not either uncovered in the due diligence or included in your offer memorandum, you pick up the bill. The buyer may well expect a sum to be set aside to cover any such eventuality for a period of months – or even up to six years.

If the due diligence uncovers problems, there are usually only four options: if the buyer is very keen to buy, they can be asked to live with it; if they are less keen, the price can be adjusted to reflect the potential problem; specific guarantees or indemnities can be offered to protect the buyer from such problems. This may include retention of some of the purchase monies; the deal is off. •

If you can break the business into parts, separating off, say, the property, you may be able to get some additional value from the sale.

14 To avoid horrors being uncovered in the due diligence, you may need to clean up the company beforehand. A change of auditors may be necessary, if you have been using a sleepy small local firm, especially if they have become particularly friendly. In preparing for a sale, you would be wise to select a more inquisitive and thorough firm, with a reputation that is likely to be known to, and respected by, potential buyers.

Private businesses do tend to run expenses through the business that might be frowned upon under different ownership. One firm, for example, had its sale delayed

PROS AND CONS OF SELLING UP

✓ You will be able to invest your money in a spread of businesses rather than just in your own business.

✓ You will have the time to pursue new business or personal interests.

✓ You will achieve financial security for yourself and your family.

✗ Once having been your own boss, it is hard to be anything else.

✗ The new owners will want to do things differently, which may be distressing to watch.

✗ You may find it more difficult than you imagine to stop working long hours.

✗ Selling a business can result in a sense of bereavement or loss.

✗ If family members work in your business, they may lose their jobs.

for three years while the chairman's yacht was removed from "work-in-progress". There can also be problems when personal assets are tucked away in the company, or when staff have been paid rather informally, free of tax. The liability rests with the company, and if the practice has continued for many years the financial picture can look quite messy.

The years before you sell up can be used to good effect by improving the performance of your business relative to others in your industry. Going down the profit and loss account and balance sheet, using ratios, will point out areas for improvement. Once the business is firmly planted on an upward trend, your future projections will look that much more plausible, and therefore encouraging, to a potential buyer.

You should certainly have a business plan and strategic projections for at least three years. This will underpin the strength of your negotiations by demonstrating your management skills in putting together the plan, and showing that you believe that the company has a healthy future.

CLOSING DOWN

If your business is not insolvent, but consists largely of yourself and your relationships with customers and suppliers, then in truth you may have little to sell. It may be that a family member or an employee could take over from you and pay you out of a share of future profits. If that is the case, then a much-slimmed-down version of the process described above is all that needs to be gone through.

If neither of those conditions prevail, then you need to close the business down in an orderly fashion, disposing of assets and paying off liabilities. Subject only to any possible capital gains tax demands that may arise, the surplus is yours.

If you are in a partnership, you may be advised to take public leave of that relationship. That will prevent any misunderstandings with people doing business with any remaining partners, if some parts of the business are to continue trading after you have gone. Once again, professional advice should be sought.

GOING UNDER

Many businesses do not enjoy the luxury of a dignified exit. They are forced into failure, usually with unpleasant repercussions. Something can usually be salvaged from the wreckage, but that requires you to know something of the likely events that lie ahead.

The ways in which small (and, for that matter, not so small) businesses go under are:

▨ **BANKRUPTCY** This is a way of dealing with your financial affairs if you cannot pay your debts. While it is not a criminal offence to get into debt, becoming a bankrupt has serious implications. You can be declared bankrupt if you own £750 or more and fail to pay within three weeks of receipt of a statutory demand, or if you fail to satisfy a judgement debt.

Under these circumstances, a creditor can apply to the court for an order of bankruptcy.

Alternatively, the debtor can apply themselves. If the debtor has paid the bill(s) in question, or the court feels that they have made a reasonable offer to their creditors, which has been unreasonably refused, a bankruptcy order will not be made.

As soon as the bankruptcy order is made, the debtor becomes an undischarged bankrupt. With the exception of the tools of the bankrupt's trade, as well as clothing, bedding, and household equipment – all of a basic nature – all of the bankrupt's personal and business assets come under the control of the official receiver, who becomes their trustee in bankruptcy.

A bankrupt cannot: act as a director or be involved in the management of a company; be an MP, counsellor, or JP; obtain credit of more than £250 without revealing that they are an undischarged bankrupt; or engage directly or indirectly in any business other than in the name they were adjudged bankrupt without disclosing their bankruptcy. Any money a bankrupt earns belongs to their trustee in bankruptcy, less anything the trustee feels is necessary to maintain or motivate them. The trustee uses all the bankrupt's assets to pay off first the secured creditors (the bank), then the preferential creditors (PAYE, VAT, National Insurance, and wages), and then everyone else.

On the bright side, bankruptcy frees the debtor from financial worry and allows them to make a fresh start. In addition, unless the bankrupt makes a habit of this offence, the effects are short-lived. If the debts are less than £20,000, the bankrupt is discharged after two years. In all other cases, a bankrupt will be discharged after three years.

These conditions apply only to people who have not been bankrupted before in the last 15 years. Those that have will have to wait five years or longer for their discharge.

▨ **VOLUNTARY ARRANGEMENTS** These were brought into being by the Insolvency Act 1986. Until then, it was not possible for a debtor to make a legally binding compromise with all their creditors. Any single creditor could scupper the plans.

Now a debtor can make a proposal to their creditors to pay all or part of the debts over a period of time. The mechanics are simple. The debtor applies to the court for an interim order stating that they intend to make a proposal naming a qualified insolvency practitioner who will be advising them. The position is then frozen, preventing any bankruptcy proceedings until the insolvency practitioner reports back to the court. A meeting will be called, notifying all creditors, and if the proposal is approved by more than 75 per cent (by value) of them, it will be binding on all creditors.

This course of action avoids all the less attractive features of bankruptcy, but it will work only if you have something credible to offer your creditors.

▓ **Receivership** This occurs when a borrower (a company) fails to meet its obligations to a mortgagee. The most usual scenario is where a company gives a charge over assets (such as property or equipment) to its bankers. This in turn allows the banker to advance funds to the company.

In these circumstances, if the company fails to meet its obligations to its bankers, for example by not repaying money when due, then the bank can appoint a receiver. The receiver has wide powers to step in and run the business or to sell off its assets for the benefit of the person who appointed them. The existing directors' authority will be suspended, and existing contracts with the company have to be carried out by the receiver only if they believe it worthwhile to do so.

Money generated by the receiver goes first to paying the costs of selling assets (auctioneers' fees), then to paying the receiver's own fees. Only then will the person appointing the receiver get his debt paid. Once that, too, has been discharged, others further down the pecking order, such as preferential debts (see p. 157), may get paid.

▓ **Winding Up and Liquidation** This is to limited companies what bankruptcy is to sole traders and partnerships. A limited company is considered to be unable to pay its debts if a creditor leaves a demand for a debt of £750 or more, in a certain prescribed form at its registered office, and that debt is not paid within 21 days. Once this position is reached, an application can be made for the company to be wound up. The company itself can ask to be wound up, as can any creditor, or in some circumstances government officials can ask for this to happen.

Before a winding-up order is made, the court appoints a provisional liquidator, known as the official receiver. Once the order is made, all court proceedings against the company are stopped, all employees' contracts terminated, and all its directors dismissed. The liquidator's job is to realize the company's assets and pay off the creditors. The order of payment is the same as for receivership outlined above.

▓ **Administration** The Insolvency Act 1986 introduced legislation to help companies in serious financial difficulties trade their way back to financial health. The thinking here is similar to that behind voluntary arrangements, although Administration usually involves much more substantial sums.

During Administration, the company is protected from its creditors while an approved rescue plan is implemented. Administration orders will be made only where the court is satisfied that the company has cash available from either shareholders or lenders to finance the rescue plan. It follows that not many Administrations are granted, and not many are successful.

FINANCIAL MATTERS

Taxation is many people's bête noire: *we do not like paying it and we do not like working out how much we have to pay. If you are an employee, then you will almost certainly be on a PAYE scheme, and your employer will be responsible for calculating and deducting your taxes. If you are running a small business, however, you need to know how to deal with the various taxes that apply to business in your area, because the responsibility for their calculation and collection will almost certainly fall on you. If you do not declare your taxable income, you are breaking the law.*

As a source of funds, tax has proved irresistible to governments the world over. Since 1842, when income tax was reintroduced into Britain, everyone in business has been required to account for their income and profits. The same is true in almost every other country, though both the amounts and methods of assessment vary widely. In the US, for example, tax revenues amount to a third of its GDP (gross domestic product), while in Sweden it amounts to about half.

Calculating Tax Due

The more successful a small business is, the greater its exposure to tax liabilities. Its exact tax position will depend on the legal nature of the business. A limited company will be subject to corporation tax at a set rate announced each year by the government. If the business is not a limited company, its proprietor is likely to be subject to income tax as well as to tax rates applying to the general public.

Simply monitoring pre-tax ratios, which in themselves are satisfactory measures of trading performance only, is not enough. The owner-manager is concerned with the net profit after tax. This, after all, is the money available to help the business to grow, or to meet unforeseen problems.

Managing the tax position is one area where timely professional advice is essential. This is made even more important because tax rules can change every year. Good advice can both help to reduce the overall tax bill and so increase the value of profits to the business.

The various types of business are treated differently for tax purposes, so this section looks at each of the following in turn:
■ sole traders
■ partners
■ limited companies

SOLE TRADERS AND PARTNERSHIPS

Partnerships are treated as a collection of sole traders for tax purposes, and each partner's share of that collective liability has to be worked out. Sole traders (self-employed) have all their income from every source brought together and taxed as one entity. In the UK, the taxes that need to be calculated are:
■ income tax, on profits
■ Class 4 National Insurance, on profits
■ capital gains tax, on the disposal of fixed assets at a profit, or when the business is sold
■ inheritance tax, paid on death or when certain gifts are made

Neither of the last two taxes are likely to occur on a regular basis, so they are not detailed here. When those taxes do come into play, the sums involved are likely to be significant, so take professional advice from the outset.

▓ **INCOME TAX** The profit and loss account structure, while more than adequate for the purpose of running the business, is not quite sufficient for working out the likely tax due. Some perfectly proper expenses that need to be accounted for in deciding how well or badly the business is running are not allowed for tax purposes, or at any rate not in the way we have treated them so far.

The rate of depreciation, for example, is a broadly a matter for each businessperson to decide for themselves. In the management accounts, you can decide, for example, to depreciate an asset over one year or five years. The nominal effect on profits can be significant. The accounts for Fast Food have been used again to illustrate this point (see below). Only the second year's figures have

THE EFFECTS OF DEPRECIATION
By setting a low rate of depreciation, so that only £2,000 is claimed for this, Fast Food achieved a high profit before tax figure of £21,950. If the depreciation had been set higher, so that £15,000 were claimed, the profit would have been much lower at £8,950.

FAST FOOD'S DEPRECIATION OF PROFITABILITY

PROFIT AND LOSS ACCOUNT		YEAR 2 (£)	LOW DEPRECIATION (%)	YEAR 2 (£)	HIGH DEPRECIATION (%)
SALES		130,000	100	130,000	100
COST OF SALES	Materials	43,000	33	43,000	33
	Labour	25,000	19	25,000	19
	COST OF GOODS SOLD	68,000		68,000	
GROSS PROFIT		62,000	48	62,000	48
EXPENSES	Rent, rates, etc.	20,000		20,000	
	Wages	13,000		13,000	
	Advertising	3,000		3,000	
	Depreciation	2,000		15,000	
TOTAL EXPENSES		38,000		51,000	
OPERATING OR TRADING PROFIT		24,000	18.5	11,000	11
DEDUCT INTEREST ON: BORROWINGS		2,050		2,050	
NET PROFIT BEFORE TAX		21,950	16.8	8,950	6.88

been used, and in an abbreviated form. They show that the higher the rate of depreciation set, the lower the rate of profit. Were that the case, then the tax due would also be much lower. Unfortunately, the taxman does not see it quite like that.

In practice, certain business expenses are disallowed, partially disallowed, or allowed for but in a different way. Such are the ways of tax authorities the world over. Some are a little less obscure in their workings than others, but few are opaque.

The profit computation is a process that has to be gone through after you have produced your management accounts showing what you understand to be the income and expenditure for the period and a record of assets bought. This computation will adjust that profit figure to meet the tax authorities' needs. Unsurprisingly, this is usually a higher figure, and so a higher tax liability, than the one you had arrived at.

Fast Food's year 2 figures demonstrate how these adjustments are made to the accounting profit to arrive at the profit for taxation purposes (see right). The expense section has been expanded to include extra details needed for this example, i.e. motoring expenses have been separated from rent/rates.

In the computation, some of the expenses are disallowed. These include depreciation, which is replaced by capital allowances. Capital allowances are an incentive allowed by governments to encourage investment in new equipment and technology. The rate is changed in the annual budget to reflect the foibles of the government of the day. In this example, the writing-down allowance, as this is known, is 25 per cent. For the first year in

which the assets are bought, however, as an incentive to invest, the rate is 40 per cent (see p. 162 for detailed calculation). Also, any private element of expenses charged in the accounts is added back.

While you may dispute that you use your car for any purpose other than for business because you have a second car, in practice it will be easier to succumb to the norms that require you to say a certain percentage (in this example, 25 per cent) is private usage.

ADJUSTMENT TO FAST FOOD'S ACCOUNTS TO ARRIVE AT TAXABLE PROFITS		
PROFIT AND LOSS		(£)
GROSS PROFIT		62,000
EXPENSES	Rent, rates, etc.	10,000
	Motoring	10,000
	Wages	13,000
	Advertising	3,000
	Depreciation	2,000
TOTAL EXPENSES		38,000
OPERATING OR TRADING PROFIT		24,000
DEDUCT INTEREST ON: BORROWINGS		2,050
NET PROFIT BEFORE TAX		21,950
ADD BACK	25% motoring	2,500
	Depreciation	2,000
TOTAL		26,450
LESS CAPITAL ALLOWANCES		10,169
ADJUSTED PROFIT		16,281

PROFIT ADJUSTMENT

Depreciation and 25% of motoring expenses have been disallowed as expenses on these accounts, bringing the net profit before tax up to £26,450. The deduction of capital allowances totalling £10,169 gives Fast Food an adjusted profit figure of £16,281.

CALCULATING FAST FOOD'S CAPITAL ALLOWANCES		
FIXED ASSETS	**YEAR 1 (£)**	**YEAR 2 (£)**
EXPENDITURE ON FURNITURE AND FIXTURES	12,500	17,610
25 PER CENT YEAR 1 FIXED ASSETS	3,125	
40 PER CENT YEAR 2 FIXED ASSETS		7,044
TOTAL CAPITAL ALLOWANCE YEAR 2		10,169

CAPITAL ALLOWANCE FOR YEAR 2
The fixed assets bought in the first year are written down to 25% of their cost. This figure is then added to the allowance for the cost of the fixed assets bought during the second year, which are written down to 40% of their cost, to give the total capital allowance figure for year 2 of £10,169.

You can see that the changes that have to be made to the management accounts to arrive at the profit for tax purposes can have a significant effect on the end result.

We have included only a few of the adjustments needed, by way of illustration. Other changes an owner-manager may have to make include:

▪ Adjustment to telephone charges if business and personal telephone use overlap; mobile phone calls also come under this heading.
▪ Heating, lighting, and other property charges if the business is run from home.
▪ Use of stock for personal use, for example food products if you run a grocery outlet, or motor parts if you run a garage

You will need to ensure that any expense that may have seemed reasonable in the management accounts meets the more stringent requirements of the tax authorities. You are generally allowed to set an expense against your income if it is:

▪ Incurred wholly and exclusively for the purposes of trade properly charged against income (not, for example, purchase of a property lease, which is capital).

TAX FOR A SOLE TRADER
Were Fast Food to be a sole-trader-run business, the final tax position could look something like this. The £16,281 adjusted profit now has deducted from it the owner's personal allowance to give a taxable figure of £12,081. The tax due on this figure is £2,658. The addition of two National Insurance payments brings the tax bill to £5,398.

▪ Not specifically disallowed by statute (for example, you cannot set entertainment of customers against your tax, although it is a perfectly legitimate accounting expense).
▪ **NET TAXABLE PROFIT** Under the self-assessment tax system in the UK, the basis of a period of a year of assessment is the accounting year ending within that tax year. So if you made up your accounts to 31 December, the basis period for income tax year 2002/2003 would be 6 April 2002 to 5 April 2003. There are special rules that apply for the first year and the last year of trading that should ensure that tax is charged fairly.

CALCULATING A SOLE TRADER'S ANNUAL TAX DUE	
YEAR 2	**£**
ADJUSTED PROFIT	16,281
LESS PERSONAL ALLOWANCE	4,200
	12,081
TAX AT 22%	2,658
CLASS 2 NATIONAL INSURANCE	2,500
CLASS 4 NATIONAL INSURANCE	240
TOTAL TAX DUE	5,398

DEDUCTING A DIRECTOR'S PAY

The director's pay of £13,000 is added to Fast Food's other expenses and deducted from the gross profit. Once corporation tax of £3,256 has been paid, the remaining profit belongs to the shareholders: £4,000 is paid to them in dividends, leaving £9,025 to be ploughed back into the business to help it grow.

If your turnover is low, currently in the UK less than £15,000 per year, you can put in a three-line account: sales, expenses, and profit. If it is over whatever the current low figure is, then you have to summarize your accounts to show turnover, gross profit, and expenses by main heading.

You will have a personal allowance, that is the current threshold below which you do not pay tax. That amount is deducted from the profit figure. Then a figure is added for Class 4 National Insurance based on taxable profits between a certain band. In the UK that band is currently between about £8,000 and £26,000 and the tax rate is 6 per cent. This is paid in addition to the flat rate Class 2 contributions of about £7 per week.

All these rates and amounts are constantly changing, but the broad principles remain.

COMPANY TAXATION

Companies have a separate legal identity from those who work in them, whether or not they are shareholding directors. Everyone working in the business is taxed as an employee. The company is responsible in the UK, through the PAYE (Pay As You Earn) system, for collecting tax and passing it to the tax authorities.

Directors' pay is a business expense, just as any other wages are, and it is deducted from the company's revenues during the process of arriving at its taxable profits. The chart above shows how this works in practice. Companies in the UK pay tax in three main ways:

■ **ON THE COMPANY'S PROFITS** for the year, as calculated in the tax adjusted profits. This is called corporation tax. The rate of corporation tax in the UK, and in many other countries, depends on the amount of

FAST FOOD'S COMPANY TAXATION		
YEAR 2		£
GROSS PROFIT		62,000
EXPENSES	Rent, rates, etc.	10,000
	Motoring	7,500
	Director's pay	13,000
	Advertising	3,000
	Capital allowances	10,169
TOTAL EXPENSES		43,669
OPERATING OR TRADING PROFIT		18,331
DEDUCT INTEREST ON: BORROWINGS		2,050
NET PROFIT BEFORE TAX		16,281
CORPORATION TAX		3,256
PROFIT AFTER TAX		13,025
DIVIDEND		4,000
RETAINED PROFIT		9,025

profits made; they are also subject to annual review. If the profits are less than £300,000, the small companies' rate of 20 per cent applies. Above £1.5 million, the full rate of 30 per cent is charged. For figures in between, a taper applies. Corporation tax is payable nine months after the end of the accounting period.

■ **ON THE DISTRIBUTION OF PROFIT** to the shareholders in the dividend payment. This gives the appearance of taxing the same profit twice, but through a process of tax credits

THE PROS AND CONS OF TRADING, FROM A TAX PERSPECTIVE, AS A SOLE TRADER/PARTNERSHIP OR A LIMITED COMPANY

SOLE TRADER/PARTNERSHIP	LIMITED COMPANY
Statutory audit not required	Statutory audit required if turnover over £350,000
Annual returns need not be submitted or statutory books kept	Annual returns must be submitted and statutory books kept
Income tax charged at rates from 10 per cent to 40 per cent, depending on profits	Corporation tax for small companies is charged at 20 per cent. This tax increases as a company grows and depends on profits. At present the top rate is 30 per cent.
"Current year" basis of assessment (except in opening and closing years of trading)	"Actual" basis of assessment
Lower total NI contributions (but fewer benefits)	Higher total NI contributions by company as well as by directors (if employees), but better benefits
Relief for personal pension premiums	Relief for personal pension premiums
Single charge to capital gains tax on disposal of assets and subsequent withdrawal of capital, for example, on liquidation	Possible double charge to capital gains tax on disposal of assets and subsequent withdrawal of capital, e.g. on liquidation
No capital duty on formation	Capital duty payable on formation
Interest relief on money borrowed to invest in business, as capital or as a loan	Interest relief to individuals only on money borrowed to invest in company as share capital or by way of a loan

this double taxation does not generally occur. When a shareholder gets a dividend from a company, it comes with a tax credit attached. This means that any shareholder on the basic rate of tax will not have to pay any further tax. Higher rate tax payers, however, will.

■ **ON CAPITAL GAINS** If an asset, say a business property, is sold at a profit, then the company will have made a capital gain. This gain will be taxed along the general lines of corporation tax, with lower rates applying to smaller companies.

Tax itself is also a business expense for a company, so an allowance for tax must be included in the accounts. Before it is paid, you accrue for it by showing it as a creditor in the balance sheet. (See pp. 97–9 for details of accrual.) When it is paid, it will appear in the profit and loss account.

WHICH STRUCTURE IS BEST?

The most important rule is never to let the tax tail wag the business dog. If you want to keep your business's finances private, then the public filing of accounts required of companies will not be for you. On the other hand, if you feel that you want to protect your private assets from creditors in the event that things go wrong, then being a sole trader or partner is probably not the best route to take.

Company profits and losses are locked into the company, so if you have several lines of business using different trading entities, you cannot easily settle losses in one area against profits in another. But because sole traders are treated as one entity for all their sources of income, there is more scope for netting off gains and losses. Some points to bear in mind regarding structure are:

- ▨ **IF YOUR PROFITS ARE LIKELY TO BE SMALL**, say below £50,000, for some time, then from a purely tax point of view you may pay less tax as a sole trader. This is because as an individual you get a tax-free allowance, so your first few thousand pounds of income are not taxable. This amount varies according to personal circumstances.

- ▨ **IF YOU EXPECT TO BE MAKING HIGHER RATES OF PROFIT** (above £50,000) and want to invest a large portion of those profits back into your business, then you could be better off forming a company. That is because companies do not start paying higher rates of tax until their profits reach £300,000. Even then, they do not pay tax at 40 per cent, whereas a sole trader would be taxed at 40 per cent by the time their profits had reached about £30,000, taking allowances into account. So, a company making £300,000 taxable profits could have £54,000 more to reinvest.

- ▨ **NON-SALARY BENEFITS** are more favourably treated for the sole trader. You can generally get tax relief on the business element of costs that are only partly business-related, such as the costs of running a vehicle. A director of a company will be taxed on the value of the vehicle's list price and will not be allowed to claim the cost of travel to and from work as a business expense.

Minimizing the Taxes You Pay

There is no reason to arrange your financial affairs in such a way as to pay the most tax possible. While staying within the law by a safe margin, you should explore ways to avoid, as opposed to evade, tax liability. This is a complex area and one subject to frequent change. The tax authorities try most years to close loopholes in the tax system, while highly paid tax accountants and lawyers try even harder to find new ways around the rules.

This is a field in which timely professional advice can produce substantial benefits in the form of lower tax bills. The summary of legal tax-saving measures shown on p. 166 provides an indicative list of areas to explore.

Value Added Tax (VAT)

This tax system on consumer spending applies across Europe, although most countries have significant variations in VAT rates, starting thresholds, and the details of the schemes themselves.

VAT is a complicated tax. Essentially, you must register if your taxable turnover – that is, sales (not profit) – exceeds a certain figure (£51,000 in November 2000) in any twelve-month period, or looks as though it might reasonably be expected to do so. This rate is reviewed each year in the Budget and is frequently changed.

The general rule is that all supplies of goods and services are taxable at the standard rate (17.5 per cent) unless they are specifically stated by the law to be zero-rated or exempt. In deciding whether your turnover exceeds the limit, you have to include the zero-rated sales (things like most food, books, and children's clothing) because they are technically taxable; it is just that the rate of tax is nought per cent. You leave out exempt items.

AREAS TO CONSIDER WHEN ASSESSING YOUR TAX LIABILITY

1 Make sure you have included all allowable business expenses.

2 If you have made losses in any tax period, these may under certain circumstances be carried forward to offset future taxable profits or backwards against past profits.

3 Capital gains tax can be deferred if another asset is to be bought with the proceeds.

4 Pension contributions will reduce your taxable profits.

5 If you intend to buy capital assets for your business, bring forward your plans so as to maximize use of the writing down allowance.

6 Identify non-cash benefits that you and employees could take instead of taxable salaries, such as a share option scheme.

7 Examine the pros and cons of taking your money out of a limited company in salary or dividends. These are taxed differently and may provide scope for tax reduction.

8 If your spouse has no other income from employment, they could earn a sum equivalent to their annual tax-free allowance (currently about £4,000) by working for your business.

9 Any pre-trading expenses, such as designing a product or buying a computer, incurred at any stage over the seven years before you started up can probably be treated as if they had been incurred after trading started.

10 If you bought any business assets on hire purchase, you may be able to include the full purchase price of the items in your capital allowances calculation.

TAX SAVING: TAKING LEGAL AVOIDANCE MEASURES

		WITHOUT TAKING AVOIDANCE MEASURES (£)	TAKING AVOIDANCE MEASURES (£)
ADJUSTED TAXABLE PROFITS		50,000	50,000
ADJUSTED TAXABLE PROFITS, LESS:	Pension contributions		7,000
	First year writing-down allowance on £10,000 worth of new equipment (40%)		4,000
	Pre-start-up expenses		3,000
	Employing spouse		4,200
	Offsetting last year's loss		2,500
TOTAL TAX AVOIDANCE MEASURES		0	20,700
FINAL TAXABLE PROFIT		50,000	29,300
TAX PAID AT 40%		20,000	11,720

AVOIDING TAX
This example illustrates the impact on taxable profits that taking some of the above measures could have on a business. By deducting sums for pension contributions, writing-down allowance, pre-start-up expenses, an employed spouse, and last year's loss, the business saved itself £9,280 on its tax bill.

There are three free booklets issued by Customs & Excise: a simple introductory booklet called *Should You be Registered for VAT?* and two more detailed booklets called *General Guide* and *Scope and Coverage*. If in doubt (and the language is not always easy to understand), ask your accountant or the local branch of Customs & Excise; after all, they would rather help you to get it right in the first place than have to sort it out later when you have made a mess of it.

VAT RECORDS

The bookkeeping system that you started out with (see pp. 74–83) may need to be extended to accommodate VAT records. As a result of these changes, the analyzed cash book, if you are using a simple system, would replace the single figure for the amount paid used in the pre-VAT registration bookkeeping system with three columns. The first would show the amount before VAT has been charged; the second, the amount of the VAT; and the third column would show the gross amount, including VAT. The analysis columns would contain the net amounts. You can cross-check the arithmetic by totalling the three columns of analysis and seeing that they add up to the total of the net amount.

The same layout can be used for the receipts side of the bookkeeping record.

DOING THE SUM

Calculating the VAT element of any transaction can be a confusing sum, but these simple rules will help you to get it right. Take the gross amount of any sum – that is, the total including any VAT – and divide it by 117.5 (if the VAT rate is 17.5 per cent) or a figure that corresponds to the VAT rate plus 100. This means that the bill you receive is made up of 100 per cent of the net bill, with another 17.5 per cent on top.

Now take the resulting figure and multiply it by 100 to get the pre-VAT total, then multiply it by 17.5 to arrive at the VAT element of the bill.

COMPLETING THE VAT RETURN

Each quarter, you will have to complete a VAT return, which shows your purchases and the VAT you paid on them, and your sales and the VAT you collected on them. The VAT paid and the VAT collected are offset against each other and the balance sent to Customs & Excise. In effect, every business over a certain size becomes a tax collector. There is no reward for carrying out this task, but there are penalties for making mistakes or for making late VAT returns. For businesses, VAT is a zero-sum game, because the end consumer picks up the tab.

If you have paid more VAT in any quarter than you have collected, you will get a refund. For this reason it sometimes pays to register even if you do not have to – if you are selling mostly zero-rated items, for example. Also, being registered for VAT may make your business look more workmanlike to potential customers.

A computer-based bookkeeping system is invaluable when it comes to completing VAT returns, because the calculations are automatically generated by the accounting package. All you have to do is enter the current VAT rate. If you take web-enabled software updates, you may not even have to do this.

Basically, the VAT inspectors are interested in five figures: how much VAT you have collected on their behalf on sales of goods and services, how much VAT you have paid on purchases, the VAT due to be paid or reclaimed (that is, the difference between the two figures), the value of your sales, and the value of your purchases, both net of VAT.

The VAT return has to be signed by the person registered for VAT. It is important to remember that a named person is responsible for VAT, a limited company being treated as a person in this instance. Your VAT records have to be kept for six years, and periodically you can expect a visit from a VAT inspector.

CASH ACCOUNTING

If your business has a turnover greater than £350,000 a year, then you have no option but to account for VAT in the usual way. This means that the VAT you claim on a sale will be recognized as income when you raise the invoice rather than when you get paid. Unfortunately, the VAT will have to be paid when your next return is due, whether you have been paid or not.

If your turnover is less than £350,000, then you can elect to pay VAT on a cash basis. This means that you are not liable for the VAT until your customers pay up, but equally you cannot reclaim VAT on any purchases until you pay for them. In the early years, when cash flow is particularly tight, or if you have a small number of customers who buy a large proportion of your output on credit, this might be worthwhile.

Other Matters

Only the outline of VAT has been sketched here. There are a number of special schemes for retailers, adjustments to be made for any private usage, different ways of handling certain second-hand goods, and scale charges to be applied to the use of motor vehicles. It is advisable to get the free booklets mentioned on p. 167 and take professional advice if you have any doubts.

Handling Employment Taxes

Employing people requires you to manage a PAYE (Pay As You Earn) system. If your business is a limited company, the owner is also liable for PAYE. You will also have to deduct National Insurance. Both these tasks will involve some additional record keeping because, once again, owner-managers are being asked to be unpaid tax collectors and, once again, there are penalties for getting it wrong.

In this area you are also handling your employees' tax affairs, so getting it wrong could hurt them financially and generate ill will among people whose high morale is important to you.

As an employer you have to:

▓ make the appropriate deductions of tax from your staff's wages

▓ keep a suitable record of the amounts paid to your staff and the amounts deducted

▓ account to the Collector of Taxes for the amounts of tax due each month

▓ prepare the returns at the end of the tax year, detailing the payments made to each of your staff and showing the amounts deducted

PAYE

Income tax is collected from employees through the PAYE system. The employees' liability to income tax is collected as it is earned, rather than being collected by tax assessment at some later date. If the business is run as a limited company, then the directors of the company are employees. As such, PAYE must be operated on all salaries and bonuses paid to them, yourself as owner included.

The Inland Revenue now issues booklets, explaining how PAYE works. The seven main documents you need to operate PAYE are:

1 A deductions working sheet (Form P11) for each employee.

2 The PAYE Tables. There are two books of tax tables in general use, which are updated in line with the prevailing tax rates. These are:

▓ Pay Adjustment Tables. These show the amount that an employee can earn in any particular week or month before the payment of tax.

▓ Tables B to D and LR – Taxable Pay Tables. These show the tax due on an employee's taxable pay.

3 Form P45, which is given to an employee when transferring from one job to another.

4 Form P46, which is used when a new employee does not have a P45 from a previous employment (for example, a school leaver starting work for the first time).

5 Form P60, which is used so that the employer can certify an employee's pay at the end of the income tax year in April.

6 Form P35 – the year-end declaration and certificate. This is used to summarize all the tax and National Insurance deductions from employees for the tax year.

▨ Form P6 – the tax codes advice notice issued by the Inspector of Taxes telling you which tax code number to use for each employee.

NATIONAL INSURANCE

As an employer, you must also deduct National Insurance (NI) contributions. There are three rates of contributions for NI purposes:

▮ Table A – the most common rate, used in all cases except those mentioned below

▮ Table B – used for certain married women who have a certificate for payment at reduced rate

▮ Table C – used for employees who are over pension age

For Tables A and B there are two amounts to calculate: the employee's contribution and the employer's contribution. For Table C there is no employee's contribution.

The amounts of contributions are recorded on the same deduction working sheets as used for income tax purposes. The amounts of NI due are found on the appropriate table. The tables show both the employee's liability and also the total liability for the week or month. Both these figures must be recorded on the deduction working sheet.

ACCOUNTING RECORDS

When you pay out wages and salaries to your staff, you need to record the net pay in your cash book. This will also record the PAYE and NI paid to the Collector of Taxes.

If you have only one or two employees, then the record of the payments in the cash book, together with the other PAYE documentation itemized above, will probably suffice. But if you have more than two employees, you should keep a simple wages book, an example of which is shown on p. 170.

The deductions working sheet (Form P11) gives you a record of the payments made to each employee throughout the year. You will also need to keep a summary of the payments made to all employees on one particular date (i.e. the totals on the chart on p. 170), so that an analysis of the business's finances can be made at any point in time.

In a full double-entry bookkeeping system, you will need to transfer these totals into your nominal ledger.

PAYSLIPS

The law requires that employers *must* provide their staff with itemized pay statements. These need to show the following three figures:

▮ gross pay
▮ net pay
▮ any deductions (stating the amounts of each item and the reason why they are made)

HOW TO CALCULATE THE TAX DEDUCTION FOR AN EMPLOYEE

▨ Add this week's/month's gross pay to the previous total of gross pay to date, so as to show the total gross pay to and including this week/month of the tax year.

▨ By checking the tax code number of the employee on Table A, arrive at the figure of tax-free pay for that particular week/month.

▨ Deduct the amount of tax-free pay from the total pay to date, to get the amount of taxable pay.

▨ By using Table B, work out the tax due on the total taxable pay for the year to date. Then make the appropriate deduction to allow for the tax due.

▨ Deduct the amount of tax already accounted for in previous weeks from the total tax due, to work out the tax due for the week/month.

Surviving a Tax Investigation

With good bookkeeping and accounting systems, you should avoid any disputes over tax and other matters. Complete records are vital if you are to defend yourself successfully from mistaken allegations of wrongdoing.

	A WAGES BOOK EXAMPLE					
	WEEK ENDING 8TH JUNE					
NAME	GROSS PAY (£)	TAX (£)	EMPLOYEE'S NI (£)	DEDUCTIONS (£)	NET PAY (£)	TOTAL NI (£)
P. HARTLY	262.00	39.30	20.84	60.14	201.86	46.64
I. GALLITLEY	301.00	45.15	21.90	67.05	233.95	48.76
S. SAUNDERS	228.00	34.20	22.94	57.14	170.86	50.84
TOTALS	791.00	118.65	65.68	184.33	606.67	146.24

There are some factors that will help you understand how tax inquiries get started and what might happen if one does.

WHY TAX INVESTIGATIONS HAPPEN

The Revenue get their information from three sources. Their own investigations and tips from the public account for the vast majority of their information received. However, an increasingly effective measure is to ask people to inform on themselves. Crazy as that may sound, it seems to work. While this does not quite amount to an amnesty, those self-employed who have strayed across the boundary between tax avoidance and tax evasion can contact tax authorities anonymously and get confidential advice on how to sort themselves out.

Sometimes the tax authorities look closely at whole industries. Recently they have looked long and hard at the amusement arcade business, construction, betting and gaming, commodities dealing, and some doctors and dentists.

Tax inspectors may also do any of the following in their search for tax evaders:
- ■ Drive around exclusive residential areas and look carefully at any expensive-looking renovation work.
- ■ Use the services of pubs, restaurants, hotels, copy shops, and other cash businesses, while looking carefully at each business's cost structure.
- ■ Read local newspapers and use press-cutting

DETAILING WAGES

The employees' tax and NI contributions (totalled under "Deductions") for the week are deducted from their gross pay. That leaves the amount of the net payment made to each employee for the week. The final column shows the total NI contributions for each employee, including the employer's portion.

agencies to cross-check people's claimed lifestyle with their actual one.
- ■ Access company databases and on-line records from Companies House.
- ■ Check up on local authority parking permits in certain areas.
- ■ Examine the Land Registry to monitor house purchases and property prices and sales and to keep an eye on the yachting register.

The tax authorities put all the information that it gathers into its computers, where all these sources of data are cross-correlated with each other. They have a skilled project team looking specifically at the uses of IT for tax investigations, and they can usually uncover anything that does not look quite right. For example, if someone is claiming to make no profit from their business, but, rather surprisingly, owns a yacht, has a residence parking permit for inner-city parking in an area they do not appear to live in, and is having a new swimming pool installed at their home, alarm bells ring.

What is much more likely, however, is that someone tips the tax inspectors off. Informers are often aggrieved spouses or employees, competitors, jealous neighbours, or jilted lovers. Some of this information is second-hand and dangerously wrong, but that is how gossip works. Some people like to brag about how they load their expenses or take cash payments that are not entered in the books, so it is not exactly surprising that gossip starts. If that gossip reaches a tax inspector's ears, then an investigation may begin.

How You Know It Has Started

It is not too difficult to know when a tax investigation is underway. You will probably get a standard letter from the Special Compliance Office, or your accountant will. It will state that inquiries have begun under Code of Practice 8 for less serious matters, or Code of Practice 9 for serious matters. Booklets will accompany the letter, to explain the procedure. By this stage you can be sure that a lot of information has already been gathered.

The Tax Authorities' Powers

The Inland Revenue have sweeping powers to demand documents from the taxpayer and from third parties under section 20 or section 745 of the Taxes Management Act. They are always entitled to obtain papers and documents under a notice if that notice is valid, and they can go back as much as 20 years into a person's affairs in cases of suspected fraud. That is way beyond the six years that you are required to keep your own accounting records. So, if you have stuck strictly to the six-year rule, you may be at something of a disadvantage in the event of a tax inquiry.

What they are not entitled to do is to insist upon an interview with the taxpayer or third parties. They cannot force people to speak.

The Revenue are allowed to search premises and remove documents if they have a warrant. If they raid your premises, do not obstruct them, but do follow a few simple rules:

- ▨ Make sure your professional adviser gets round to the premises as fast as possible.
- ▨ Read the warrant and make sure that you understand it.
- ▨ Remember you are under no legal obligation to talk.
- ▨ Make sure that your staff are also aware that they are under no legal obligation to talk.
- ▨ Ask what is the purpose of the search.
- ▨ Obtain a receipt for any materials that they take away.
- ▨ Get the name and office of the investigator in charge.

Confidentiality

The Revenue understand the real world and the fact that some people have complex financial, commercial, and personal lives. They go to great lengths to protect confidences and save unnecessary embarrassments.

This means, in practice, that disclosures can be made on a managed basis. Two spouses can go through one joint disclosure as appropriate, and then have separate meetings with the Revenue in which they can make disclosures of which the other is unaware. Likewise, directors can make disclosures of which fellow directors are unaware.

The Revenue is governed by the Official Secrets Act, but they do, however, have a number of obligations to share information with HM Customs & Excise and with the police. The Revenue lay down their rules on confidentiality in Code of Practice 2. In short, they will give information to people not authorized by the taxpayer only in the very restricted cases where it is allowed by law.

The Code specifically says that you do not have to discuss your personal tax affairs in front of other people.

Privilege

In theory, whatever you disclose to your lawyer is privileged, but in practice this is not always so. For example:

- ▨ Original documents recording a transaction are never covered.
- ▨ Any communication intended to facilitate a crime is excluded.

■ Documents that get into the hands of a third party are usually no longer privileged.

What you reveal to your tax adviser is also covered by the privilege law, but less so. The law on privilege is not clear-cut, and you should always ask your adviser about which disclosures are covered and which are not. As a result of a recent case, the law now seems to be that a formal notice under section 20(I) of the Taxes Management Act imposes a duty on taxpayers to produce communications with lawyers.

Meetings

Meetings with the Revenue can be tense and contentious affairs. The atmosphere is similar to that in a court between two opposing lawyers. Both parties' main task is to put their own position in the most believable light. In the process, the truth can get left behind.

In Code 8 cases there is usually no need for you to meet the Revenue, but in Code 9 cases you usually have to meet at least twice – once in a formal interview and once again at the final settlement. Exceptions are made by the Revenue in the case of ill health or age, or if a person has left the country.

If you have to have a meeting with the Revenue, then there are some issues to consider beforehand to make the meeting less onerous:

Do not overdress; if anything be casual. The more natural you look and behave, the better you come across.

Do not hold meetings in the Revenue's own offices; opt for your adviser's office. There are even occasions when holding meetings in your own home can be advantageous. The Revenue are going to have a good look at the home anyway. But if they do come, make sure that the rest of the family is out for the day.

The better prepared you are, the better the outcome. People who just go straight into meetings with a tax inspector generally come unstuck. They tend to make guesses when under pressure, out of an urge to answer the questions. If these answers given on the hoof prove wrong later, their credibility evaporates.

The best approach is to think carefully about the questions likely to be asked, and to rehearse both questions and answers with your adviser.

Penalties

The penalties can theoretically be as high as 100 per cent of the unpaid tax, but in practice they are nearly always dwarfed by the amount of tax to be paid.

If you can bring the tax figure down, you get a lower interest figure too (since that is statutorily determined), while another 5 or 10 per cent off the penalty does not materially affect most settlements. Note that penalties are imposed on the tax only, not on the interest.

In the worst-case scenario you would go to jail. In practice, however, the Revenue prosecute very rarely, so the number of investigations that end up with someone in prison is relatively small. It is, of course, of no benefit to the Revenue if someone who owes them tax is in jail and so cannot earn any money.

If the Revenue say that they are going to prosecute, the consequences can be very serious. You must seek professional advice *immediately*. Each year, the Revenue initiate over 100 criminal proceedings. Between 10 and 25 of these cases relate to false accounts or false claims, and a high two-thirds of these cases result in a conviction.

Bargaining

Bargaining is inevitable in most cases. The revenue's main aim is to ensure that taxpayers pay the right amount of tax. But what is the right amount of tax is open to discussion. They are also concerned with hitting their own "sales targets" in an efficient manner. They have goals as to how much unpaid tax they have to collect each year and deadlines to meet along the way. Anyone with a goal and a deadline is someone with whom you can negotiate.

At the end of the day, the Revenue is also influenced by the total conduct of the case – by the quality of the taxpayer's disclosure and by the co-operation that they receive during their investigation. Good conduct of a case can only reflect in the taxpayer's favour.

Negotiation starts at the very beginning of the process. The adviser contacts the Revenue – on a no-names basis if the approach by the tax payer is a voluntary one – to discuss the terms and scope of the inquiry and the code of practice under which it is to be handled.

The Revenue has two Codes of Practice for tax fraud. Cases of suspected serious fraud are pursued under Code of Practice 9; other (less serious) cases follow Code of Practice 8. The Revenue's position on Code of Practice 9 is laid down in what is known as the Hansard Rules.

HANSARD RULES

In answer to a parliamentary question in 1990, the Chancellor of the Exchequer confirmed long-standing rules on the Revenue's bargaining powers in cases of tax fraud. He made three points, known as the Hansard Rules (named after the official published report of British parliamentary proceedings):

1 The Inland Revenue may accept a money settlement instead of instituting criminal proceedings in cases where fraud is alleged to have been committed by a taxpayer.

2 The Revenue can give no undertaking that it will accept such a settlement even if the case is one in which the taxpayer has made a full confession and has fully co-operated in the investigation of the facts. The Revenue has full discretion in all cases as to the course it chooses to pursue.

3 In considering whether to accept a money settlement or to institute criminal proceedings, however, the Revenue is influenced by the taxpayer making a full

confession and fully co-operating in the investigation by, for instance, allowing the Revenue to examine whatever books, papers, or documents that they see fit.

In practice, this means that as long as the taxpayer is upfront with the Revenue during the course of the investigation, they can be assured that the settlement will remain confidential and will be a civil one. There will be no recourse to criminal law.

The Revenue's powers are unique in this respect and differ greatly from those of HM Customs & Excise and those of the police.

TIME

The duration of an investigation varies according to the complexity of the case and the availability of information. It would, however, be surprising if a case has not been cleared within 18 months from beginning to end. With a technically based case, however, it can take much longer, if, for example, both sides need to seek tax counsel's advice. When parts have to be taken to the Commissioners, a case can stretch for years.

What is as worrying to the owner-manager as the length of time is the distraction the procedure makes. This can eat into time that could have been spent getting more customers, improving products, or introducing new equipment.

The other problem is the cost. Apart from any fine, you will have to bear the cost of your own advisers answering the tax inspector's questions. This can run into a substantial four-figure sum, even for a relatively trivial case, and even if you win you will not get those costs back. You can, however, insure against a tax, VAT, or NI investigation, which will ensure that you get good, timely advice at no additional cost.

GLOSSARY OF ACCOUNTING TERMS

Cross-references at the end of entries are shown in bold type.

Account
Page in the ledger recording the common aspects of different transactions; for example, cash books, and sales and purchase budgets.

Account payable
Money owed by a business, for example to a supplier.

Account receivable
Money owed to a business, for example by a customer.

Accounting
Art of preparing reports from bookkeeping records, based on accounting concepts and measurement conventions.

Accounting concepts
Practical rules that enable bookkeeping records of transactions to be converted into accounting reports.

Accounting language
Special accounting meaning of various words and phrases, rather than the usually accepted layman's meaning.

Accounting period
Period of time from one balance sheet to the next, usually a month, quarter, or year. Period of the profit and loss account.

Accounting reports
Balance sheet, profit and loss account, and cash-flow forecasts.

Accrual
A provision made for an event that has occurred but for which no written evidence is available yet. For example, an estimate of tax liability would be accrued for the peiod to which it applies, because you know the bill will come in at some point in the future.

Accumulated depreciation
Extent to which the fixed asset cost has been allocated to depreciation expense since the asset was originally acquired. This is deducted from the fixed assets.

Accumulated profit
Balance of profit retained in the business over its entire life rather than being paid out to shareholders. Also known as retained earnings.

Administrative expense
Cost of directing and controlling a business, which includes directors' fees, office salaries, office rent, lighting, heating, legal fees, auditors' fees, accounting services, etc. It does not include research and development costs, manufacturing, sales, or distribution expenses.

Amortization
A US alternative to the word "depreciation", sometimes used in the UK.

Appropriation account
Statement of accumulated profit.

Asset
Something owned by the business that has a measurable cost.

Authorized capital
Share capital of the business authorized by law. May be only partly issued for cash.

Bad debt
Debtor who fails to pay. The amount may be written off to expenses.

Balance
Difference between the debits and credits in a ledger account.

Balance sheet
Accounting report. A statement of the assets owned by a business and the way they are financed from liabilities and the owner's equity. Does not indicate the market value of the business.

Bonds
Long-term loans, often secured on the assets. Also known as debentures.

Bookkeeping
Recording of financial transactions. Posting of transactions from journals to ledgers to provide data for accounting reports.

Book value
The value of the assets owned by a business after depreciation has been deducted from the total.

Buildings
Fixed assets unless acquired for resale, they are depreciated to expense over their working life.

Capital allowance
An allowance given against taxable profit by the Inland Revenue instead of depreciation.

Capital reserve
This is created, for example, when a fixed asset is revalued. So, while the business is clearly better off with the higher valuation, no more cash is available, unless, of course, that asset is sold.

Cash
The money asset of a business, which includes both cash in hand and cash held at the bank.

Cash discount
Discount allowed to a debtor for early payment of the debt. Terms may be "2 per cent for payment within ten days or net (no discount) for payment within one month".

Cash flow
The pattern and extent of cash payments and receipts by a business over a particular period. Also used to describe the differences between total cash inflow and toal cash outflow for a specific project.

Cash transactions
Receipts or payments of cash.

Claims
The owners' or creditors' claims against the assets of a business. Owners' claims are called owners' equity. Creditors' claims are called liabilities.

Closing stock
Stock at the end of the accounting period. Part of the computation of cost of goods sold.

Collateral see **security**.

Company
Legal entity, limited or unlimited, regulated by the Companies Acts.

Conservatism
If there is a choice as to the amount of certain figures when preparing accounts, it is conservative to opt to use the lower figure for assets and the higher for liabilities.

Consistency
Accounting methods are not changed frequently. If they are changed, it is only for good stated reasons.

Contingent liability
A liability not yet recorded on the balance sheet. It may or may not become an actual liability.

Co-operative
A legal business structure, where the members who own the business must also work in the business. Each member of a co-operative has one vote.

Cost
Any expense of a business.

Cost accounting
Recording of cost data and preparation of cost statements.

Cost concept
Assets are to be valued at cost, not market value. Current assets, such as stock, are normally valued at the lower cost or the market value.

Cost of goods sold
Cost of goods actually sold during the accounting period. Excludes cost of goods left unsold. Also excludes all overheads except manufacturing overheads.

Creditor
Someone to whom a business owes money.

Credit transaction
A transaction that incurs (accrues) liability. No cash is paid or received until later.

Cumulative preference shares
Preference shares whose unpaid dividends accumulate until they are eventually paid by the company. Some preference shares are specifically non-cumulative.

Current asset
Something owned by a business that is either cash, can be turned into a known amount of cash quickly, or is owned with the intention of selling it for cash within one year of buying.

Current liability
Liability due for payment within one operating period, normally within one year.

Current tax liability
Income tax due within one year.

Debenture
A document that shows that the debenture owner has lent money to the business for a specific period of time, at an annual rate of interest. In some cases the capital sum is secured against certain of the business's assets.

Debt capital
Money loaned to a business for more than a year.

Debtor
Money due to a business, usually from a customer.

Deferred income
Income received in advance of being earned and recognized. It is normally left as a theoretical current liability in the balance sheet until the sale is made and the income recognized.

Deferred shares
Shares of a company ranking for dividend after preference and ordinary shares. Also known as deferred stock.

Depreciation
Allocation of the cost of a fixed asset (such as a building, car, or equipment, such as a photocopier) to each accounting period over its working life.

Depreciation expense
Depreciation (at cost) during the accounting period; not the same as accumulated depreciation, except in the first year of the fixed asset.

Diminishing balance depreciation
Depreciation method charging off the cost of a fixed asset by a level percentage of the reducing balance over its working life. The percentage remains the same but the depreciation charge decreases over time.

Director
An officer of a limited company. A member of the board of directors. Not a partner.

Dual aspect
The two aspects of each transaction – debit and credit – that form the basis of double-entry bookkeeping.

Earnings
Another way of describing profit.

Entity
A business has an entity that is legally separate from the owners or managers. It is to this entity that the accounting reports are addressed.

Equipment
This is regarded as a fixed asset if it is acquired for long-term use and not for resale. It is recorded in the balance sheet at cost less depreciation, not at market value.

Equity
The capital of a business that comes from the issue of shares.

Expenditure
Money paid for cost, expenses, assets, or other purposes.

Expense
Any payments properly chargeable to the profit and loss account, for example, manufacturing, selling, or administrative expenses. Expenses are "matched" against revenues during the accounting period to compute the figure of profit.

Face value
Normal value of shares, not the book value or market value.

Fixed assets
Assets, such as land, plant, and equipment acquired for long-term use in the business and not for resale. These are charged to overhead expenses periodically as depreciation. They are recorded in the balance sheet at cost less depreciation, not at market value. See also **expense**.

Fixtures and fittings
Fixed assets if acquired for use and not for resale.

Furniture and fixtures
Fixed assets if acquired for use and not for resale.

Future tax liability

Reserve for future income tax computed on the current year's profit and not due for payment until a future date. It normally becomes the current tax liability in the following year.

Gearing

The relationship between a firm's debt capital and its equity. The higher the proportion of debt, the more highly geared is the business.

General expense

Expense of the business that is not part of manufacturing, selling, and administrative expense. It includes audit fees, legal expenses, etc., and is sometimes grouped with administrative expense in the income statement.

General reserve

Part of the accumulated profit set aside in the owner's equity section of the balance sheet, so that it is not distributed to the shareholders as dividends. It is neither an asset nor cash, merely part of the owner's equity, which is shown separately on the claims side of the balance sheet.

Going concern

All accounting reports and values assume that a business is a "going concern"; that is, that the business will continue to trade and is not about to liquidate (end). Market values are therefore based upon those expected in the normal course of business.

Goodwill

The value of the name, reputation, or intangible assets of a business. In accounting it is recorded (at cost) only when it is purchased. It is not depreciated and often written off to nil. It is never valued at market price. It is generally a hidden asset of the business.

Gross profit

The difference between sales and cost of goods sold. The profit computed before selling and administrative expenses etc. are charged.

Income

The profit of a business.

Income statement

A term commonly used in the US instead of "profit and loss account".

Income tax liability

See **current tax liability** or **future tax liability**.

Incomplete transaction

A transaction that is incomplete at the end of the accounting period and consequently a cause of uncertainty in accounting. The concept of profit recognition must be employed to determine in which accounting period the profit is earned or the loss sustained.

Inflation accounting

Accounts are based on historical values, assuming the purchasing power of money to be stable from one year to the next. However, because of inflation this is untrue, and various methods of accounting attempt to reconcile this with useful accounting information.

Intangible asset

Asset that cannot actually be touched, for example goodwill.

Inventory

A term used in the US instead of stock.

Investment

Amount invested in stocks, shares, bonds, debentures, or any asset. See also **trade investment.**

Issue price of a share

Price at which a share is first sold by a company. It is normally the nominal value plus share premium or less share discount.

Issued capital

Share capital actually issued by a company. See also **authorized capital.**

Land

Freehold or leasehold property owned by a business. It is normally a fixed asset and is not depreciated.

Leverage

A term used in the US instead of **gearing.**

Limitations of accounting

Accounting reports show a limited picture of a business because: (a) some important facts cannot be stated in money terms; (b) accounting periods at fixed intervals involve uncertainty due to incomplete transactions; (c) accounting reports depend on concepts; and (d) accounting is not scientific but depends upon judgment.

Limited company
Company whose shareholders have limited their liability to the amounts they subscribe to the shares they hold. Limited companies are regulated by the Companies Acts.

Liquidity
Availability of cash or assets easily turned into cash.

Loan capital
See **debt capital**.

Long-term liability
Liability not due for payment within one year, such as bonds, debentures, or loans. Holders of these are creditors and receive interest; they are not shareholders.

Loss
Opposite of profit or income. The excess of costs and expenses over sales. Reduces the owner's equity.

Loss on disposal of fixed assets
Loss due to the sale or disposal of fixed assets, treated as "other income and expense" in the income statement. Significant losses or profits are sometimes charged to capital reserve.

Machinery
Fixed asset if acquired for use and not for resale. Valued at cost less depreciation. Machinery manufactured or acquired for resale is stock. See **depreciation**.

Maintenance cost
The expense of maintaining or repairing the fixed assets of the business. Such costs are charged as expense in the income statement.

Manufacturing expenses
Overheads for manufacturing. Part of the cost of goods sold. It does not include sales or administrative expense.

Matching
Costs and revenues in the accounting period should be "matched" in order that the computed profit may be certain to be true and fair. Matching means "appropriate to" not "equal to".

Mortgage
Long-term loan normally secured on a fixed asset. It is a long-term liability rather than a current one.

Net
(a) Figure after deduction; for example, gross sales less sales returns equals net sales.
(b) Payment of the full amount with no allowance for cash discount.

Net current assets
Another term used to describe working capital.

Net profit
Profit for the accounting period after income tax.

Net worth
Balance sheet value of owner's stake in the business. It consists of both the money put in at the start, and any profits made since and left in the business.

Nominal value
Face value of shares rather than the book or market value. Authorized and issued share capital in the balance sheet shows the nominal value of the shares separately from any premium or discount.

Non-operating expense
Expense not directly related to normal operations; for example, loss on sales of fixed assets, interest paid, etc.

Non-operating income
Income not arising from normal operations; for example, profit on sale of fixed assets, dividends received, etc.

Notes to financial statements
Notes attached to the balance sheet and income statement that explain (a) significant accounting adjustments or (b) information required by law, if not disclosed in the financial statements.

Opening stock
Inventory at the beginning of the accounting period.

Operating expenses
All overheads of the business. The term is sometimes restricted to mean only selling, administrative, and general expenses.

Operating profit
Gross profit less operating expense in the income statement.

Order
Purchase order to a supplier for delivery of goods and services.

Ordinary shares
Normal shares in the business used to apportion ownership. See also **deferred shares**.

Other assets
Assets that are not fixed or current assets; for example, goodwill, research cost carried forward, trade investments, etc. These are valued at cost not market value, unless losses are exceptional.

Other creditors
Creditors or accruals for services, not trade creditors for purchase of material and supplies.

Overhead
As in overhead expense: indirect cost that cannot be conveniently associated with a unit of production.

Owner's equity
Amount due to owners of the business, increased by profits, reduced by losses and dividends. N.B. Assets less liabilities equal owner's equity.

Package of accounting reports
Set of financial statements prepared for a business. This will include a balance sheet for the start and end of the period in question, plus the intervening profit and loss account.

Partnership
When two or more people agree to carry on a business together, intending to share the profits they make.

Patent
The legal right to exploit an invention. This is recorded at cost less depreciation under the heading "Other assets" on the balance sheet.

Plant
Equipment and machinery. This is regarded as a fixed asset if acquired for use and not for resale.

Preference share
Share that entitles the holder to fixed dividends (only) in preference to the dividends for ordinary shares. On liquidation, the holder is normally entitled only to the nominal value and has no right to share in any excess profits.

Prepaid expense
Expense paid in advance for more than one accounting period.

Profit
The excess of sales over costs and expenses during an accounting period. Does not necessarily increase cash – it may be reflected in increased assets or decreased liabilities. See also **net profit**.

Profit and loss account
Statement showing sales, costs, expenses, and profit for an accounting period.

Profit and loss appropriation account
Statement of accumulated profit or retained earnings. Balance of profit and loss account.

Profit before tax
Operating profit less non-operating expenses plus non-operating income, as shown in the income statement.

Provision
Setting a sum aside to meet a future liability.

Published financial statements
Balance sheet, profit and loss account, and statement of accumulated profit, with comparative figures and notes disclosing the information required under the Companies Acts. See **notes to financial statements**.

R & D
Research and development cost of the business. This is normally regarded as an expense but is sometimes treated as an "other asset".

Redeemable preference shares
Preference shares that may be repurchased by the company from the shareholders. Part of the owner's equity, not ordinary shares.

Research cost
Cost of research listed either as a separate overhead or as part of manufacturing overhead. It is sometimes carried forward as an "other asset" if it is of specific future benefit for a future limited period.

Reserve
Strictly means accumulated profit. See **revenue reserve**, **capital reserve**, **provision**.

Retained earnings
The profits that have been earned and kept in the business to help finance growth.

Revaluation
Sometimes fixed assets are revalued from cost

to current values. The difference between the two is credited to capital reserve.

Revenue
Earnings. Sometimes also used to mean sales.

Revenue reserve
The profit made from trading, which has not been distributed. Distinct from a capital reserve, which usually arises from the sale of a fixed asset at a price higher than its cost.

Sales
Total of amounts sold, recognized normally when goods are shipped to customer, or the service is executed, and the invoice has been raised.

Sales allowance
Special allowance to a customer against the amount due for goods sold. This is often allowed for damaged goods or shortages.

Sales discount
Trade or cash discount on sales.

Sales expense
The cost of promoting sales and retaining custom. This is an indirect cost and an overhead expense, not a manufacturing, administrative, or general expense. Sales expense includes advertising, sales literature, sales salaries, cars, travelling expenses, depreciation of sales, etc.

Security
Assets claimable by some creditors in priority to others.

Share
Document certifying ownership of shares in a company.

Share capital
Money put into a business by the owners of the business in return for a stake in the venture.

Share premium
The excess of the original sales price of a share over its face or nominal value.

Shareholder
Owner of part of the share capital and owner's equity. Also known as a stock holder.

Sleeping partner
One who puts capital into a partnership but who does not intend to take an active part in running the business.

Sole trader
The simplest type of business: there are no shareholders – just the owner's money and borrowings.

Stock
Goods on hand for resale or held in raw materials or as work in progress. In the US referred to as inventory.

Straight line depreciation
Depreciation method that involves charging off the cost of a fixed asset equally over all the years of its working life. See also **diminishing balance depreciation**.

Tangible asset
Asset that can be physically identified or touched. It sometimes refers only to those assets that have a definite value; that is, it excludes intangible assets such as goodwill, as well as research and development expenditures carried forward.

Trade creditor
Money owed for credit purchases.

Trade discount
Deduction from the selling price of an invoice because the buyer is in the same trade as the seller. It is not a cash discount.

Trade investment
Investment in shares or debentures of another company in the same trade or industry. It is a long-term investment and not a marketable security. Valued at cost unless there is a substantial loss.

Transaction
May be sale, purchase, cash receipt, cash payment, or accounting adjustment. Translated into debits and credits in the bookkeeping records.

True and fair
The balance sheet and income statement show a "true and fair" view of the business, in accordance with generally accepted accounting principles.

Uncertainty
A limitation of accounting. Uncertainty at the end of each accounting period makes it difficult to determine the "true and fair" position.

Uncertainty arises from: (a) incomplete transactions; (b) the market value of stock; (c) the working life of fixed assets for depreciation calculations; (d) the realizable values of current assets; (e) contingent liabilities not yet known or calculable.

Unpaid dividends

Dividends declared as due to shareholders but not yet paid in cash. They are shown as a current liability in the balance sheet and are deducted from accumulated profit in the owner's equity.

Value

This is one of those difficult accounting words that sounds very normal but rarely means what you would think. For example, look at the definition of book value. There is nothing in the name to suggest that the book value of an asset is the amount of money you might actually get for it.

Work-in-progress

Items for sale that are only partially ready for sale. For example, a carpenter's half-finished table would have consumed some raw materials and some labour. These would be accounted for in arriving at the value assigned to work-in-progress. Valued at the lower of manufacturing cost or market value. Real value is not known in accounting.

Working capital

Has a special meaning of current assets less current liabilities. It is not the same as "capital".

USEFUL CONTACTS

SOURCES OF FINANCE

Association of British Credit Unions
Holyoak House
Hanover Street
Manchester
M60 0AS
Tel: 0161 832 3694
Fax: 0161 832 3706
Infor@abcul.org

British Venture Capital Association
Essex House
12–13 Essex Street
London
WC2R 3AA
Tel: 0207 240 3846
Fax: 0207 240 3849
http://www.bvca.co.uk/
This site provides extensive information on venture capital in the United Kingdom and on the services of the British Venture Capital Association, which represents every major source of venture capital in the country.

Factors and Discounters Association
Administration Office
2nd Floor, Boston House
The Little Green
Richmond
Surrey
TW9 1QE
Tel: 0208 332 9955
Fax: 0208 332 2585
http://www.factors.org.uk

Finance and Leasing Association
Imperial House
15-19 Kingsway
London
WC2B 6UN
Tel: 0207 836 6511
Fax: 0207 420 9600
info@fla.org.uk
http://www.fla.org.uk

London Stock Exchange
Old Broad Street
London
EC2N 1HP
Tel: 0207 797 4404
Fax: 0207 797 2001
http://www.londonstockexchange.com

National Business Angels Network
40–42 Cannon Street
London
EC4N 6JJ
Tel: 0207 329 2929
Info@BestMatch.co.uk
This commercial site provides information on LINC, an organization sponsored by several UK banks that aims to introduce investors to businesses seeking growth and start-up capital, including details on its services and regional offices.

Prince's Trust
18 Park Square East
London
NW1 4LH
Tel: 0207 543 1234
Fax: 0207 543 1200
http://www.princes-trust.org.uk
The business start-up arm of the Prince's Trust helps young people, aged between 18 and 30, who are unemployed, underemployed, or of limited means, to start their own business. A last-resort funder, it offers low-interest business loans, test marketing grants, advice, and other assistance, such as discounted exhibition space.

Small Firms Loan Guarantee Section
SME Policy Directorate
Department of Trade and Industry
Level 2, St. Mary's House
c/o Moorfoot
Sheffield
S1 4PQ
Tel: 0114 259 7308/9
Fax: 0114 259 7316

Ulster Factors Ltd
7 North Street
Belfast
BT1 1NH
Tel: 0123 232 4522
Fax: 0123 223 0336
Venture Capital Report
Magdalen Centre
Oxford Science Park
Oxford
OX4 4GA
Tel: 0186 578 4411
Fax: 0186 578 4412
http://www.vcr@vcrnet.unet.com
This commercial site aims to link investors with entrepreneurial businesses seeking capital. It includes a list of current investment opportunities, as well as details of how to have your project featured in the report.

ACCOUNTANCY BODIES AND SOFTWARE PROVIDERS

Association of Chartered Certified Accountants
29 Lincoln's Inn Fields
London
WC2A 3EE
Tel: 0207 242 6855
Fax: 0207 831 8054
http://www.ACCA.org.uk
Chartered Institute of Management Accountants
63 Portland Place
London
W1N 6AB
Tel: 0207 637 2311
Fax: 0207 631 5309
http://www.cimaglobal.com
Institute of Chartered Accountants in England and Wales (ICAEW)
PO Box 433
Chartered Accountants Hall
Moorgate Place
London
EC2P 2BJ
Tel: 0207 920 8100

Fax: 0207 920 8699
http://www.icaew.co.uk/
The Institute of Chartered Accountants in England and Wales (ICAEW) provides accountancy news and information, together with the full text of ICAEW reports on accounting in business, self-assessment taxation, and other subjects.
Institute of Chartered Accountants of Scotland
27 Queen Street
Edinburgh
EH2 2LA
Tel: 0131 225 5673
Fax: 0131 225 3813
http://www.icas.co.uk
Institute of Company Accountants
40 Tyndalls Park Road
Bristol
BS8 1PL
Tel: 0117 973 8261
Fax: 0117 923 8292
Intuit
Full range of accounting software for small firms.
London Society of Chartered Accountants
15 Basinghall Street
London
EC2V 5BR
Tel: 0207 726 2722
Fax: 0207 776 6930
http://lsca.co.uk
Sage Group plc
Sage House
Benton Park Road
Newcastle upon Tyne
NE7 7LZ
Tel: 0191 255 3000
Fax: 0191 255 0308
http://www.sagesoft.co.uk
Comprehensive range of accounting software for small firms.

General Business Advice

British Chamber of Commerce
Manning House
22 Carlisle Place
London
SW1P 1JA
Tel: 0207 565 2000
http://www.britishchambers.org.uk/
The British Chamber of Commerce provides information about its activities, as well as press releases and links to local chamber of commerce sites.

Business in the Community
44 Baker Street
London
W1M 1DH
Tel: 0207 224 1600
Fax: 0207 486 1700
http://www.bitc.org.uk

Business Link London
6 New Bridge Street
London
EC4V 6AB
Tel: 0207 557 7300
Fax: 0207 557 7301
info@London.businesslink.co.uk
http://bll.org.uk
This site offers an overview of the Business Link network of advice centres, including location details for local offices, details of available services and advice, and a search engine that is based on an index of accredited UK business sites.

Confederation of British Industry
Centre Point
103 New Oxford Street
London
WC1A 1DU
Tel: 0207 379 7400
Fax: 0207 240 1578
http://www.cbi.org.uk/
The official web site of the Confederation of British Industry (CBI) provides information on business in Great Britain and the organization itself, including press releases, trend surveys, and a searchable database of articles from CBI News.

Institute of Directors
116 Pall Mall
London
SW1Y 5ED
Tel: 0207 839 1233
Fax: 0207 930 9060
http://www.iod.co.uk

NewLenta
28 Park Street
London
SE1 9EQ
Tel: 0207 403 0300
Fax: 0207 403 1742
mail@gle.co.uk
http://www.gle.co.uk.

Government Departments

Board of Inland Revenue
Press Office
Somerset House
Strand
London
WC2R 1LB
Tel: 0207 438 6692
Fax: 0207 438 7541
Companies House
P O Box 29019
21 Bloomsbury Street
London
WC1B 3XD
Tel: 0292 038 0801
Fax: 0292 038 0517
http://www.companies-house.gov.uk/
The register of companies in the UK provides details about itself and its services, together with extensive information and guidance for anyone setting up and running a limited company. Companies House is responsible for company registration in the UK. It also has a key role in providing information about British companies. The web site contains a free information section of company names and addresses and disqualified directors. There are numerous guidance notes covering a wide range of topics, and many of the administrative forms are available on-line.

Department of Trade and Industry
1 Victoria Street
London
SW1 0ET
Tel: 0207 215 5000
Fax: 0207 215 6446
http://www.dti.gov.uk/
The Department of Trade and Industry provides information about its activities and resources for UK business and industry, including news, advice, and regulatory guidance.

GENERAL FINANCIAL HELP

Business Credit Management UK
Mariners House
24 Nelsons Gardens
Hedge End
Southampton
SO30 2NE
Tel: 0148 978 7541
http://www.creditman.co.uk/
This commercial site provides a comprehensive resource for business credit, including news, information on company formations and insolvencies, and legal resources.

Business Money Ltd
Strode House
10 Leigh Road
Street
Somerset
BA16 OHA
Tel: 0145 884 1112
Fax: 0145 884 1286
http://business-money.com/
The on-line version of *Business Money*, an independent review of finance and banking for business, offers articles from the current edition plus links to pages supplying current financial news.

Business Names Registration plc
Somerset House
Temple St.
Birmingham
B2 5DN
Tel: 0121 643 0227
Fax: 0121 678 9001

http://www.bnr.plc.uk
For a small fee, the Business Names Register will search more than 3,000,000 business names and 600,000 registered trade marks to ensure that your name does not conflict with any other. It will also help you to ensure that your own business name is legal and protected. It publishes a newsletter to communicate any changes in UK/EEC legislation that may affect names and ownership. It will obtain permission if your name contains a restricted word or phrase, and it will pay litigation costs in order to protect your name if required.

HELPFUL WEB SITES

Accounting Web
http://www.accountingweb.co.uk/
Accounting Web offers a range of accountancy resources, including an on-line weekly newsletter, a company information search-tool, access to Key Note Executive Summaries, and a directory of over 2,000 accountancy firms in the UK.

Business Clubs UK
http://www.businessclub.co.uk/bcuk/
Business Clubs UK provides contact information for over 600 business clubs, groups, and associations throughout the UK, as well as links to other business sites.

CCTA Government Information Service
http://www.open.gov.uk/
Maintained by the Central Computer and Telecommunications Agency, this site provides access to over 400 UK public-sector web sites, including the G7 Information Network for Small and Medium-Sized Enterprises.

Companies Act 1989 (c. 40)
http://194.128.65.3/acts/summary/01989040.htm
Her Majesty's Stationery Office provides a summarized version of the Companies Act 1989, together with an order form for the full printed version.

Enterprise Advisory Service
http://www.govgrants.com/
This commercial site provides information on business grants for UK companies, including news, advice, and regulatory guidance.

Her Majesty's Stationery Office
http://www.hmso.gov.uk/
Her Majesty's Stationery Office provides summaries of Acts of Parliament, together with the full text of all Acts and Statutory Instruments published from 1997 onwards and detailed copyright information.

Inland Revenue Online
http://www.inlandrevenue.gov.uk/home
The Inland Revenue provides information on UK taxation, including on-line versions of advice leaflets and tax forms, details on self-assessment, and answers to frequently asked questions. The web site features news and information on tax and National Insurance matters in the UK. It is easy to use and has a whole section devoted to "Tax for Business", which contains information on self-assessment and corporation tax self-assessment, the construction industry scheme, rates, allowances, press releases, tax offices, helplines, and orderlines. You can also access the New Business Starter Pack containing forms, help sheets, leaflets, and booklets.

Kelly's
http://www.kellys.co.uk/
The official web site of the business directory Kelly's offers a searchable database of over 12,000 UK companies, together with useful contacts and links to other business information; registration required.

Scottish Enterprise
http://www.scotent.co.uk/
The economic development agency for Scotland provides a wealth of information for businesses in Scotland, including information on business-improvement schemes, trade and export, and local advice centres.

Small Business
http://www.natwest.co.uk/nav_sbs/sbs/
This commercial site from the UK's National Westminster Bank provides news and information for small businesses, together with a business start-up planner and a business angels service linking businesses with potential investors.

Venture Site
http://www.venturesite.co.uk/
This commercial site provides an on-line marketplace for small companies needing investors. Registration and a small fee is required to place an advertisement for investors, but it is free to browse the lists of ventures and business angels.

http://www.dosh.co.uk
This small business specializes in accounting software for the self-employed and businesses with less than ten employees. DO$H Cashbook assumes no bookkeeping knowledge, but provides help through on-screen steps and a comprehensive manual. The software prints the reports on A4 paper. Trial versions of the software can be downloaded from the web site.

OTHER USEFUL WEB SITES

HM Customs & Excise
www.hmce.gov.uk

Health and Safety Executive
www.hse.gov.uk

Office of Fair Trading
www.oft.gov.uk

Trading Standards
www.tradingstandards.gov.uk

SUGGESTED READING

The Business Plan Workbook
Colin Barrow, Kogan Page, London, 1998
Explains each step in the business planning process, with illustrative case examples and useful checklists to ensure that everything is coverered. Templates for the financial reports needed in a business plan are provided.

The Cash Flow Challenge
Phillip Ramsden, Gower Publishing, London, 1997
Provides comprehensive coverage of all aspects of cash flow. It shows how each area that impacts on cash flow can be managed more effectively.

Setting up a Limited Company
Robert Browning, How to Books, Plymouth, 1999
Offers a detailed explanation of how to form a company as well as step-by-step advice on dealing with the formalities.

Guide to Venture Capital
British Venture Capital Association (BVCA), London, 2000
Provides the most comprehensive guide to sources of venture captital in the UK. Updated each year. Lists all major venture capital providers and describes their preferred investment categories, covering size and sector.

Sage Guide to Setting up and Managing Your Own Business
Edited by Colin Barrow, Kensington West Productions, London, 2000
Covers all aspects of starting up or running a recently established small business. Topics covered include raising finance, finding premises, recruiting staff, administration, and planning.

Managing Your Business Accounts
Peter Taylor, How To Books, Plymouth, 1999
Provides a step-by-step guide for the small business to carry out double-entry bookkeeping and accounting procedures.

Understanding Your Accounts
A. St. John Pice, Kogan Page, London, 1999
Offers simple and practical advice on making sense of a profit and loss account and balance sheet, managing cash flow, pricing your time and your product, controlling stock, and using budgets to plan for profits.

Budgeting for Non-financial Managers
Ian Maitland, Financial Times, Prentice Hall, London, 1999
A step-by-step guide to the whole budgeting process, from making the initial sales projections through to detailed profit and loss summaries.

The Vest Pocket Guide to Business Ratios
Michael Tyran, Prentice Hall, 1991
Demystifies 200 of the most important financial ratios. Designed for instant access and written in a non-technical style.

Lloyd's Bank Tax Guide
Sara Williams and John Williams, Penguin, London, 2001
A comprehensive source of information for anyone needing to learn the ins and outs of the British tax system. An essential resource for everyone wanting help through the tax maze.

Law for the Small Business
Patricia Clayton, Kogan Page, London 1998
Sets out the law as it applies to small businesses, for those wanting to get to grips with legal basics.

INDEX

ACKNOWLEDGMENTS

AUTHOR'S ACKNOWLEDGMENTS

This book owes its existence to the insight and enthusiasm of Stephanie Jackson and to Adèle Hayward who courageously took it over half-way through. I owe much to Alison Bolus, who continously pushe for greater clarity, and to Jane Laing and all the editorial and design staff who worked on the book. I also indebted to my colleagues at Cranfield and elsewhere, on whose wisdom and information I have drawn, and to the students, on whom much of the material used in the book has been tested.
The following sources are thanked for their permission to reproduce bar charts: European Observator for SME Research (p. 47), European Franchise Federation, Arthur Andersen, and World Franchising Council (p. 49), and Cranfield Working Papers (p. 46 and p. 119).

PUBLISHER'S ACKNOWLEDGMENTS

Grant Laing Partnership thank the following for their help and participation in producing this book:
Design: Graham Curd
Proofreading: Nikky Twyman
Index: Kay Ollerenshaw

Dorling Kindersley thank the following for their help and participation in producing this book:
Editorial: Mary Lindsay, Daphne Richardson, Mark Wallace
Design: Sarah Cowley
DTP: Jason Little, Amanda Peers

PICTURE CREDITS

2: Telegraph Colour Library 5 top: Telegraph Colour Library 5 centre: Powerstock Zefa 5 centre belov Powerstock Zefa 5 below: gettyone stone 8-9: Telegraph Colour Library 10: Robert Harding Picture Library 14: Robert Harding Picture Library 20: gettyone stone 23: Canon Colour Copier CLC 1130 courtesy of Canon 25: The Stock Market 26: The Image Bank 27: gettyone stone 28: Robert Hardir Picture Library 29: Rex Features 32: Robert Harding Picture Library 36: Pictor 40: The Image Bank 42: gettyone stone 43: Pictor 44: The Stock Market 46: Richard T Nowitz/Corbis 48: Rex Features 53 above: Gail Mooney/Corbis 55: TheImage Bank 58: The Image Bank 60: The Stock Market 62: Robert Harding Picture Library 64: Robert Harding Picture Library 68: Robert Harding Picture Libra 71: gettyone stone 72-73: Powerstock Zefa 74: Robert Harding Picture Library 80: Robert Harding Picture Library 98: Telegraph Colour Library 101: Robert Harding Picture Library 102-103: Powerstoc Zefa 107: Robert Harding Picture Library 121: Sally and Richard Greenhill 144: gettyone stone

AUTHOR'S BIOGRAPHY

Colin Barrow is Head of the Enterprise Group at Cranfield School of Management and Director of the Business Growth and Development Programme. He was educated at Sandhurst and took his MBA at Cranfield. Colin has taught on Business School MBA programmes and on management development programmes in countries throughout the world. In addition to his work at Cranfield, he is a strategic consultant and a non-executive director of a number of companies.